THE EDGE OF WISDOM

The Edge of Wisdom

A SOURCE BOOK

OF RELIGIOUS AND SECULAR WRITERS

ROBERT S. WICKS

Chairman, Department of Religion

Lawrenceville School

CHARLES SCRIBNER'S SONS

New York

COPYRIGHT NOTICES AND ACKNOWLEDGMENTS

The Editor thanks the following publishers and copyright owners for permission
to reprint from the works indicated below:

Appleton-Century—From "The Methods of Science and Religion" by Ian Barbour, in *Science Ponders Religion*, Harlow Shapley, ed.

Doubleday and Company, Inc.—From *Doing the Truth* by James A. Pike. Copyright © 1955 by James A. Pike. From *Hardness of Heart* by E. La B. Cherbonnier. Copyright © 1955 by E. La B. Cherbonnier. From *The Precarious
Vision* by Peter L. Berger. Copyright © 1961 by Peter L. Berger.

Eiseley, Loren—From "An Evolutionist Looks at Modern Man" by Loren Eiseley, in *Adventure of the Mind*, eds. Richard Thruelsen and John Kobler, published by Alfred A. Knopf, Inc., 1959. As appeared in *The Saturday Evening Post*.
© 1958 by The Curtis Publishing Company.

Farrar, Straus & Company, Inc.—From *Judaism & Modern Man* by Will
Herberg. Copyright 1951 by Will Herberg.

Harcourt, Brace & World, Inc.—From *The Human Comedy* by William Saroyan.
Copyright 1943 by William Saroyan.

Harper & Row, Publishers, Incorporated—From *Dynamics of Faith* by Paul
Tillich. Copyright © 1957 by Paul Tillich. From *The Art of Loving* by Erich
Fromm. Copyright © 1956 by Erich Fromm. From *Radical Monotheism and
Western Culture*, With Supplementary Essays. Copyright © 1943, 1952, 1955,
1960 by H. Richard Niebuhr.

Holt, Rinehart and Winston, Inc.—From *The Sane Society* by Erich Fromm.
Copyright © 1955 by Erich Fromm.

The opposite page constitutes an extension of the copyright page.

TO MY FATHER

CONTENTS

Contents

Contents

PREFACE

I would like to make quite clear at the outset what this book is not. It is not an answer book. In fact it may produce more questions than answers. It is not a balanced survey of contemporary secular and religious thought. This book does not give a reader the pleasure of discovering *the* Christian, or *the* Jewish, or *the* Humanist point of view, nor does it do full justice to the entire thought of the writers whose work is represented here.

How then is one expected to approach the book? I would suggest that the reader imagine himself as sitting in on an extended conversation with a number of sensitive and articulate thinkers, both secular and religious, as each endeavors to interpret some aspect of the human situation and point the way to a fuller life for man. And as in any good conversation, not all positions are represented, not all speakers get equal time, nor do all give their attention to the same problems. Perhaps the host's friends take up more time than seems quite fair, but then, real conversations are seldom impartial. In defense I can say only that by and large these are men who have broken new ground and taken fresh approaches to religion that have captured the attention of intelligent people both within and without the church. They have helped many in our day to recapture the vitality and power residing in an ancient tradition and to discover again the perennial relevance of the Bible. There are other voices to be heard in this dialogue—creative artists, scientists, sociologists, psychiatrists. They may or may not be at home with the language and symbols of the Judeo-Christian faith, yet perhaps they clarify for modern man some issues that are obscured in the traditional language of religion.

I emphasize the image of this book as a conversation in order to remind the reader of a fact we often overlook. When a thought has made the printed page, it has not thereby ceased to be the thought of a man, a living human being, who wrestled with his world, who struggled more or less successfully to remain open to what he encountered and who sought within the limits of a reluctant language to give a name to what had happened to him. Since this task is and should be the concern of any educated man, I have tried through these various samplings to entice the reader into the conversation, not for the purpose of indoctrination or with the intention of providing final answers, but to enlist him in that continuing search for the next small step toward maturity and toward a heightened sensitivity to what is going on in himself and in his world. Hopefully, those with whom he will be conversing in the course of the book will assist him as he experiments with a vocabulary that will give shape to his intuitions and structure to his awareness, like the woman who said, "I have to speak in order to find out what I think." The vocabulary is no easier than any other technical vocabulary, nor is it an absolute necessity for living a full and rewarding life. But it is helpful, just as knowledge of the language of mathematics can be helpful, in giving one access to a community of thought which can sharpen a man's perception of reality and enhance his ability to evaluate and recreate his world.

It is to be hoped that as the reader comes to feel at home in this conversation he will become a little uneasy with the labels "secular" and "religious," a little less confident of his skepticism, a little more embarrassed to speak of God, a little less certain that he needs no guidance along the way of truth. To those who are joining the circle for the first time let me offer a word of encouragement. Do not be dismayed to find real life deeper and more of a mystery than expected; do not be alarmed if the crucial questions of existence turn out to be questions we must live with rather than answer. Plato long ago remarked in the Phaedo, "How hard or rather impossible is the attainment of any certainty about questions such as these in the present life. And yet he would be a poor creature who did not test what is said about them to the uttermost, or who abandoned the task before he had examined them from every side and could do no more."

Robert S. Wicks

PART I

Basic Definitions

JOHN UPDIKE

[*This conversation occurs in a poorhouse for old people. Hook is one of the inmates and Conner is the young man in charge of the place.*]

"What makes you think God exists?" As soon as he pronounced the ominous hollow noun, Conner knew absolutely he could drive the argument down to the core of shame that lay heavily in any believer's heart.

"Why, there are sever-al sorts of evidence," Hook said, as he held up one finger and then added a second, "there is what of Cre-ation I can see, and there are the inner spokesmen."

"Creation. Look at the smoke of your cigar; twisting, expanding, fading. That's the shape of Creation. You've seen, in the newspapers you've just said you read, photographs of nebulae: smears of smoke billions of miles wide. What do you make of their creation?"

"I know little of astronomy. Now a flower's creation—"

"Is also an accident."

"An ac-cident?" Hook smiled softly and he touched the fingertips together, better to give his attention.

"Lightning stirred certain acids present on the raw earth. Eventually the protein molecule occurred, and in another half-billion years the virus, and from then on it's evolution. Imagine a blind giant tossing rocks through eternity. At some point he would build a cathedral."

"It seems implausible."

"It's mathematics. The amounts of time it takes is the factor that makes it seem implausible. But the universe has endless time."

"Not according to Scripture."

"Not according to Scripture, no."

"I do not quite see how any amount of time can generate something from nothing."

"Presumably there was always something. Though relatively, very little. The chief characteristic of the universe is, I would say, emptiness. There is infinitely more nothing in the universe than anything else."

"Indeed, you propose to extinguish re-ligion by measuring quantities of nothing. Now why would no matter how much nothing be imposing, when my little fingernail, by being something, is of more account?"

"Yes, but there is something. Stars; many of such size that were one placed in the position of the sun we would be engulfed in flame. The issue is, can any sane mind believe that a young carpenter in Syria two thousand years ago *made* those monstrous balls of gas?"

For the first time, Hook was slow in answering. He shifted his position, and the old dry leather audibly protested. "As to being a carpenter, it has often struck me that there is no profession so native to holy and constructive emotions, or so appropriate for God-made flesh to assume."

"The truth is, Mr. Hook, that if the universe was made, it was made by an idiot, and an idiot crueler than Nero. There are no laws. Atoms and animals alike do only what they can't help doing. Natural history is the study of horrible things. You say you read the papers; but have you ever walked around the skeleton of a brontosaurus? Or watched microbes in a drop of water gobble each other up?"

"No, but I have seen a lobster being cooked."

"These are our fathers, Mr. Hook. Monsters. We are mostly monsters. People speak of loving life. Life is a maniac in a closed room."

"Now it has never been claimed," Hook said, "that the Creator's mind is a book open for all to read. This I do know, that that part of the uni-verse which is visible to me, as distinct from that which is related to me, is an unfailing source of consolation. Dumb creatures are more than their skeletons. Even a spider may set us a lesson. As to the stars that so repel you, they are to me points of light arranged at random, to give the night sky adornment. I have sometimes thought, had you and your kind arranged the stars, you would have set them geometrically, or had them spell a thought-provoking sentence."

Conner waved his hand impatiently. "As a student of debate you know how little humor proves. What was your second piece of evidence? Inner spokesmen? The truth here is, there is no door where these spokesmen could get in. We've sifted the body in a dozen directions, looking for a soul. Instead we've found what? A dog's bones, an ape's glands, a few quarts of sea water, a rat's nervous system, and a mind that is actually a set of electrical circuits. An experiment that might interest you, Mr. Hook, was conducted several years ago by a team of Latin-American scientists. They took a young Indian girl from the mountains of Peru who had been educated entirely by Catholic nuns. By means of a series of precisely directed electrical shocks, administered while she was under drugs, she was induced to have a vision of Christ as real to her as I am to you."

With this he knew that he had indeed succeeded, had touched the core of shame and shaken Hook. All the old man could say was, "That was a very cruel experi-ment."

"I don't know why. The girl was ecstatic. He spoke to her in Quechua."

"He spoke?"

Conner paused. "I think the report said the appearance told her not to be afraid."

The fire had failed to take Fuller's large logs; and the rain continued more quietly outside, infrequently pattering on the ashes as a few drops found their way down the chimney. Hook was silent for a moment, but might have spoken again, had not an interruption occurred. "Mr. Hook," Buddy said sharply, and he stepped forward, lithe and clean in his crisp shirt and his skin quickened by indignation. "I'll tell you my own experience with

5

popular religion." Conner realized that, however long Buddy had been listening by the door, he did not comprehend the situation, that Conner stood among the ruins of a venerable faith; helplessly Conner perceived that in the boy's brain the grotesque idea of a rescue had taken form. "I watched a friend die," Buddy continued quickly, speaking solely to Hook. "It took a long time. His bones were riddled with cancer. Every time he'd turn over in his sleep, he would break a bone; this was toward the end; at first it was just his joints, one by one, stiffening, and not obeying. He and I were very young; we prayed. We prayed for years, yet the pain came on, and in the end we prayed simply that he die now, before the disease was through playing with him. It would have been such a little thing for God to do, yet it was not done, even that little thing. At last the doctors themselves did it, and killed my twin brother with drugs, on his fifteenth birthday."

...Hook...now pronounced tiredly, "That is a ver-y terrible tale. Let an old fella say one thing more, and then he'll hold his peace. When you get to be my age—and I shall pray that you never do, I wish it on no one, but if you do—you shall know this: There is no goodness, without belief. There is nothing but busy-ness. And if you have not believed, at the end of your life you shall know you have buried your talent in the ground of this world and have nothing saved, to take into the next." [1]

---

[1] JOHN UPDIKE, *The Poorhouse Fair* (New York, 1959), pp. 112–116.

INTRODUCTION

There are few people, young or old, who have not been drawn into such an argument as John Updike describes in The Poorhouse Fair. If we are believers, then we surely have known something of what he calls "the core of shame" that lies in any believer's heart, the doubt that assails us under an attack like Conner's, the inadequacy of the words we marshal to our defense. Or if we have been the attacker, the rational unbeliever, then perhaps we have known that strange triumph of the brain where the logic of chaos wins the day but brings a curious sense of loss, a half-formed awareness of our own defeat. For the one who "proves" that God is dead thereby announces that all is permissible, "anything goes." If we are ultimately accountable to nothing or no one, if all is accident and smear of gas, then, as Conner says, "We are mostly monsters.... Life is a maniac." Yet very few of the Conners of this world are willing to live with the implications of such a position. It is hard to escape the conclusion that this jingle represents Conner's view.

> Lizzie Borden took an ax
> And gave her mother forty whacks;
> When she saw what she had done,
> She gave her father forty-one!

To say this, does not make Hook's argument much more effective. Rather, it points up the importance of intellectual honesty and the need for the humility to listen with more than our ears to what the other one says. Too often we find ourselves more concerned with winning than with learning. Too often we would blind the other rather than look with him at what he sees, as if we were frightened of the possibility of a truth we could not control or explain. The religious are as guilty of this tendency as the irreligious. Men like Hook are the victims of a frightened

7

piety that feels it has to choose between Darwin and the Bible, that worships at the altar of a deus ex machina who for the virtuous brings victory in the basketball game, miraculous deliverance from the plane crash, and guarantees success in business. (Too many Conners simply lost the ball game, or a job, or a friend, and the religious whispered something about punishment.) Maybe such a god is dead. Maybe he never was more than the pleasant rationalization of the insecure. Maybe such a god should be attacked. This is about the level at which the debate between the "secular" and the "religious" or science and religion usually proceeds. Maybe it is only the small minds that get trapped in logic and the shriveled spirits that are afraid of truth. Actually, when one reads the work of men who have hungered after wisdom, who have had the courage to face the mystery of life as it comes to them in their particular discipline, he finds that the usual stereotypes do not apply; he begins to realize that thoughtful people in all disciplines and faiths are not as far apart as their words seem to suggest. If theologians are not talking about "Somebody up there," then the skeptic must in all honesty make sure he knows what they mean before he concludes that he does not believe in God. In order to understand a view of life, whether it be scientific, philosophical, or religious, one must try to discern the assumptions on which it is based. One must try to grasp the special meanings of the terms used to express each view and recognize that men who may stand within the same general community (i.e., the Christian Church) may use the same words in quite different ways. One must also give attention to the kinds of questions a writer is seeking to answer. The inability of Conner and Hook to understand each other is due to their failure to recognize that each is really answering a different question. Hook tries to use religion to answer a scientific question; Conner tries to use science to answer a religious question.

These are the kinds of problems that are discussed in this part. Notice, for instance, the two ways in which Tillich defines

8

Introduction

religion. Obviously it would make a great deal of difference in any discussion to know which way the word was being used. Many people would say they were not religious and mean that they did not go to church or accept the creeds and doctrines of some specific historical faith. Yet these same people might be deeply concerned about the meaning of their lives and ask themselves what the world was for, what they should be doing in the world, and to whom or to what they were accountable. In this connection Tillich's broader definition of religion as "living in the dimension of depth" may be helpful in making people more conscious of the religious implications of their daily decisions and practical judgments. The questions, "Why get an education?" or "What about pre- or extra-marital sex?" or "Would you welcome Negroes in your school?"—these can be answered on many different levels. If pursued in "depth" they bring a person face to face not only with himself but also with his god, his ultimate concern and sense of value. This is precisely what is meant by the religious dimension of man's nature. As Tillich sees it, our predicament today is that not enough people are willing to ask these questions seriously.

If religion, then, has to do with the meaning and purpose of life, we have to face other questions: "How is meaning discovered or known?" "How can it be expressed?" "How can one believe and by what authority?" The readings in these three sections of Part I deal with some aspects of these questions but by no means exhaustively. Through them we get a sense of the style and tone of theological and philosophical writing. Since many of these writers are addressing their remarks to people who they assume have done considerable reading in this field, it is necessary to be attentive to the special ways they raise questions, the levels of experience that interest them, the care with which they seek to control the meaning of a word they use. Take, for example, a word like "myth." To the average man myth suggests something that is untrue, a product of wishful thinking or self-delusion, a childish fairy story. Yet many of these writers consider

9

myth one of the highest and most profound forms of human expression. Is a myth true? If so, in what sense? Or take the apparently simple question, How do we know? Not many people have explored this issue in any disciplined way, yet many of the fundamental assertions of faith stand or fall on the way this question is answered. Is definite knowledge possible only of things that can be measured with instruments or observed with the senses? Can we know what water is made of with greater certainty than we know we ought to do good rather than evil? What is this "I" that does the knowing? Can it be observed and located? Does it exist? Do we really need absolute certainty in order to believe? There seem to be fundamental distinctions involved in discovering the truth about objects and the truth about persons, and to blur these distinctions is to become entangled in the so-called conflict between science and religion.

Notice how conscious all of these writers are of the problems of communication and of the limitations and dangers of language. Catholics, Protestants, and Jews all make the same point. Certain kinds of language are appropriate for communicating some levels of our experience and not others. It is clear that we cannot dismiss the language of myth, symbol, poetry, and drama without cutting ourselves off from some of the deepest sources of insight and wisdom.

THE NATURE OF RELIGION

AND

SOME PROBLEMS OF RELIGIOUS LANGUAGE

PAUL TILLICH

The decisive element in the predicament of Western man in our period is his loss of the dimension of depth. Of course, "dimension of depth" is a metaphor. It is taken from the spatial realm and applied to man's spiritual life. What does it mean?

It means that man has lost an answer to the question: What is the meaning of life? Where do we come from? Where do we go to? What shall we do? What should we become in the short stretch between birth and death? . . . Man in our period of history . . . has lost the courage to ask such questions with an infinite seriousness—as former generations did—and he has lost the courage to receive answers to these questions, wherever they may come from.

I suggest that we call the dimension of depth the religious dimension in man's nature. Being religious means asking passionately the question of the meaning of our existence and being willing to receive answers, even if the answers hurt. Such an idea of religion makes religion universally human, but it certainly differs from what is usually called religion. It does not describe religion as the belief in the existence of gods or one God, and as a set of activities and institutions for the sake of relating oneself to these beings in thought, devotion and obedience. No one can deny that religions which have appeared in history are religions in this sense. Nevertheless, religion in its innermost nature is more than religion in this narrower sense. It is the state of being concerned about one's own being and being universally.

There are many people who are ultimately concerned in this way who feel far removed, however, from religion in the narrower sense, and therefore from every historical religion. It often happens that such people take the question of the meaning of their life infinitely seriously and reject any historical religion just for this reason. They feel that the concrete religions fail to express their profound concern adequately. They are religious while rejecting the religions. It is this experience which forces us to distinguish the meaning of religion as living in the dimension of depth from particular expressions of one's ultimate concern in the symbols and institutions of a concrete religion.... If we define religion as the state of being grasped by an infinite concern we must say: Man in our time has lost such infinite concern. And the resurgence of religion is nothing but a desperate and and mostly futile attempt to regain what has been lost.

How did the dimension of depth become lost? Like any important event, it has many causes, but certainly not the one which one hears often mentioned from minister's pulpits and evangelist's platforms—namely, that a widespread impiety of modern man is responsible. Modern man is neither more pious nor more impious than man in any other period. The loss of the dimension of depth is caused by the relation of man to his world and to himself in our period, the period in which nature is being subjected scientifically and technically to the control of man. In this period, life in the dimension of depth is replaced by life in the horizontal dimension. The driving forces of the industrial society of which we are a part go ahead horizontally and not vertically. In popular terms this is expressed in phrases like "better and better," "bigger and bigger," "more and more." One should not disparage the feeling which lies behind such speech. Man is right in feeling that he is able to know and transform the world he encounters without a foreseeable limit. . . . The predominance of the horizontal dimension over the dimension of depth has been immensely increased by the opening up of the space beyond the space of the earth.

If we now ask what does man do and seek if he goes ahead in the horizontal dimension, the answer is difficult. . . . For on his way into space and time man changes the world he encounters. And the changes made by him change himself. He transforms everything he encounters into a tool; and in doing so he himself becomes a tool. But if he asks, a tool for what, there is no answer. . . . Our daily lives in office and home . . . are in themselves continuous examples of a life which has lost the dimension of depth. It runs ahead, every moment is filled with something which must be done or seen or said or planned. But no one can experience depth without stopping and becoming aware of himself. Only if he has moments in which he does not care about what comes next can he experience the meaning of this moment here and now and ask himself about the meaning of his life. As long as the preliminary, transitory concerns are not silenced, no matter how interesting and valuable and important they may be, the voice of the ultimate concern cannot be heard.

If the dimension of depth is lost, the symbols in which life in this dimension has expressed itself must also disappear. I am speaking of the great symbols of the historical religions in our Western world, of Judaism and Christianity. The reason that the religious symbols became lost is not primarily scientific criticism, but it is a complete misunderstanding of their meaning; and only because of this misunderstanding was scientific critique able, and even justified, in attacking them. The first step toward the non-religion of the Western world was made by religion itself. When it defended its great symbols, not as symbols but as literal stories, it had already lost the battle. In doing so the theologians helped to transfer the powerful expressions of the dimension of depth into objects or happenings on the horizontal plane. There the symbols lose their power and meaning and become an easy prey to physical, biological, and historical attack.

If the symbol of creation which points to the divine ground of everything is transferred to the horizontal plane, it becomes a story of events in a removed past for which there is no evidence, but which contradicts every piece of scientific evidence. If the symbol of the Fall of Man, which points to the tragic estrangement of man and his world from their true being, is transferred to the horizontal plane, it becomes a story of a human couple a few thousand years ago in what is now present day Iraq. One of the most profound psychological descriptions of the general human predicament becomes an absurdity on the horizontal plane. If the symbols of the Saviour and the salvation through Him which point to the healing power in history and personal life are transferred to the horizontal plane, they become stories of a half-divine being coming from a heavenly place and returning to it. Obviously, in this form, they have no meaning whatsoever for people whose view of the universe is determined by scientific astronomy.

If the idea of God (and the symbols applied to Him) which expresses man's ultimate concern is transferred to the horizontal plane, God becomes a being among others whose existence or non-existence is a matter of inquiry. Nothing perhaps is more symptomatic of the loss of the dimension of depth than the permanent discussion about the existence or non-existence of God—a discussion in which both sides are equally wrong, because the discussion itself is wrong and possible only after the loss of true dimension of depth.

When in this way man has deprived himself of the dimension of depth and the symbols expressing it, he then becomes a part of the horizontal plane. He loses his self and becomes a thing among things. . . . He becomes an element in the process of manipulated production and manipulated consumption. . . . The influence of gang mentality on adolescents, of the corporation's demands on the executives, of the conditioning of everyone by public communication, by propaganda and advertising under the guidance of motivation research, et cetera, have all been described in many books and articles.

Under these pressures, man can hardly escape the fate of becoming a thing among the things he produces, a bundle of conditioned reflexes without a free, deciding and responsible self. The immense mechanism, set up by man to produce objects for his use, transforms man himself into an object used by the same mechanism of production and consumption.

But man has not ceased to be man. He resists this fate anxiously, desperately, courageously. He asks the question, for what? And he realizes that there is no answer. He becomes aware of the emptiness which is covered by the continuous movement ahead and the production of means for ends which become means again without an ultimate end. Without knowing what has happened to him, he feels that he has lost the meaning of life. . . .

Out of this awareness the religious question arises and religious answers are received or rejected. Therefore, in order to describe the contemporary attitude toward religion, we must first point to the places where the awareness of the predicament of Western man is most sharply expressed. . . .

It is the religious question which is asked when the novelist describes a man who tries in vain to reach the only place which could solve the problem of his life, or a man who disintegrates under the memory of a guilt which persecutes him, or a man who never had a real self and is pushed by his fate without resistance to death. . . .

It is the religious question which is asked when the poet opens up the horror and the fascination of the demonic regions of his soul . . . or if he shows the physical and moral mud under the surface of life, or if he sings the song of transitoriness, giving words to the ever present anxiety of our hearts. . . .

It is the religious question which is asked when the painter breaks the visible surface into pieces, then reunites them into a great picture which has little similarity with the world at which we normally look, but which expresses our anxiety and our courage to face reality. . . .

The existential philosophers have much to say about the problems of human existence. They bring into rational concepts what the writers and poets, the painters and architects, are expressing in their particular material. What they express is the human predicament in time and space, in anxiety and guilt and the feeling of meaninglessness. From Pascal in the seventeenth century to Heidegger and Sartre in our time, philosophers have emphasized the contrast between human dignity and human misery. And by doing so they have raised the religious question.

. . . Is there an answer? There is always an answer, but the answer may not be available to us. We may be too deeply steeped in the predicament out of which the question arises to be able to answer it. To acknowledge this is certainly a better way toward a real answer than to bar the way to it by deceptive answers. And it may be that in this attitude the real answer (within limits) is given. . . . It is given by the awareness that we have lost the decisive dimension of life, the dimension of depth, and that there is no easy way of getting it back. Such awareness is in itself a state of being grasped by that which is symbolized by the term, dimension of depth. . . . What we need above all—and partly have—is the radical realization of our predicament, without trying to cover it up by secular or religious ideologies. . . .

This does not mean that the traditional religious symbols should be dismissed. They certainly have lost their meaning in the literalistic form into which they have been distorted. . . . If the resurgence of religion would produce a new understanding of the symbols of the past and their relevance for our situation, instead of premature and deceptive answers, it would become a creative factor in our culture and a saving factor for many who live in estrangement, anxiety, and despair. The religious answer has always the character of "in spite of." In spite of the loss of the dimension of depth, its power is present, and most present

16

in those who are aware of the loss and are striving to regain it with ultimate seriousness.[2]

Both Tillich and Niebuhr reject the customary notion of supernaturalism which seems to suggest another world peopled by supernatural beings. Instead they talk about the eternal as a dimension of this world that can be expressed only symbolically. Take particular note of Niebuhr's illustration of the portrait artist who distorts reality in order to express its meaning. The artist has to paint a moment in the life of his subject in such a way as to suggest what Tillich would call the "depth" of the person which is not contained in any single facial expression. The portrait artist is not really interested in what the person "looks like." If he were, he would use a camera. This is a useful analogy for recognizing the basically different, though not conflicting, approaches of religion and science to an interpretation of reality.

When Niebuhr speaks of the "childlikeness of an adequate religion" he does not mean childish but rather the absolute openness to life, the sense of "awe, hope, and fear" which is another way of describing the appropriate humility of the creature in the face of an unfinished creation.

REINHOLD NIEBUHR

Christianity does not believe that the natural, temporal and historical world is self-derived or self-explanatory. It believes that the ground and the fulfilment of existence lie outside of existence, in an eternal and divine will. But it does not hold, as do many forms of dualism, that there is an eternal world separate and distinct from the temporal world. . . . The eternal is revealed

[2] PAUL TILLICH, "The Lost Dimension in Religion" in *Adventures of the Mind*, Richard Thruelsen and John Kobler, editors (New York, 1959), pp. 48–56.

and expressed in the temporal but not exhausted in it. . . . The relation of time and eternity cannot be expressed in simple rational terms. It can be expressed only in symbolic terms.

Before analysing the deceptive symbols which the Christian faith uses to express this dimension of eternity in time, it might be clarifying to recall that artists are forced to use deceptive symbols when they seek to portray two dimensions of space upon the single dimension of a flat canvas. . . . The necessity of picturing things as they seem rather than as they are, in order to record on one dimension what they are in two dimensions is a striking analogy, in the field of space, of the problem of religion in the sphere of time.

Time is a succession of events. Yet mere succession is not time. Time has reality only through a meaningful relationship of its successions. Therefore time is real only as it gives successive expressions of principles and powers which lie outside of it. Yet every suggestion of the principle of a process must be expressed in terms of the temporal process, and every idea of the God who is the ground of the world must be expressed in some term taken from the world. The temporal process is like the painter's flat canvas. It is one dimension upon which two dimensions must be recorded. This can be done only by symbols which deceive for the sake of truth.

Great art faces the problem of the two dimensions of time as well as the two dimensions of space. The portrait artist, for instance, is confronted with the necessity of picturing a character. Human personality is more than a succession of moods. The moods of a moment are held together in a unity of thought and feeling, which gives them, however seemingly capricious, a considerable degree of consistency. The problem of the artist is to portray the inner consistency of a character which is never fully expressed in any one particular mood or facial expression. This can be done only by falsifying physiognomic details. Portraiture is an art which can never be sharply distinguished from caricature. A moment of time in a personality can be made to express what transcends the moment of time only if the moment is not recorded accurately. It must be made into a symbol of something beyond itself.

This technique of art explains why art is more closely related to religion than science. Art describes the world not in terms of its exact relationships. It constantly falsifies these relationships, as analysed by science, in order to express their total meaning.

Religious literalism seeks to preserve childlike profundity in religion by giving simple and childlike answers to childlike questions. It thinks that the mythical answers to childlike questions are adequate scientific answers. It tries to insist that, because the idea of creation is true, it is also true that God created the world in six days; and that because the story of the Fall is true, therefore the account of the serpent and the apple in the garden is actual history. Thus it corrupts ultimate religious insights into a bad science. It tries to make mythical explanations of the ultimate "why" into scientific explanations of the immediate "how." This is a form of cultural primitivism as baneful as the social primitivism of reactionary politics.

The culture of modernity is a reaction to this kind of primitivism. It is unfortunately a new childishness which imagines that superficial answers to profound questions are sufficient. The child asks questions without claiming to know the answers. The adolescent thinks he knows the answers. The adolescent sophistication of modernity expresses itself in finding scientific answers for religious questions; in thinking that analyses of historical sequences and natural causation are an adequate approach to the problem of the meaning of life. It believes that the world is self-derived and self-explanatory because it is always possible to find a previous cause for every subsequent event.

The childlikeness of an adequate religion lies not on this but on the other side of sophistication. It is not the childlikeness of primitive ignorance but the childlikeness of a wisdom which has learned the limits of human knowledge. It therefore approaches life with awe, hope and fear. With awe, because it knows that the mystery of life is something more than an unknown region not yet explored by an advancing science; with hope because "it doth not yet appear what we shall be" and no record of past history gives us an adequate clue of what creative omnipotence may bring forth out of the infinite possibilities of existence; with fear, because it knows the possibilities of evil, which appear at each new turn in history, are never adequately anticipated by any analysis of the past.[3]

Too many non-Catholics look at the Catholic faith as a form of brainwashing in which an authoritarian priesthood hands out the answers to all questions and demands total conformity from their sheeplike followers, who obey out of fear of eternal damnation. The two Catholic theologians, Karl Adam and Gustave Weigel, whose writings appear in this part, help to dispel this outrageous image. There are major differences between Catholic and Protestant understanding of Christianity, but here again the reality does not in the least resemble the stereotype. Notice what Adam has to say about the continual need for reform, the emphasis on the impossibility of capturing truth in human conceptions, and the frank acknowledgment of the "servile forms which disfigured the Church" in the past.

KARL ADAM

As long as Catholicism lasts, it will feel the need for reform, for a more perfect assimilation of its actuality to the ideal which illumines its path.... [What are the causes] of this continual conflict between the ideal and the real?... The first and most obvious cause of these conflicts lies in the very nature of revelation.... We can grasp the actuality of the absolute and infinite and incomprehensible, the essence and existence of God, only by

[3] REINHOLD NIEBUHR, *Beyond Tragedy* (New York, 1937), pp. 4-6, 147-149.

20

means of conceptions borrowed from the world of our experience. No man has ever seen God. We have no immediate perception of the essence of God. . . . No assertion that we make about God is an exhaustive assertion. It contains truth but not the whole truth, and therefore possesses only an analogous value. We can speak of God only by comparisons. We are therefore aware that all our conceptions of God's being lag infinitely behind the reality. . . .

But even God's supernatural revelation, even those truths which go beyond the data of nature and are directly taught us by divine revelation . . . do not enter our consciousness in their original and in their self-evident force and immediacy, but are mediated through human conceptions and notions. The dogmas, in which these supernatural truths have been authoritatively formulated by the Church, denote the Absolute, but are not themselves the Absolute. The conceptual forms in which they are stated belong to specific periods of time, being borrowed mostly from Greek philosophy, and express the supernatural truths truly and aptly and in a form intelligible in every age, but by no means exhaustively or perfectly. . . . So there lies over the whole of our supernatural knowledge, and over the life which is rooted in this knowledge, an air of insufficiency. . . . We walk not in the sun, but in semi-darkness. It is true that our faith gives us the strongest certainty that the world of the supernatural is no mere dream, but absolutely genuine reality, the reality of God and His eternal life. And therefore our goal is clear, and the way is clear. But we see this sublime reality only through a veil and from afar, like a mountain wrapped in clouds. . . .

We have seen that the Divine, the Absolute, can in the nature of the case be conveyed to us mortal men only in adequate human conceptions and notions. And in the second place those instruments, by whom our faith is conveyed to us, are men, that is to say intelligences conditioned by space and time, restricted by the limitations of their age and of their individuality. Above all they are conditioned by the limitations of their age. Every period of time has its special character, its "spirit," i.e. a characteristic way, conditioned by its special circumstances, of seeing, feeling, judging, and acting. The eternal light of revelation is differently reflected in the prism of each age, with different angles of refraction. The supernatural is not manifested in naked truth, as it is in itself, but enters into the particular age and therefore in a form determined by that age. In this way it becomes an enkindling and fruitful and present force; but at the same time it loses in the process something of the austerity and majesty of its supernatural being. It suffers a sort of "emptying," it despoils itself, and takes the form of a slave, as the Divine Word despoiled Himself when He became man. And supernatural truth may sometimes be so far "emptied" and so much modified by time and circumstance, that the eternal is scarcely visible any more through the veils of time and we are puzzled and distressed by the "servile" forms which disfigured the Church in certain periods of the Middle Ages.[4]

[4] KARL ADAM, *The Spirit of Catholicism* (Doubleday Image Book), pp. 224–227.

THE NATURE OF FAITH

Again, in this passage, we see the way theologians resist the average man's approach to the question of God and the problem of belief. Since the theologian does not himself think of God as "Someone up there somewhere, with edges," he does not raise the question, "Does such a being exist?" As Roberts puts it, "Conceptions of God are attempts to characterize the ultimate context in which natural and human events take place." To return to Niebuhr, this is what he meant by the analogy to the portrait artist. Notice how Roberts uses the word "beyond." Perhaps this will provide at least the starting point for a new understanding of the "transcendent" or the "supernatural." Faith, then, involves man's response to what he believes are the "healing, life-giving, transforming" powers of being.

DAVID E. ROBERTS

Let us agree, for the sake of argument, that if a question can be settled by means of scientific evidence, historical research or philosophical reflection, it should not be settled by faith. What remains? Many will say that the only questions which remain are in principle unanswerable because we can never hope to have verifiable knowledge in connection with them. Yet it does not follow that since we cannot operate on the basis of verifiable knowledge we therefore remain practically neutral in relation to such questions. On the contrary, our basic orienta-

23

tions of trust or despair toward the meaning of life will go beyond knowledge, no matter what attitude we adopt. . . . Even if one declares that attempts to formulate an over-all view on such matters are fruitless, the declaration itself rests upon an "over-all" view.

[Therefore] it would be helpful if we could reserve the word "faith" for the responses a man makes to ultimate questions which *in principle* cannot be answered by means of knowledge. Frequently discussions of both faith and "religious knowledge" sound as though God were one entity among others, distinct from the world and man. Belief then takes the form of affirming that this entity exists, and unbelief takes the form of denying that it does. This manner of stating the issue obscures the fact that religion essentially is an acceptance of life as grounded in whatever evokes unreserved devotion; it is characterized by a sense of internal harmony, and of oneness with nature, humanity and the "ground of being." . . . Much confusion could be removed in both theology and philosophy if we could recognize that conceptions of God are attempts to characterize the ultimate context in which natural and human events take place; and that other characterizations of the object or objects of religious devotion are competing attempts of the same order. So long as theologians persist in talking about the "supernatural" as though it were a second world, either hermetically sealed off from or interacting with the world in which human beings exist, naturalists and humanists are entirely right in replying that they prefer to confine their interests to the one world which we indubitably have on our hands. Unless attention is fixed upon the relationship between the object of religious concern (however conceived) and the meaning of human life (its possibilities and limits), the ensuing debate can wander endlessly at crosspurposes, without ever bringing to light the venture of faith which underlines the naturalistic or humanistic position.

. . . So long as we regard human beings as divided into two groups—those who follow "faith" and those who follow "reason"—the issues are being wrongly conceived. "Faith" and "reason" are names for two different capacities which can operate in any man; insofar as they are at odds with each other, the man is at odds with himself. . . .

At the center of vital religion stands the awareness that reality is wider and richer than any conceptual system we can build in attempting to grasp it. Even more important is the discovery, in personal experience, that some aspects of reality and some ways of coming to terms with existence which have been excluded from conscious thinking are healing, life-giving and transforming. When powers are unleashed which put an end to conflict and enable a person to achieve wholeness and internal harmony on a whole new level, religion speaks of those powers as coming from "beyond" the individual's own thought and will—and the religious description is quite accurate.

Often the profoundest form of faith comes to a man only when, despite the fact that he has given up on himself, "something" does not give up on him. Positive faith has not been reached so long as despair predominates; but, in our age especially, many of us cannot find a faith that will stand up except by passing through despair and receiving a stable orientation toward life—cleansed of illusions and defensiveness—on the other side. When that happens the work of healing power (grace) which bestows beatitude as a gift (though not without participation on our part), has a compelling and inescapable quality that is utterly different from the "You must believe" of authoritarian threats.[5]

Tillich spells out the meaning of faith in some detail. He defines it as "the state of being ultimately concerned." By this he means being unconditionally committed to or loyal to that which one believes is the ultimate. In the examples of ultimate concern that he gives, i.e. the extreme nationalisms of our

[5] DAVID E. ROBERTS, *Psychotherapy and A Christian View of Man* (New York, 1950), pp. 73–76.

century, the Old Testament faith in God as expressed in Deuteronomy 6:5, the concern with success, social standing, and economic power, he describes two important facets of this concern: (a) it makes an unconditional demand for the sacrifice of all other concerns, (b) it promises ultimate fulfillment.

In the last part of the selection he speaks about the "awareness of the holy." What one identifies as ultimate becomes holy and sacred. A simple illustration of this experience would be a small boy in the presence of his athletic hero. It would even cover the fascinating and at the same time threatening aspect of the holy. Notice what he says about the role of language in the act of faith. Finally, it is important to note what he calls "the Protestant principle" which is a clue to the way Protestantism differs from Catholicism in its understanding of the Church.

PAUL TILLICH

Faith is the state of being ultimately concerned: the dynamics of faith are the dynamics of man's ultimate concern. Man, like every living being, is concerned about many things, above all about those which condition his very existence, such as food and shelter. But man, in contrast to other living beings, has spiritual concerns—cognitive, aesthetic, social, political. Some of them are urgent, often extremely urgent, and each of them as well as the vital concerns can claim ultimacy for a human life or the life of a social group. If it claims ultimacy it demands the total surrender of him who accepts this claim, and it promises total fulfillment even if all other claims have to be subjected to it or rejected in its name. If a national group makes the life and growth of the nation its ultimate concern, it demands that all other concerns, economic well-being, health and life, family, aesthetic and cognitive truth, justice and humanity, be sacrificed. The extreme nationalisms of our century are laboratories for the study of what ultimate concern means in all aspects of human existence, including the smallest concern of one's daily life. Everything is centered in the only good, the nation—a god who certainly proves to be a demon, but who shows clearly the unconditional character of an ultimate concern.

But is not only the unconditional demand made by that which is one's ultimate concern, it is also the promise of ultimate fulfillment which is accepted in the act of faith. The content of this promise is not necessarily defined. It can be expressed in indefinite symbols or in concrete symbols which cannot be taken literally, like the "greatness" of one's nation in which one participates even if one has died for it, or the conquest of mankind by the "saving race," etc. In each of these cases it is "ultimate fulfillment" that is promised, and it is exclusion from such fulfillment which is threatened if the unconditional demand is not obeyed.

An example—and more than an example—is the faith manifest in the religion of the Old Testament. It also has the character of ultimate concern in demand, threat and promise. The content of this concern is not the nation—although Jewish nationalism has sometimes tried to distort it into that—but the content is the God of justice, who, because he represents justice for everybody and every nation, is called the universal God, the God of the universe. He is the ultimate concern of every pious Jew, and therefore in his name the great commandment is given: "You shall love the Lord your God with all your heart, and with all your soul, and with all your might" (Deut. 6:5). This is what ultimate concern means and from these words the term "ultimate concern" is derived. They state unambiguously the character of genuine faith, the demand of total surrender to the subject of ultimate concern. . . .

Another example—almost a counter-example, yet nevertheless equally revealing—is the ultimate concern with "success" and with social standing and economic power. It is the god of many people in the highly competitive Western culture and it does what every ultimate concern must do: it demands unconditional surrender to its laws even if the price is the sacrifice of genuine human relations, personal conviction, and creative *eros*. Its threat is social and economic defeat, and its promise—indefinite as all such promises—the fulfillment of one's being. It is the breakdown of this kind of faith which characterizes and makes religiously important most contemporary literature. Not false calculations but a misplaced faith is revealed in novels like *Point of No Return*. When fulfilled, the promise of this faith proves to be empty.

Faith is the state of being ultimately concerned. The content matters infinitely for the life of the believer, but it does not matter for the formal definition of faith. And this is the first step we have to make in order to understand the dynamics of faith.

... What concerns one ultimately becomes holy. The awareness of the holy is awareness of the presence of the divine, namely of the content of our ultimate concern. The awareness is expressed in a grand way in the Old Testament from the visions of the patriarchs and Moses to the shaking experiences of the great prophets and psalmists. It is a presence which remains mysterious in spite of its appearance, and it exercises both an attractive and a repulsive function on those who encounter it. In his classical book, *The Idea of the Holy*, Rudolf Otto has described these two functions as the fascinating and the shaking character of the holy. They can be found in all religions because they are the way in which man always encounters the representations of his ultimate concern. The reason for these two effects of the holy is obvious if we see the relation of the experience of the holy to the experience of ultimate concern. The human heart seeks the infinite because that is where the finite wants to rest. In the infinite it sees its own fulfillment. This is the reason for the ecstatic attraction and fascination of everything in which ultimacy is manifest. On the other hand, if ultimacy is manifest and exercises its fascinating attraction, one realizes at the same time the infinite distance of the finite from the infinite and, consequently, the negative judgment over any finite attempts to reach the infinite. The feeling of being consumed in the presence of the divine is a profound expression of man's relation to the holy. It is implied in every genuine act of faith, in every state of ultimate concern.

... At the present point the obvious and yet significant assertion must be made that the act of faith, like every act in man's spiritual life, is dependent on language and therefore on community. For only in the community of spiritual beings is language alive. Without language there is no act of faith, no religious experience! This refers to language generally and to the special language in every function of man's spiritual life. The religious language, the language of symbol and myth, is created in the community of the believers and cannot be fully understood outside this community. But within it, the religious language enables the act of faith to have a concrete content.

... How can a faith which has doubt as an element within itself be united with creedal statements of the community of faith? The answer can only be that creedal expressions of the ultimate concern of the community must include their own criticism. It must become obvious in all of them—be they liturgical, doctrinal or ethical expressions of the faith of the community— that they are not ultimate. Rather, their function is to point to the ultimate which is beyond all of them. This is what I call the "Protestant principle," the critical element in the expression of the community of faith and consequently the element of doubt in the act of faith. Neither the doubt nor the critical element is always actual, but both must always be possible within the circle of faith. From the Christian point of view, one would say that the Church with all its doctrines and institutions and authorities stands under the prophetic judgment and not above it. Criticism and doubt show that the community of faith stands "under the Cross," if the Cross is understood as the divine judgment over man's religious life, and even over Christianity, though it has accepted the sign of the Cross. In this way the dynamic faith which we first have described in personal terms is applied to the community of faith. Certainly, the life of a community of faith is a continuous risk, if faith itself is understood as a risk. But this is the character of dynamic faith, and the consequence of the Protestant principle.[6]

Erich Fromm is a humanist who approaches the human situation from the perspective of psychiatry. As a psychiatrist he has had to cope with many forms of irrational faith which can sometimes cause considerable damage to a personality. He is attacking any faith that becomes for the believer a way of retreating from himself, his world, or from life itself. He is against any faith that is used to condone injustice and cruelty and to relieve the believer of moral responsibility. He has little respect for a faith that does not spring from the inner integrity of the person but which is imposed from outside by threat or arbitrary authority. In this he is in agreement with the theologians.

ERICH FROMM

Objectivity . . . is the faculty to see people and things *as they are*, objectively, and to be able to separate this objective picture from a picture which is formed by one's desires and fears.

The faculty to think objectively is *reason*; the emotional attitude behind reason is that of *humility*. To be objective, to use one's reason, is possible only if one has achieved an attitude of humility, if one has emerged from the dreams of omniscience and omnipotence which one has as a child.

. . . This process of emergence, of birth, of waking up, requires one quality as a necessary condition: *faith*. . . . What is faith? . . . Is faith by necessity in contrast to, or divorced from, reason and rational thinking? . . . Rational faith is a conviction which is rooted in one's own experience of thought or feeling. Rational faith is not primarily belief in something, but the quality of

[6] PAUL TILLICH, *Dynamics of Faith* (New York, 1957), pp. 1–4, 12–13, 23–24, 29.

certainty and firmness which our convictions have. Faith is a character trait pervading the whole personality, rather than a specific belief.... How does the scientist, for instance, arrive at a new discovery? Does he start with making experiment after experiment, gathering fact after fact, without having a vision of what he expects to find? Rarely has a truly important discovery in any field been made in this way.... At every step from the conception of a rational vision to the formulation of a theory, faith is necessary: faith in the vision as a rationally valid aim to pursue, faith in the hypothesis as a likely and plausible proposition, and faith in the final theory, at least until the general consensus about its validity has been reached.

... While irrational faith is the acceptance of something as true only *because* an authority or the majority says so, rational faith is rooted in an independent conviction based upon one's own productive observing and thinking, *in spite of* the majority's opinion.[7]

In a time when all faiths are seeking to draw closer together in order to present a common front against aggressive evil, it is important to be clear about our differences. Non-Catholic Christians would like to join together with Catholics but tend to become resentful when the Catholic insists that the unity be on Catholic terms. What the Protestant is inclined to overlook is that he implicitly counts on the Catholic to settle for a Protestant conception of the Church.

In this passage Gustave Weigel describes the different meanings for the Catholic of faith, the relation of the Bible to the Church, and the place of man's encounter with God. The Church as the "Mystical Body of Christ" by definition does not sin. In this sense of the Church no Catholic could assent to Tillich's notion of the "Protestant principle." Yet Weigel can

---

[7] ERICH FROMM, *The Art of Loving* (New York, 1956), pp. 118–120.

say "many of its members, high and low" may be "grievous sinners who by that very fact reduce the vital activity of the Mystical Body of Christ."

GUSTAVE WEIGEL

Faith has different meanings for a Catholic and a Protestant. To the Protestant, faith means a trusting self-surrender of the complete man to the revealing God. For a Catholic, however, this act of cordial surrender is called faith, hope, and charity. To a Catholic the word "faith" conveys the notion of an intellectual assent to the content of revelation as true because of the witnessing authority of God the Revealer.

Consequently the Catholic understands faith intellectually and supernaturally. Faith is the Catholic's response to an intellectual message communicated by God. For the Catholic, God reveals Himself through the medium of the teaching of the living holy community called the Church. It is so important for non-Catholics to appreciate this from the outset. A Christian of the Reform tradition believes that God makes Himself and His truth known through a collection of books called the Bible. This book is the teacher, and all other teaching is commentary, good or bad. The divine message itself is restricted to the Book.

In the light of these basic observations we can see the great difference between the Catholic and Protestant conceptions of the God-encounter. For the Catholic, the locus of meeting is the Church, which for its task of bringing men to God uses many means: the teaching of authorized masters, that is, the bishops and their primate the Pope; the liturgy; books written by men of the Church under divine inspiration, the Scriptures; the common beliefs and practices of the Catholics stretched out over time and space.[8]

[8] GUSTAVE A. WEIGEL, S.J., *Faith and Understanding in America* (New York, 1959), pp. 1–2.

REVELATION AND KNOWLEDGE:
HISTORY AS LIVED AND OBSERVED

Fromm clearly suggests that there is "a satisfactory answer" to the problem of human existence. The criterion for determining this answer is not found in public opinion but in what he calls the "characteristics and laws of human nature." The "truth" about man would be revealed either through the negative consequences flowing from conditions contrary to his nature or in the positive form of mental health. Anyone who wants to say that a man can achieve real happiness any way he chooses is going to have to get around Fromm's premise that man has a law to his nature which cannot be safely ignored.

ERICH FROMM

The approach of *normative humanism* is based on the assumption that, as in any other problem, there are right and wrong, satisfactory and unsatisfactory solutions to the problem of human existence. Mental health is achieved if man develops into full maturity according to the characteristics and laws of human nature. Mental illness consists in the failure of such development. From this premise the criterion of mental health is not one of individual adjustment to a given social order, but a universal one, valid for all men, of giving a satisfactory answer to the problem of human existence.

What is so deceptive about the state of mind of the mem-

33

bers of a society is the "consensual validation" of their concepts. It is naively assumed that the fact that the majority of people share certain ideas or feelings proves the validity of these ideas and feelings. Nothing is further from the truth. Consensual validation as such has no bearing whatsoever on reason or mental health. . . . The fact that millions of people share the same vices does not make these vices virtues, the fact that they share so many errors does not make the errors to be truths, and the fact that millions of people share the same forms of mental pathology does not make these people sane.

. . . The statement that man can live under almost any condition is only half true; it must be supplemented by the other statement, that if he lives under conditions which are contrary to his nature and to the basic requirements for human growth and sanity, he cannot help reacting; he must either deteriorate and perish, or bring about conditions which are more in accordance with his needs.[9]

Many people, especially the young, are afraid of tradition. This is understandable in view of the way tradition is often used as a weapon to prevent the curious from asking why or to hold back new creation on the notion that what was good enough for grandfather is good enough. Rollo May emphasizes another side of tradition which is not usually seen. Soaking oneself in tradition, far from making one a conformist contributes to the uniqueness of the self. Why can the classics speak to contemporary man?

ROLLO MAY

The greater a person's awareness of himself, the more he can acquire the wisdom of his fathers to make it his own. It is the persons who are weak in the sense of their own personal identity who are overcome by the power of tradition, who can-

[9] ERICH FROMM, *The Sane Society* (New York, 1955), pp. 14–15, 19.

not stand its presence, and who therefore either capitulate to it, cut themselves off from it, or rebel against it. . . . One of the distinguishing marks of strength as a self is the capacity to immerse one's self in tradition and at the same time be one's own unique self.

This is what the classics, in literature or ethics or any field, should do for one. For the essence of a classic is that it arises from such profound depths in human experience that like the works of Isaiah, or Oedipus, or The Way of Lao-Tze, it speaks to us who live centuries later in vastly different cultures as the voice of our own experience, helping us to understand ourselves better and enriching us by releasing echoes within ourselves which we may not have known were there. . . . The more profoundly one delves into his own experience, the more original are his reactions and productions. Here is the seeming paradox, which no doubt everyone knows to be true in his own experience, that the more profoundly he can confront and experience the accumulated wealth in historical tradition, the more uniquely he can at the same time know and be himself.[10]

Pay particular attention to Richard Niebuhr's discussion of the two ways of viewing history, the external and the internal, the way of the dispassionate observer and the way of the involved participant. In his illustration of the blind man one can see how two different levels of the same event can be expressed in totally different ways and yet both be true. To interpret the significance and meaning of events involves more than simply recording what happens. It requires a selection and raises the question, "By what criterion does one determine the important things to select?" In this connection, if we are looking at history, past or present, with the intention of finding those causal factors that explain the twist and turn of succeeding events, we will be primarily interested in the impersonal levels of life. So the

[10] ROLLO MAY, *Man's Search for Himself* (New York, 1953), p. 208.

Romans of the first century find nothing worth mentioning in the death of Jesus. Likewise, the escape of the Hebrews from Egypt is an unremembered event in Egyptian annals.

Revelation is concerned with persons and from this perspective events are significant and remembered when they disclose to those who have eyes to see and ears to hear, "certainties about fundamental, indestructible relations between persons." Revelatory history tells us who we are, gives us a vision of reality, and a purpose for our being. In other words, it is God's disclosure of Himself to us, the encounter with the "ground and power" of our being.

H. RICHARD NIEBUHR

Christian faith cannot escape from partnership with history, however many other partners it may choose. . . . But though this is true the question remains, how can it be true? How can revelation mean both history and God?

We may be helped toward a solution of the problem of history and faith by reflection upon the fact that the history to which we point when we speak of revelation is not the succession of events which an uninterested spectator can see from the outside but our own history. It is one thing to perceive from a safe distance the occurrences in a stranger's life and quite a different thing to ponder the path of one's own destiny, to deal with the why and whence and whither of one's own existence. Of a man who has been blind and who has come to see, two histories can be written. A scientific case history will describe what happened to his optic nerve or to the crystalline lens, what technique the surgeon used or by what medicines a physician wrought the cure, through what stages of recovery the patient passed. An autobiography, on the other hand, may barely mention these things but it will tell what happened to a self that had lived in darkness and now saw again trees and the sunrise, children's faces and the

eyes of a friend. Which of these histories can be a parable of revelation, the outer history or the inner one, the story of what happened to the cells of a body or the story of what happened to a
self? When we speak of revelation in the Christian church we
refer to our history, to the history of selves or to history as it
is lived and apprehended from within.

. . . The distinctions between the two types of history cannot
be made by applying the value-judgment of true and false but
must be made by reference to differences of perspective.

In external history value means . . . strength. The objective
historian must measure the importance of an event or factor by
the effect it has on other events or factors in the series . . . . as a
scientific historian he is bound to suppress his own value-judg-
ments as much as possible. Not what is noblest in his sight but
what is most effective needs to be treated most fully. So Alex-
ander may have a larger place in his account than Socrates. . . .

In internal history, however, value means worth for selves;
whatever cannot be so valued is unimportant and may be
dropped from memory. . . . Value here means quality, not
power; but the quality of valued things is one which only selves
can apprehend.

. . . There is no continuous movement from an objective inquiry into the life of Jesus to a knowledge of him as the Christ
who is our Lord. Only a decision of the self, a leap of faith,
a . . . revolution of the mind can lead from observation to participation and from observed to lived history.

Revelation means for us that part of our inner history which
illuminates the rest of it and which is itself intelligible. Sometimes when we read a difficult book, seeking to follow a complicated argument, we come across a luminous sentence from
which we can go forward and backward and so attain some understanding of the whole. Revelation is like that. . . . The special
occasion to which we appeal in the Christian church is called
Jesus Christ, in whom we see the righteousness of God, his

power and wisdom. But from that special occasion we also derive the concepts which make possible the elucidation of all the events in our history. Revelation means this intelligible event which makes all other events intelligible.

... Revelation is like a classic drama which, through the events of one day and place, makes intelligible the course of a family history. Or it is like a decisive moment in the common life of friends. In the face of some emergency a man may act so as to reveal a quality undisclosed before. Through that revelatory moment his friend is enabled to understand past actions which had been obscure and to prophesy the future behavior of the revealer. But the revealing moment not only disclosed constant features of conduct which had previously been hidden; it also introduced a new relation between the persons and remains a unique point in their history.

... When we speak of revelation we mean that something has happened to us in our history which conditions all our thinking and that through this happening we are enabled to apprehend what we are, what we are suffering and doing and what our potentialities are. What is otherwise arbitrary and dumb fact becomes related, intelligible and eloquent fact through the revelatory event. To the extent that revelation furnishes the practical reason with an adequate starting point it may be said to be validated.

... We mean ... that something has happened which compels our faith and which requires us to seek rationality and unity in the whole of our history .... revelation proves itself to be revelation of reality not only by its intrinsic verity but also by its ability to guide men to many other truths.

... The most important fact about the whole approach to revelation ... is that we must think and speak in terms of persons. In our history we deal with selves, not with concepts ... [our] certainties [are] about fundamental, indestructible relations between persons. We need, therefore, to put our question in the following form, "What persons do we meet in the revelatory event and what convictions about personal relations become our established principles in its presence?" [11]

In this selection Father Weigel discusses two aspects of the Catholic position which tend to embarrass Catholics in their efforts to make themselves understood by those who are not Catholics. One he calls the Church's antimodernism, which he attributes to her deep sense of history and her affirmation of the community of the past with the present. She is not inclined to accept the new simply because it is new. The other obstacle in the Catholic's attempts to communicate with non-Catholics is his belief in the authority of the Church. Non-Catholics are inclined to see little difference between the arbitrary, externally imposed authority of either a military system or a totalitarian government and the nature and practice of Catholic authority. To the Catholic, however, the claim of authority is part of his faith and therefore not an alien power. Second, he is required by this same authority to follow his own conscience even if it leads him out of the Church. In considering the implications of such authority, one might well ask whether in fact the scientific community does not operate under a similar notion, though not so clearly defined.

GUSTAVE WEIGEL

Modernity is atomistic. Catholicism is a continuum. Hence, the Church is always antimodern. This makes communication difficult in the modern moment, which, of course is any actual moment. . . . It is a hard and awkward task to be ever forced to be uncommitted to the passing superstitions and frenzies of the moment we live in. Contemporaries see in such an aloofness a

[11] Richard Niebuhr, *The Meaning of Revelation* (New York, 1941), pp. 59–60, 63, 67–68, 83, 93, 129, 138, 143.

refusal to belong—and that is always an exasperating thing for the one who enthusiastically belongs. Nor is it an easy thing to hold dialogue with an exasperated man.

The difficulty is intensified by the presence of a traditional vocabulary of long standing. The Catholic language was formed gradually over the centuries, keeping the points of view of past moments of history. The completely modern man does not know this symbolic system nor does he feel any desire to learn it. When he does hear it spoken, he is prone to misunderstand it. In consequence, the Catholic is always bilingual; he must speak his own traditional tongue, for only by it can he live his own traditional life, and he must also translate this language to the men of his day. . . .

[Weigel next turns to the problem of Catholic authority.]

The Catholic, qua Catholic, is socially specified because the Church is a society. To be social puts man under authority, for anarchism simply liquidates all social bonds. Now authority is restrictive, even when the restrictions are life-giving. And there are revolutionary moments in history when authority is resented and freedom extolled. We are in such a moment and the word "authoritarian" is for us a bad word. . . . Any religious statement rests on some authority. . . . The Christian evangelists gave witness to God's good news in Jesus. Witness was the only thing they could give. . . . Christianity today is far removed in time from the witness of the associates of Jesus. The authority of their witness can only be mediated to us. . . . The Catholics believe that their society, as a living and structured organism, mediates the testimony. In Catholicism it is not a book [Protestantism] which has the ultimate authority nor yet the floating traditions of a loosely conjoined fellowship [Eastern Orthodoxy]. It is the living community itself, acting as a society with the proper hierarchical architechtonic of a mystical body. . . .

What prejudices contemporary man against the Catholic

form of authority is that it is juridical. If an organized society itself is to be the decisive mediation of the Gospel, it must be jurisdictionally operative. Yet the consequence will be that belief seems to be imposed by fiat and bureaucracy. Both in the Reform churches and Eastern Orthodoxy there is fullest possibility for a personal reconstruction of the gospel. In Catholicism this possibility is severely restricted. This restriction seems to many to be an assault on freedom. Consequently, the witness of the Church grates on the sensitivities of our time.

The non-Catholic Christian has two questions: what does the Church say, and what does God say? These questions are for him two, and the answer to the one is not necessarily the answer to the other. For the Catholic, the two questions are identical in scope, because he believes that God speaks exclusively through the Church, so that what God says and what the Church says in his name are necessarily one. He believes this because he believes that only the Church can tell us what God communicates to the world and time. But in dialogue with non-Catholic Christians this basic assumption cannot be shared by the non-Catholic. . . . The Catholic must always begin his dialogue with an exposition of the meaning of the Church. Nor will he consider this a question permitting any answer except the affirmation of the Catholic Church. That is his Christian faith. There he stands; he cannot do otherwise. . . . The Protestant begins his conversation unconsciously supposing that the Catholic comes to Christianity in a Protestant way. . . . It will take much reflection for the Protestant to realize that he is as authoritarian as the Catholic but in a different way. Although, like the Catholic, he follows an authority and a tradition, he will accuse the Catholic of authoritarianism and traditionalism without realizing that he too bases his beliefs on these two grounds.[12]

The Jewish thinker, Will Herberg, understands revelation in the same way as Richard Niebuhr, though for him the Exodus-

[12] WEIGEL, *op. cit.*, pp. 56–61.

Sinai event becomes the event through which the meaning of all events is discerned. It is the "contemporaneity" of the crucial events of biblical history that leads the man of this faith to speak of the content of revelation in terms of eternal "Life" (personal, dynamic, concrete) rather than in terms of timeless truths (impersonal, static, abstract). If it is seen as a drama, then when we are drawn into the story so that it becomes our story—we are spoken to.

WILL HERBERG

The Bible is the word of God, but it is also the work of man: neither side of this double affirmation may be suppressed or ignored. It is, however, necessary to define biblical revelation a little more closely from another direction. Biblical revelation . . . is ineradicably particularistic. This particularism . . . is a scandal to the modern mind as it was to the mind of Greek antiquity, for to both, truth is somehow identified with the time-less and the universal. . . . The particularism of the biblical out-look insists not only that God's dealings with Israel as recorded in Scripture reveal his will and ways in a uniquely significant manner, but that certain events within that history are uniquely significant as revelation. . . . In Jewish faith . . . this crucial event is the "event at Sinai," understanding by this term the whole complex of events beginning with the call of Moses and culmi-nating in the "reception of the Torah." . . . Exodus-Sinai is, for the Jew, the interpretive center of redemptive history, as Calvary is for the Christian. Revelation is thus . . . "once and for all," not in the sense, of course, that God thereafter no longer reveals himself in his encounter with men, but in the sense that all other "visitations" of God, both before and after, yield their meaning only when seen with the eyes of faith from the perspec-tive of this central event. . . . In the biblical view, nothing that confronts man with the claim to authority as living truth can stand unless justified in terms of the central revelatory event.

* * *

42

The true redemptive history for the Jew—and in rather a different way for the Christian as well—is the sacred history of Israel.... Every believing Jew *in his own life* stands in the place of Abraham our father and *in his own life* re-enacts the historical encounter between Israel and God.... "All this I do," the Passover Haggadah represents the Jew as saying in explanation of the order of service, "all this I do because of what God did for *me* in bringing me forth from Egypt." For *me*, not for my ancestors. ..."Hear, O Israel ... the Lord our God made not his covenant with our fathers, but with *us*, even *us*, who are all of us here alive this day." (Deut. 5:5)

[The three great festivals of Judaism—Passover, Pentecost, and Tabernacles] are for us the living re-enactment of the formative events in the redemptive history of Israel. Just as Israel became Israel through the events to which they refer, so the individual Jew becomes a Jew-in-faith by "repeating" these events in his own life. It is neither past time nor timeless eternity in which we live in faith, but *contemporaneity*.[13]

Ian Barbour holds degrees in both theology and physics and so brings unusual competence to the discussion of that perennially thorny issue, the relation between science and religion. Take special note of what he has to say about communities and their tendency to forget the symbolic character of their special language. See how he deals with the question of certainty. Notice the particular type of knowledge science aims at—"reproducible relations expressible in general laws." Science is not interested in the unique, the singular, which is to say, the person. This is not to say that scientists are not interested in people, but rather that the personal dimension of reality is excluded from the possibility of scientific investigation employing laboratory techniques. Barbour makes an interesting point near the end on the problem of commitment in religion. "Too tenta-

[13] WILL HERBERG, *Judaism and Modern Man* (New York, 1951), pp. 250–252, 288–289.

tive an attitude may deny one the very sorts of experience which are most crucial in understanding religion."

IAN BARBOUR

Experience does not come to us already organized. Every philosophy of life selects some aspect of experience as a key organizing principle, as the most significant category of interpretation. Though every such world view is in part a venture of faith not deducible from science alone, it need not be an irrational choice unsupported by evidence.

Both science and religion involve these two basic factors: the interaction of experience and interpretation. In science experience takes the form of observation or experiment, and the interpretive aspect is called hypothesis or theory. Science is often misunderstood as being just a matter of precise observation. But no one has seen an atom. Scientific concepts are symbolic mental constructs by which we try to organize and correlate complex laboratory experiences....

Turning to religion, we find the same basic components: experience and interpretation. Man's *religious experience* includes his wonder and gratitude at creation, his response of reverence before what is to him holy and sacred, his sense of dependence and finitude. It includes prayer and worship, as well as moral experience, the obligation he acknowledges to choose good rather than evil, his guilt when he falls short. It includes his reflection on the basic structures and conditions of existence. ... The men who wrote the Bible were writing of what happened to them, attempting to interpret their own experience.

THE ROLE OF COMMUNITY AND ANALOGY

Both science and religion depend not only on individual experience, but on the experience of communities. There is no one-man science, for science is a cooperative venture. A physicist is dependent on his predecessors, and on the whole group of physicists which has its own institutions and journals and meetings. The physics community has its own jargon; its own norms and loyalties.

Similarly the religious community is central. Religious experience has its corporate aspects, a group that worships and acts together, bound by common loyalty to God, attempting to be a community of love and forgiveness. The religious community, too, draws upon the past experience of its historic life.

Moreover each community has its own *symbolic language* in terms of which it interprets its experience, and these symbols have little meaning for the outsider until he enters into the life of the community. Mechanical models seen as literal representations of nature have been replaced in modern physics by abstract mathematical symbolisms which could never be visualized. These are symbolic representations whose function is to allow us to coordinate experimental relationships. But note that the community itself is not consciously aware that its language is symbolic. Both science and religion arise as unreflective and spontaneous responses—a response of curiosity about nature on the one hand and of worship of God on the other, or in the case of the Christian community, response to the events surrounding the life of Christ. There is an assumed realism on the part of the working scientist or the worshipper. In practical operation they use language as if it were a literal description of reality and only in their more reflective moments is its symbolic and interpretive character recognized.

It is instructive to analyse the role of analogy in both fields. Analogy can be defined as the extension of concepts drawn from some relation within experience to suggest a possible mode of coordinating other experiences.... Thus Maxwell's theory of electromagnetic transmission was conceived by analogy with waves in solids (a very fruitful analogy, though, like all analogies, one with limitations for it seemed to imply a medium, the hypothetical ether).... In religion man uses analogies drawn from other areas of experience to describe the responses through which he conceives his relation to the transcendent.... One of the central modes of biblical communication is the parable, whose analogical character is always clear.

PRIMACY OF RELATIONSHIPS RATHER THAN OBJECT

Both science and religion see reality in terms of processes and relationships rather than in terms of objects.... In religion man is man, not as an individual alone, but in a fabric of social relationships.... so too, the biblical tradition does not talk about God as a separate object, does not try to describe him as if he were a thing in itself. The important questions are about God's relation to man and man's relation to God. Sin means man's violation of his true relationships, means being alienated from God and one's neighbor; love means reunion overcoming these divisions. In both science and religion, then, we are interpreting experience of relationships.

TESTING OF INTERPRETATIONS

In both areas testing requires the full use of reason, applying criteria of consistency and comprehensiveness. Yet in neither area is final and complete certainty possible. In science certainty is never achieved, and no formulation is final and irrevocable. ... In religion too, we cannot claim certainty. We must test our interpretations, for we are all prone to wishful thinking.... Our religious beliefs must reflect the most adequate, consistent and comprehensive interpretation of all human experience.

Now in this approach there is a significant place for the concept of *revelation*. In interpreting our total experience we need clues, crucial ideas and categories of interpretation.... For the Christian community the life of Christ is such a key event which illuminates the rest of human experience and helps us understand ourselves and what has happened to us.

SCIENCE AND RELIGION: DIFFERENCES IN METHOD

Science and religion ask essentially different questions, even about the same event. Suppose you are asked, "Why is that man climbing the mountain?" You can give a detailed scientific explanation about the construction of his leg muscles and the way energy from his lunch activates those muscles. But someone else may say, "The reason he is climbing the mountain is to see the view from the top." Both answers may be correct. The explanation in terms of scientific mechanisms and the explanation in terms of purposes are both important. Again, science asks about *means* but not about the *ends* for which those means should be used. In its questions science is necessarily selective. . . . (Science tends to deal only with the measurable and the quantitative, though not exclusively.) But the scientist does limit himself to publicly verifiable sense data, and he purposely disregards other aspects of experience.

In religion the central question is about man's ultimate allegiance, the objects of his trust and loyalty. It asks about the powers operating in the world for good or evil, the forces of fulfillment and destruction in human life. It is concerned about the goals and values men serve.

Science aims at a particular type of knowledge namely reproducible relations expressible in general laws. Scientific understanding is concerned only about repeatable phenomena and considers prediction one test of understanding. Science is not interested in individual events or objects except as instances of general laws. . . . Consider by way of contrast what a history teacher means when he says he wants to help his students understand a historical event—say the French Revolution. His primary interest is not the formulation of universal laws but the understanding of a unique pattern among the various social factors and personalities contributing to the French Revolution. . . . Understanding a work of art or of music is primarily a ques-

47

tion of insight into the relationship among its parts. A similar approach is called for by a novel or a drama. . . . So also religion asks about the significance of my own unique life—the only one in the universe I experience from the inside—and about my relation to the unique God, who is never one of a general class of objects.

There are dangers in seeking the security of guaranteed dogmas that close the door to new understanding; tentativeness concerning all our formulations is desirable. Nevertheless religion does require involvement and commitment. . . . The scientist may have to accept tentatively an hypothesis and act on the basis of its assumed truth if he is to test it. But in religion testing means living in accordance with a choice in which not just a theory but the man himself and the significance of his life is at stake . . . too tentative an attitude may deny one the very sorts of experience which are most crucial in understanding religion. . . . It is not easy to hold beliefs for which you would be willing to die, and yet remain open to new insights; but it is precisely this combination of commitment and inquiry which constitutes religious maturity.

Either science or religion alone affords a partial view. . . . no single type of language exhausts the description of even one event. Scientist and theologian both depend on experience and interpretation and both use their minds. Asking different types of questions, they will not expect the same types of answer. Science and religion thus reflect different aspects of our experience. Whether the power of science contributes to good or evil depends on man's goals, values, and motives, which are central concerns of religion. Understanding the relation of science and religion is no longer an interesting speculation for philosophers only, but a practical necessity, perhaps even for the survival of civilization.[14]

[14] IAN BARBOUR, "The Methods of Science and Religion," in *Science Ponders Religion,* edited by Harlow Shapley (New York, 1960).

PART II

The Nature of Man
and the Human Situation

INTRODUCTION

No matter where you turn these days, you hear people expressing concern over the state of the world and the condition of man. Theologians, psychiatrists, teachers, writers, artists, historians, all seem to be raising in one way or another the question, "What is man?" The very real prospect of the end of man apparently has impelled many thoughtful people to cast a critical eye on the structures of society, the goals and values of contemporary man, and most of them have voiced dismay at what they have discovered. The crisis has made scientists talk like religious prophets, theologians involve themselves in politics and economics, psychiatrists take another look at faith, and optimists think again about the problem of evil and the sinfulness of man. All of them are wondering whether man has lost control of himself and his world, whether the pressures and dangers of modern life are too much for his emotional and spiritual resources, or whether his new-found knowledge and power will enable him not only to survive but to create a new age in which men are free of the horrors of war, poverty, disease, and hunger. Some people are prepared to blame the present state of affairs on the Russians or the welfare state or some other specific cause; others see the situation in terms of a perennial predicament of man. The latter recognize that both the source and the solutions require an understanding of human nature, a doctrine of man.

In this part it will be seen that both secular and religious writers place great emphasis on the concept of the self. Man has lost himself; he is against himself; he searches for himself; he is sure or unsure of himself; he is curiously the subject—the seeker, and the object—the one sought. He may define his plight in the form of such questions as, "Who am I?" "Where do I belong?" "Where am I going?" "What kind of a world am I in?" "To whom or to what am I accountable?" It is these questions to which secular and religious faiths claim to have answers. Moreover, this concern for man's true nature or "real" self is based on the premise that man has a nature which can reasonably be defined. This means that generalizations about man have a universal relevance. It implies that human existence in every age and every culture poses essentially the same questions to which essentially the same answers could be given. Of course each age and culture has its own unique style, gives priority to some questions and ignores others, and arrives at more or less adequate answers. For example, the cave man presumably had to come to terms with the problem of how to live with his neighbor over the hill, how to get his cooperation in the hunt for food. The fact that he buried his dead with care suggests he too reflected on the mystery and meaning not only of the person but of life and death as well. The questions are the same whether they are brought to man's attention by an atom bomb or an inching glacier, by a companion mangled by a limousine or a lion.

The theme that unifies all the writers in this part is their insistence on the unique freedom of man over the natural process in which he is rooted, a freedom which enables him to have a say in what he shall become, which makes him anxious lest he miss his true destiny, and which finally, through the misuse of his freedom, gives him the power to interfere with his own growth and ultimately to cut himself off from his own fulfillment.

Obviously these questions are not readily answered. We live with them whether we ignore them, give over-simple answers to them, or insist that man is a total mystery to himself. But we should not be afraid to trust our own experience and common sense in dealing with philosophical and theological problems. Common sense is often productive of uncommon wisdom and insight

Sometimes in our encounter with people we run across someone of whom we can say, "he is a real person" or "he is a true man," and we would mean that this bit of reality is what it ought to be, or is becoming what it might be. We are saying we recognize in this person the right nature, the true properties and powers that ought to be there—that what he is and what he ought to be are identical. But to say this implies a rather curious fact about human reality. It can be less than it ought to be; it can be a denial of its own true nature.

The following statements point to several important ways in which men experience their true nature or their separation from it.*

1. Man is capable of entering into close and intimate relationships of friendship and love, or he can be deprived of them and be caught in the grip of a loneliness he is powerless to overcome.

2. He is capable of being freed from domination by other people and by external forces and of being freed for responsible living that springs spontaneously from an inner willingness of his own. Or he may be caught by this domination and resent it because he senses he is being used for purposes other than his own; he may then resent himself for giving in to these powers, yet be unable to see any way to escape this domination and become his real self.

3. He is capable of experiencing free participation in the life of a group or community in which people think and work constructively together in an atmosphere of mutual trust, acceptance, and respect. Or he may become isolated from such a relationship. Though living in a group, he may feel he doesn't belong, that he is an unrecognized nobody lost in the crowd.

4. He is capable of becoming a united self whose will power, conscience, mind are drawn together and he is able to determine from within himself the responses he will make

* I am indebted to Dr. Lewis J. Sherrill for these five points. He developed these ideas in a book called *The Gift of Power* (New York, 1955).

to what confronts him. Or he may live in a state of inward conflict, a divided self, in which one part of the self wars against another part.

5. He is capable of being a unique individual, unlike anyone else on earth, able to accept his own particular talents and interests and develop them to the full. Or he may be "just like everybody else," fitting the prevailing pattern, conforming to what is popular and expedient rather than to what he believes is right.

SELF-AWARENESS, FREEDOM, ANXIETY

WILLIAM SAROYAN

[Homer works as a delivery boy for the telegraph office. It is a time of war; so, many of the telegrams he has to deliver bring word of death to a family.]

"Yes, Homer?" Mrs. Macauley said without turning.

"I didn't talk to you last night when I came home from work," he said, "because it was like you said. I couldn't talk. All of a sudden on the way home last night I started to cry. You know I never did cry when I was little or at school when I was in trouble. I always felt ashamed to cry. Even Ulysses never cries because—well, what's the use crying? But last night I just couldn't help it. I cried, but I don't remember if I was ashamed even. I don't think I was. After I started to cry I couldn't come straight home. I rode out to Ithaca Wine and then, because I was still crying, I rode across town to the high school. On the way there I rode past a house where some people had been having a party earlier in the evening—the house was dark now. I took those people a telegram. You know the kind of telegram it was. Then I went back to town and rode all around the streets looking at everything—all the buildings, all the places I've known all my life, all of them full of people. And then I really saw Ithaca and I really knew the people who live in Ithaca, all of them good people. I felt sorry for all of them and I even prayed that nothing would happen to them. After that I stopped cry-

55

ing. I thought a fellow would never cry when he got to be grown up, but it seems that's when a fellow starts, because that's when a fellow starts finding out about things." He stopped a moment and then his voice became even more somber than it had been. "Almost everything a man finds out is bad or sad," he said. He waited a moment for some word from his mother but she did not speak and did not turn away from her work. "Why is that so?" he said.

Mrs. Macauley began to speak, but she did not turn to him. "You will find out," she said. "No one can tell you. Each man finds his own way. If it's sad, nobly or foolishly, the man himself will make it so. If it's richly sad and full of beauty, it's the man himself, so, and not the things around him. And so it is, if it's bad, or ugly, or pathetic—it is always the man himself, and each man is the world. Each man is the whole world, to make over as he will and to fill with a human race he can love, if it is love he has, or a race he must hate, if it is hate he has. The world waits to be made over by each man who inhabits it, and it is made over every morning like a bed or a household where the same people live—always the same, but always changing too." The mother was now busy on the back porch, and even though she was out of sight her son continued to speak with her.

"Why did I cry on the way home last night?" he said. "I have never felt the way I felt then. I don't understand it. And after I stopped crying why couldn't I talk? Why was there nothing for me to say—to you or to myself?"

From the porch Mrs. Macauley spoke very clearly so that he heard every word unmistakably. "It was pity that made you cry," she said. "Pity, not for this person or that person who is suffering, but for all things—for the very nature of things. Unless a man has pity he is inhuman and not yet truly a man, for out of pity comes the balm which heals. Only good men weep. If a man has not wept at the world's pain he is less than the dirt he walks upon because dirt will nourish seed, root, stalk, leaf and flower, but the spirit of a man without pity is barren and will

56

bring forth nothing—or only pride which must finally do murder of one sort or another—murder of good things, or murder even of human lives." Now Mrs. Macauley returned to the sink of the kitchen where she began new work—work which even Homer knew was unnecessary.

"There will always be pain in things," Mrs. Macauley said. "Knowing this does not mean that a man shall despair. The good man will seek to take pain out of things. The foolish man will not even notice it except in himself. And the evil man will drive pain deeper into things and spread it about wherever he goes. But each man is guiltless, for the evil man no less than the foolish man or the good man did not ask to come here and did not come alone, from nothing, but from many worlds and from multitudes. The evil do not know they are evil and are therefore innocent. The evil man must be forgiven every day. He must be loved, because something of each of us is in the most evil man in the world and something of him is in each of us. He is ours and we are his. None of us is separate from any other. The peasant's prayer is my prayer, the assassin's crime is my crime. Last night you cried because you began to know these things."

Homer Macauley poured milk over the oatmeal in the bowl and began to eat his breakfast. Suddenly he felt it was all right to eat.[1]

The following paragraphs develop the specifically human problems arising from the fact that man is aware of himself— that he can stand outside himself and his world and make value judgments about what is and what ought to be. The three tensions that characterize his existence—finite, yet aware of the infinite; conditioned, yet free; an individual, yet in need of community—represent the context in which all men must understand themselves and shape their lives.

When the word "spirit" is used to describe an aspect of hu-

[1] WILLIAM SAROYAN, *The Human Comedy* (New York, 1943), pp. 186 ff.

man nature, it generally refers to man's capacity to transcend himself, to stand outside himself, to make value judgments about himself, to make decisions. This power includes man's memory, his imagination, and his reason. It sets man apart from the rest of creation and is responsible for a number of specifically human problems. It is the ground of his hope when it shows man the indeterminate possibilities open to him, but it can also be the ground of his despair and frustration when it shows him what he actually is. It holds the key to an understanding of man's freedom and anxiety and therefore to his salvation or damnation as well. It involves him in a perplexing and perpetual dialogue (a) with himself, (b) with other people, (c) with some power or center of meaning or God beyond himself. It prevents him from being mere animal. He can be greater than animal; he can be worse than animal; but because he is self-conscious he cannot be mere animal. It does not allow him simply to be. He must be someone. It does not allow him simply to live. It requires that he have a reason for living. The spirit is therefore perhaps the most important single concept to understand in developing a doctrine of man.

Since man can and does make value judgments about himself, he may be deeply troubled by the gap between what he is and what he ought to be. To be thus disturbed is to be aware of the tension that commonly exists in the depths of our being.

First, we are never more than a limited particle of the creation, yet we must reckon with the whole of it. We are tied down to a particular time and place, involved in conflict, change, and disorder, conscious that we and our creations are mortal and come to an end. But this is not the whole story and we are never satisfied with it. The fact that we know we are limited indicates that we have in some sense transcended our limitation and have a living connection with infinitely more that is hidden beyond our horizon. Because we are aware of a potential beyond the actual, we live toward an order beyond our disorder, a harmony beyond our conflict, a perfection beyond our imperfection. We try to bring the whole of life under some system of meaning and purpose. We set for ourselves ideals, moral codes, and goals and create social and political structures that will embody them or enable us to achieve them. However, the very tools we use in this effort—our reason, our memory, our foresight—are themselves limited and distorted because they remain our reason, our memory, our foresight. Though we want to do what is right and seek to know the truth, nobody can possibly be all right or know all. We never have more than a one-sided view, for we always see life from one particular place and with some particular interest. The very structure of our being requires that "to be something is not to be something else, to be here is not to be there," to be a boy is not to think like a man, to be a man is perhaps not to think like a child. We spend our life, as it were, on the sides of a mountain whose top runs up into unreachable infinity. We are never on the top where we see the whole view. That is why in a perplexing situation we instinctively say, "God only knows." We human beings always have the view from our side of the hill where we live, and while our view may be logical, consistent, and true to us, it is never as objective as we think it is and may be diametrically opposed to the view of another man who is equally convinced that his is logical, consistent, and true. There is always our side which is partly true and partly distorted, the other man's side, which is true from his point of view and therefore distorted, and then there is the top view which is never possessed by man, which contains the total truth and the total possibilities. The last word about anything is never with limited man.

This understanding of life is not to be confused with a cynical relativism which would deny us the right to say that a free democratic society is better than a police state, and would argue that "it all depends on how you look at it." We are simply restating what the Bible points to in the line "My ways are higher than your ways," which means that man can never exhaust the possibilities for new truth and that he should continually subject the truth which he has to a higher judgment than his own. This attitude characterizes the man with an open mind. To use the word "open" in this way is to acknowledge the limitations of man's mind but at the same time to affirm his relation to a source of truth beyond him. The closed mind wants a final, definite solution to the ambiguities of life and is unable to see that every question answered creates a new situation which challenges the adequacy of the old answer.

There is a second tension which characterizes our lives. On the one hand, both our environment and impulses hidden in our subconscious have a determining effect upon the way we act. On the other hand, most of us have the ability to make decisions and determine the responses we shall make to the problems that confront us.

Our physical body imposes some limitations on our freedom which are important to consider. It ties us to the animal world and makes us subject to the laws of nature. Our body confines us to one place at a time. It wants food, clothes, shelter, and since these things cost money and are unevenly distributed in the world, we become involved in competition with our fellow men. Our body affects our freedom in another way, for its very shape and condition may keep us from doing what we would like to do. In any case, the body is normally no more than a conditioning factor, influencing but not causing the decisions we make.

This free alternative must be experienced; it can never be quite defined in abstract terms. Whenever we make a choice, we understand from the inside what it means to be free. Provided we are sane, we can always consider our conditions, measure one stimulus against another, and weigh the difference between an immediate good and a remote good. Then again after considering, we can make a decision, knowing that every decision cuts off a multitude of other decisions. It shuts many doors that might have been opened. And finally we have to commit our life in some act. Under any conditions our considered decisive action is our own idea and our own responsibility. What we make of ourselves is, of course, greatly influenced by the stuff we have to work with. That is what ties our freedom to something substantial in the practical world. Like members of an orchestra we must contribute to a combined result while confined to the particular instrument which we are able to play.

The third tension is seen in the fact that we are separate, distinct individuals but are able to fulfill our individuality only when we participate in a community. Each of us has a responsibility to himself to develop his own capacities to the full, but he cannot do this without becoming involved directly or indirectly in the lives of others. The Bible emphasizes the individual's primary allegiance to God yet defines that allegiance in terms of concern for the neighbor. What each man is or does makes a difference to the community and what the community does affects the lives of all its members.

In this paragraph Niebuhr gives a useful definition of the difference between man and animal that hinges on man's self-awareness and freedom.

REINHOLD NIEBUHR

The human self is different from other creatures in two respects: 1) It is able by its freedom to transmute nature's survival impulse into more potent and more destructive, more subtle and more comprehensive forms of self-seeking than the one-dimensional survival impulse of nature. 2) It is able to envisage a larger good than its own preservation, to make some fitful responses to this more inclusive obligation and to feel itself guilty for its failure to make a more consistent response. Every animal will run as fast as it can from a superior foe, a strategy which subjects human beings to the charge of cowardice. Naturalists may argue that human actions have been reduced to the level of "physical events" to which no praise or blame can be attached because they always have "sufficient antecedents." But the common sense of mankind has never accepted this ridiculous denial of a unique freedom in human life and of a consequent responsibility and guilt in human action.[2]

Here Fromm points to an important consequence of man's self-awareness, namely, his recognition of his aloneness, his helplessness, his disunited existence which drives him to strive for union.

ERICH FROMM

While we find love, or rather, the equivalent of love, in animals, their attachments are mainly a part of their instinctual equipment; only remnants of this instinctual equipment can be seen operating in man. What is essential in the existence of man is the fact that he has emerged from the animal kingdom, from instinctive adaptation, that he has transcended nature—although he never leaves it; he is a part of it—yet once torn away from nature, he cannot return to it. . . . Man is gifted with reason; he is *life being aware of itself*; he has awareness of himself, of his fellow man, of his past, and of the possibilities of his future. This awareness of himself as a separate entity, the awareness of his own short life span, of the fact that without his will he is born and against his will he dies, . . . the awareness of his aloneness and separateness, of his helplessness before the forces of nature and of society, all this makes his separate, disunited existence an unbearable prison. . . . The awareness of human separation, without reunion by love—is the source of shame. It is at the same time the source of guilt and anxiety.

Man of all ages and cultures is confronted with the solution of one and the same question: the question of how to overcome separateness, how to achieve union, how to transcend one's own

[2] REINHOLD NIEBUHR, *Faith and History* (New York, 1949), p. 95.

individual life and find at-onement . . . the question is the same, for it springs from the same ground: the human situation, the conditions of human existence. . . . While there are many answers—the record of which is human history—they are nevertheless not innumerable. On the contrary, as soon as one ignores smaller differences which belong more to the periphery than to the center, one discovers that there is only a limited number of answers which have been given, and only could have been given by man in the various cultures in which he has lived.[3]

Man's self-awareness is closely related to the question of his freedom. A person might ask himself whether he was living his life in the sense of acting out of his own inner integrity and conviction or he was simply driven, others living their lives through him.

Because man is able to be aware of himself, he becomes conscious of the variety of roles he might play in his world. Yet in the face of the complexities of modern life he may become confused about what to be. He may panic and become hostile if he feels himself being swept along by a society that seems neither to recognize him nor need him. Or if he finds that his feelings and desires do not seem to make the least difference in his world, he retreats from feeling and wanting into apathy. The technical term for this basic confusion about our identity and our reason for living is "anxiety." It is the feeling of being threatened without knowing how to cope with the danger. Going into a room full of strangers tends to make us "anxious"; we don't quite know how to act, and precisely because we are not sure what to expect or what is expected, we generally do something ridiculous. We try to protect "ourselves" by hiding our real feelings, or possibly by anesthetizing the problem with alcohol. Anxiety has its positive side. It is a sign of the inner life of the self struggling to acquire the courage to be a real self. If a man is

[3] ERICH FROMM, *The Art of Loving* (New York, 1956), pp. 7, 8, 9, 10.

willing to face the pain of this struggle, perhaps he can find resources by which to accept himself for what he is and begin to live his own life.

In the following passage Roberts discusses some of the problems arising from man's awareness. He points to aspects of our culture that are productive of "phony" relationships and "phony" people, that incline us to present a false front to the world rather than "be ourselves."

DAVID E. ROBERTS

One of the most ominous features of contemporary life is the feeling of fatalism on the part of the individual. He tends to assume that his future lies wholly in the hands of forces which he cannot direct at all, or can influence only to an insignificant degree. This assumption reflects another one, namely, that what determines his security or insecurity, his success or failure, the worth or futility of his life, is something outside himself. He is at the mercy of fortune. Modern man's substitute for Fate is largely to be found in those dehumanised mass forces which sweep peoples into depressions, totalitarianism and war. The greatest threat to human existence is no longer nature; to an enormous extent science has made it possible to use nature for human ends. The greatest threat is man himself—his untamed irrational drives, his cruelty, his capacity for collective self-deception and mistrust.

* * *

We cannot have the high potentialities of human nature without the attendant risks. If the goods of a cultural heritage must be transmitted through the development of each new person, then evils—emotional disorders, prejudices, unjust social and economic patterns, deeply rooted national hatreds—can be transmitted and perpetuated in the same way.

Another risk arises from the fact that human beings are

poor, as compared with animals, in instinctual equipment because intelligence is destined to play such a dominant role.... An instinct "works" for an animal only so long as the environmental conditions to which it is suited remain relatively stable; if things go wrong only a few of the higher animals can employ a measure of problem-solving in getting themselves out of the predicament. But man is able to remember the past, anticipate the future, understand causal connections, employ universal notions, follow out logical implications, adapt himself to an infinite variety of changing circumstances, identify himself as a self-conscious person distinct from others, organize his communities by means of symbols and ideas, and enrich his life through creative imagination. One cannot have these potentialities without increasing the number of ways in which things can go awry. From the point of view of producing, maintaining, and enjoying a cultural heritage, human consciousness is utterly indispensable. But from the point of view of fitting neatly into the endless round of nature's cycle—birth, struggle for survival, instinctual routine, maturation, reproduction, and death—human consciousness might almost be described as a nuisance.... [It is this "nuisance"] which makes man a center of good and evil. Nature can afford to be heedless of the individual; man injures his "human-ness" if he becomes thus heedless. Animals kill when they are hungry or threatened; but man can kill with calculated cruelty, and instead of killing physically he can violate the mind, the personality, of another. Whereas an animal can be only an animal, man, because he has the potentialities just described, can fall into physical and moral caricatures of his own nature; he can miss, in important respects, what it means to be human; he can become worse than an animal.

* * *

We have already examined some of the cultural conditions which explain why so many of us fail to discover that each person must play a decisive part in achieving (or missing) beatitude by what he *is*. We seek answers to the meaning of life by means of acquiring wealth, power, pleasure, popularity and any number of other things. All of these things, so long as they are external, leave us at the mercy of circumstances and in the power of others. If the basis for the worth of a man's existence does not lie within him, then the significance of his life can be destroyed by forces beyond his control. The net result is deep-seated anxiety. Such anxiety may cause endless attempts to tighten one's grip upon property and power; but these expedients can do no more than evade the problem; they cannot eradicate it. Usually, the more desperately one places one's eggs in such baskets, the more vulnerable he is. Feverish effort may drive a sense of emptiness and lostness out of consciousness; but the emptiness is therefore all the more acute at the core. The disruption is sure to be serious once strategies for keeping the emptiness out of sight have broken down. This sense of emptiness, lostness and isolation, which is so prevalent in contemporary life, is symptomatic of the fact that human resources for self-possession are not being adequately employed. Far too often we strive to meet the problem by *having* something significant instead of by *becoming or being* something significant.[4]

Here we can see how Reinhold Niebuhr's analysis of self-consciousness and anxiety expresses the religious dimension of the themes Fromm and Roberts have been discussing. He speaks of the "essential homelessness" of the human spirit by which he means that man must look beyond himself and the world in order to understand himself. It is this homelessness that for Niebuhr is the source of man's anxiety. As Augustine put it, "Our hearts are restless until they find their rest in Thee." When anxiety is viewed from the Biblical perspective, it is seen as the "internal description of the state of temptation." Man is anxious because he knows he is limited and dependent, a creature; yet at the

[4] DAVID E. ROBERTS, *Psychotherapy and A Christian View of Man* (New York, 1950), pp. 7, 15–16, 46–47.

same time he is anxious because he does not know the limits of his possibilities. He does not like to live in tension with a truth and purpose he cannot control. He is therefore tempted to deny his finiteness (play God) or escape from the responsibility of freedom, both of which alternatives are included in the definition of sin discussed in Section 2 of this part.

REINHOLD NIEBUHR

The obvious fact is that man is a child of nature, subject to its vicissitudes, compelled by its necessities, driven by its impulses, and confined within the brevity of the years which nature permits its varied organic forms, allowing them some, but not too much, latitude. The other less obvious fact is that man is a spirit who stands outside of nature, life, himself, his reason and the world. . . .

This essential homelessness of the human spirit is the ground of all religion; for the self which stands outside itself and the world cannot find the meaning of life in itself or the world.

. . . Man, being both free and bound, both limited and limitless, is anxious. Anxiety is the inevitable concomitant of the paradox of freedom and finiteness in which man is involved. . . . It is the inevitable spiritual state of man. . . . Anxiety is the internal description of the state of temptation. . . . Yet anxiety is not sin. It must be distinguished from sin partly because it is its precondition and not its actuality, and partly because it is the basis of all human creativity. . . . Man is anxious not only because his life is limited and dependent . . . he is also anxious because he does not know the limits of his possibilities. He can do nothing and regard it perfectly done, because higher possibilities are revealed in each achievement. . . . There are, of course, limits but it is difficult to gauge them from any immediate perspective.

Obviously, the basic source of temptation . . . resides in the inclination of man either to deny the contingent character of his existence (in pride and self-love) or to escape from his freedom (in sensuality). Sensuality represents an effort to escape from his freedom and the infinite possibilities of spirit by becoming lost in the detailed processes, activities and interests of existence, an effort which results inevitably in unlimited devotion to limited values. Sensuality is man "turning inordinately to mutable good." (Aquinas)[5]

[5] Reinhold Niebuhr, *The Nature and Destiny of Man* (New York, 1943), pp. 3-4, 14, 194-196.

MAN AGAINST HIMSELF: SIN AND EVIL

What is it that drives some sensitive souls to despair? What is it that shatters so many schemes of meaning that man has fashioned in order to make sense out of his existence? Surely it is none other than the mystery of iniquity, what Herman Melville described as "those malicious agencies some deep men feel eating in them, till they are left living on with half a heart and half a lung . . . all that most maddens and torments; all that stirs up the lees of things; all truth with malice in it; all that cracks the sinews and cakes the brain; all the subtle demonisms of life and thought; all evil. . . ."

The dilemma produced by a full awareness of evil must be faced for any adequate appraisal of the human situation. Few men have described it with such stark clarity and honesty as Dostoyevsky, and in this dialogue between Ivan Karamazov and his younger brother, Alyosha, one sees Ivan struggling, as Job struggled, with realities so terrible that although he claimed he believed in God, "His wisdom, His purpose—which are utterly beyond our ken," yet he confesses to his brother, "In the final result I don't accept this world of God's, and, although I know it exists, I don't accept it at all."

Alyosha, who is a novice in a monastery, asks Ivan for an explanation of his rejection of the world. Ivan's reply suggests something of the agony that hides beneath his good humor.

"To be sure I will, it's not a secret, that's what I've been leading up to. Dear little brother, I don't want to corrupt you or turn you from your stronghold, perhaps I want to be healed by you."

The following selections represent only a portion of Ivan's argument, which culminates in his story of "The Grand Inquisitor." Ivan is speaking.

FYODOR DOSTOYEVSKY

"You asked me just now what I was driving at. You see, I am fond of collecting facts, and, would you believe it, I even copy anecdotes of a certain sort from newspapers and books, and I already got a fine collection. . . .

"Our historical pastime is the direct satisfaction of inflicting pain. There are lines in Nekrassov describing how a peasant lashes a horse on the eyes, 'on its meek eyes,' every one must have seen it. It's peculiarly Russian. He describes how a feeble little nag had foundered under too heavy a load and cannot move. The peasant beats it, beats it savagely, beats it at last not knowing what he is doing in the intoxication of cruelty, thrashes it mercilessly over and over again. 'However weak you are, you must pull, if you die for it.' The nag strains, and then he begins lashing the poor defenceless creature on its weeping, on its 'meek eyes.' The frantic beast tugs and draws the load, trembling all over, gasping for breath, moving sideways, with a sort of unnatural spasmodic action. . . . But that's only a horse, and God has given horses to be beaten. . . . But men, too, can be beaten. A well educated, cultured gentleman, and his wife beat their own child with a birch-rod, a girl of seven. I have an exact account of it. The papa was glad that the birch was covered with twigs. 'It stings more,' said he, and so he began stinging his daughter. I know for a fact there are people who at every blow are worked up to sensuality, to literal sensuality, which increases progressively at every blow they inflict. They beat for a minute, for five minutes, for ten minutes, more often and more savagely. The child screams. At last the child cannot scream, it gasps,

'Daddy! daddy!' By some diabolical unseemly chance the case was brought into court. A counsel is engaged. The Russian people have long called a barrister 'a conscience for hire.' The counsel protests in his client's defence. 'It's such a simple thing,' he says, 'an everyday domestic event. A father corrects his child. To our shame be it said, it is brought into court.' The jury, convinced by him give a favorable verdict. The public roars with delight that the torturer is acquitted. . . . Charming pictures.

"But I've still better things about children. . . . You see, I must repeat again, it is a peculiar characteristic of many people, this love of torturing children. . . . It's just their defencelessness that tempts the tormentor, just the angelic confidence of the child who has no refuge and no appeal, that sets his vile blood on fire. In every man, of course, a demon lies hidden—the demon of rage, the demon of lustful heat at the screams of the tortured victim, the demon of lawlessness let off the chain. . . ."

[*Ivan then tells about a little girl of five who was beaten, kicked, thrashed, and finally locked in a privy all night in the frost and cold, her face smeared and her mouth filled with excrement all because she did not ask to be taken up at night. After describing the mother's sleeping while the child weeps and prays to "dear, kind God to protect her," Ivan turns on his brother and asks,*]

"Do you understand that, friend and brother, you pious and humble novice? Do you understand why this infamy must be and is permitted? Without it, I am told, man could not have known good and evil. Why should he know that diabolical good and evil when it costs so much? . . .

"One picture, only one more, because it's so curious. . . . It was in the darkest days of serfdom at the beginning of the century. . . . There was in those days a general of aristocratic connections . . . one of those men . . . who, retiring from the service into a life of leisure, are convinced that they've earned absolute power over the lives of their subjects. . . . One day a serf boy, a little child of eight, threw a stone in play and hurt the paw of the general's favourite hound. 'Why is my favourite dog lame?' He is told that the boy threw a stone that hurt the dog's paw. 'So you did it.' The general looked the child up and down. 'Take him.' He was taken—taken from his mother and kept shut up all night. Early that morning the general comes out on horse-back, with the hounds, his dependents, dog-boys, and huntsmen, all mounted around him in full hunting parade. The servants are summoned for their edification, and in front of them all stands the mother of the child. The child is brought from the lockup. ... The general orders the child to be undressed; the child is stripped naked. He shivers, numb with terror, not daring to cry. ... 'Make him run,' commands the general. 'Run! run!' shout the dog-boys. The boy runs.... 'At him!' yells the general, and he sets the whole pack of hounds on the child. The hounds catch him, and tear him to pieces before his mother's eyes! ... Well—what did [the general] deserve? To be shot? To be shot for the satisfaction of our moral feelings? Speak, Alyosha!"

"To be shot," murmured Alyosha, lifting his eyes to Ivan with a pale, twisted smile.

"Bravo!" cried Ivan delighted. "If even you say so.... You're a pretty monk! So there is a little devil sitting in your heart, Alyosha Karamazov!"

"What I said was absurd, but—"

"That's just the point, that 'but'!" cried Ivan. "Let me tell you, novice, that the absurd is only too necessary on earth.... Listen! I took the case of the children only to make my case clearer. Of the other tears of humanity with which the earth is soaked from its crust to its center, I will say nothing. I have narrowed my subject on purpose. I am a bug, and I recognise in all humility that I cannot understand why the world is arranged as it is. Men are themselves to blame, I suppose; they were given paradise, they wanted freedom, and stole fire from heaven, though they knew they would become unhappy, so there is no need to pity them. With my pitiful, Euclidian understanding, all I know is that there is suffering and that there are none guilty; that cause follows effect, simply and directly; that everything flows and finds its level—but that's only Euclidian nonsense, I know that, and I can't consent to live by it! What comfort is it to me that there are none guilty and that cause follows effect simply and directly, and that I know it—I must have justice, or I will destroy myself. And not justice in some remote infinite time and space, but here on earth, and that I could see for myself. I have believed in it. I want to see it, and if I am dead by then, let me rise again, for if it all happens without me, it will be too unfair. . . . I want to be there when every one suddenly understands what it has all been for. All the religions of the world are built on this longing, and I am a believer. But then there are the children, and what am I to do about them? That's a question I can't answer. . . . Listen! If all must suffer to pay for the eternal harmony, what have children to do with it, please? It's beyond all comprehension why they should suffer and why they should pay for the harmony. . . . It's not worth it, because those tears are unatoned for. They must be atoned for, or there can be no harmony. But how? How are you going to atone for them? Is it possible? By their being avenged? But what do I care for avenging them? What do I care for a hell for oppressors? What good can hell do, since those children have already been tortured? And what becomes of harmony if there is hell? I want to forgive. I want to embrace. I don't want more suffering. And if the sufferings of children go to swell the sum of sufferings which was necessary to pay for truth, then I protest that the truth is not worth such a price. I don't want the mother to embrace the oppressor who threw her son to the dogs! She dare not forgive him! . . . If that is so, if they dare not forgive, what becomes of harmony? Is there in the whole world a being who would have the right to forgive and could forgive? I don't want harmony. From love of humanity I don't want it. I would rather be left with the unavenged suffering. I would rather remain with my unavenged suffering and unsatisfied indignation, *even if I were wrong. . . .*"

73

"That's rebellion," murmured Alyosha, looking down.

"Rebellion? I am sorry you call it that," said Ivan earnestly. "One can hardly live in rebellion, and I want to live. Tell me yourself, I challenge you—answer. Imagine you are creating a fabric of human destiny with the object of making men happy in the end, giving them peace and rest at last, but that it was essential and inevitable to torture to death only one tiny creature—that baby beating its breast with its fist, for instance—and to found that edifice on its unavenged tears, would you consent to be the architect on those conditions? Tell me. Tell me the truth."

"No, I wouldn't consent," said Alyosha softly.

"And can you admit the idea that men for whom you are building it would accept their happiness on the foundation of the unexpiated blood of a little victim? And accepting it would remain happy for ever?"

"No, I can't admit it. Brother," said Alyosha suddenly, with flashing eyes, "you said just now, is there a being in the whole world who would have the right to forgive and could forgive? But there is a Being and He can forgive everything, all and for all, because He gave His innocent blood for all and everything. You have forgotten Him, and on Him is built the edifice, and it is to Him they cry aloud, 'Thou art just, O Lord, for Thy ways are revealed!'"

"Ah! the One without sin and His blood! No I have not forgotten Him; on the contrary I've been wondering all the time how it was you did not bring Him in before, for usually all arguments on your side put Him in the foreground." [6]

Almost anyone would be prepared to say that man isn't what he should be, but there is serious disagreement over why this is so. It is precisely around this problem of human perversity, sin, evil—whatever name you want to give it—that most

[6] FYODOR DOSTOYEVSKY, *The Brothers Karamazov* (New York, Modern Library edition), pp. 284–292.

humanist and religious thinkers part company. Furthermore one's concept of salvation or human fulfillment is pretty much determined by the way one accounts not only for the evil that men do but also for the curious unwillingness, or inability, or blindness that accompanies man's attempt to change for the better.

Some argue that man is corrupted by his social environment —slums, money, crime, comics, private property—things or conditions outside the self which twist or pull the basically good self out of shape. Others claim it is man's ignorance and limited understanding that lead him into miscalculations and errors which work injustice and evil among his fellows. Still others suggest that the evils men do are prompted by the physical, animal impulses in man and that he can scarcely be blamed for not having evolved further from his ancestors in the trees.

Theological opinion generally finds these explanations too simple. They feel that there is a profound mystery about human evil which is only partially grasped in these views. They have been led into some extreme statements in an effort to point to what they believe is the real dilemma of man, namely, that the good he knows, he will not do; but the evil he hates, that he does. Original sin, bondage of the will, total depravity are part of a difficult vocabulary which modern man has perhaps too quickly rejected. Pascal says of the doctrine of original sin, "Nothing offends us more rudely than this doctrine, and yet without this mystery, the most incomprehensible of all, we are incomprehensible to ourselves." (Pensées, 434)

The element of freedom in human nature makes man an unpredictable creature whose life must be understood in terms of "not only but also." We have seen that he is a limited creature but can partly rise above his limitations; that he is partly determined by outside influences but has a free alternative; that he is a self-centered, separate individual but at the same time a social being; and finally, that his communities offer him fulfillment but also frustrate him. It is precisely this contradictory aspect of life which made the biblical writers insist that man's creative drive toward the ideal is possible only when all of life is held under a higher judgment than man's. The Bible does not deny the importance or necessity of self-interest, but it affirms that apart from this judgment, man is tempted to claim that what is best for him is best for all men. So too must the community stand under this judgment because it is tempted by the opposite error of assuming too easily that what serves the interests of the state is best for the individual.

REINHOLD NIEBUHR

Actually there is a great mystery in the fact that man, who is so created that he can not fulfill his life except in his fellowmen, and who has some consciousness of this law of love in his very nature, should nevertheless seek so persistently to make his fellowmen the tools of his desires and the objects of his ambitions.[7]

Tillich's passage on the meaning of sin may seem strange to some who are accustomed to use the word to describe any bad act. But it is important to see what he is trying to describe with the term "sin." It is a state of being, an inner disposition of the will. His interpretation of sin as a state of threefold separation is very close to what Fromm was talking about in the last section. When he emphasizes fate, he is suggesting that all men inevitably find themselves in this state. When he emphasizes the sense of guilt that accompanies the state, he is suggesting that sin is grounded in man's freedom and that man is therefore responsible for this separation. A similar understanding of sin is expressed by Roberts at the end of this section and a similar description of the human situation is revealed in Fromm's term "alienation."

[7] Reinhold Niebuhr, *Discerning the Signs of the Times* (New York, 1946), p. 165.

Man Against Himself: Sin and Evil

PAUL TILLICH

Have the men of our time still a feeling of the meaning of sin? Do they, and do we, still realize that sin does not mean an immoral act, that "sin" should never be used in the plural, and that not our sins, but rather our sin is the great, all-pervading problem of our life? Do we still know that it is arrogant and erroneous to divide men by calling some "sinners" and others "righteous"? . . .

I should like to suggest another word to you, not as a substitute for the word "sin," but as a useful clue in the interpretation of the word "sin": "separation." Separation is an aspect of the experience of everyone. Perhaps the word "sin" has the same root as the word "asunder." In any case, *sin is separation.* To be in the state of sin is to be in the state of separation. And separation is threefold: there is separation among individual lives, separation of a man from himself, and separation of all men from the Ground of Being. This three-fold separation constitutes the state of everything that exists; it is a universal fact; it is the fate of every life. And it is our human fate in a very special sense. For *we* as men know that we are separated. We not only suffer with all other creatures because of the self-destructive consequences of our separation, but also know *why* we suffer. We know that we are estranged from something to which we really belong, and with which we *should* be united. We know that the fate of separation is not merely a natural event like a flash of sudden lightning, but that it is an experience in which we actively participate, in which our whole personality is involved, and that, as fate, it is also *guilt.* Separation which is fate and guilt constitutes the meaning of the word "sin." [8]

Here is another selection from Tillich on the nature of sin. In this more extended treatment of the subject, he suggests that

[8] PAUL TILLICH, *The Shaking of the Foundations* (New York, 1948), pp. 154–155.

aspect of the problem which has led many in the Christian tradition to speak of man's enslavement to a demonic power, a loss of self-determination, described by the phrase "bondage of the will." Melville pictured this bondage in Captain Ahab when Starbuck almost persuaded him to give up the pursuit of the white whale and return to home port. Ahab cried out:

"What is it, what nameless, inscrutable, unearthly thing is it, what cozzening, hidden lord and master, and cruel, remorseless emperor commands me; that against all natural lovings and longings, I so keep pushing and crowding, and jamming myself on all the time.... Is Ahab, Ahab? Is it I, God, or who, that lifts this arm?" *

PAUL TILLICH

We experience a power that dwells in us and directs our will against itself.

The name of this power is sin. Nothing is more precarious today than the mention of this word among Christians, as well as among non-Christians, for in everyone there is tremendous resistance to it. It is a word that has fallen into disrepute. To some of us it sounds almost ridiculous and is apt to provoke laughter rather than serious consideration. To others, who take it more seriously, it implies an attack on their human dignity. And again, to others—those who have suffered from it—it means the threatening countenance of the disciplinarian, who forbids them to do what they would like and demands of them what they hate. Therefore, even Christian teachers, including myself, shy away from the use of the word sin. We know how many distorted images it can produce. We try to avoid it, or substitute another word for it. But it has a strange quality. It always returns. We cannot escape it.... And so it would be more honest ... to face it and ask what it really is.

It is certainly not what men of good will would have us

* HERMAN MELVILLE, *Moby Dick*, Chapter CXXXII.

believe—failure to act in the right way, a failure to do the good one should and could have done. If this were sin, a less aggressive and less ugly term, such as human weakness, could have applied. But that is just what sin is *not*. And those of us who have experienced demonic powers within and around ourselves find such a description ludicrous. So we turn to Paul, and perhaps to Dostoyevski's Ivan Karamazov. . . . From them we learn what sin is. And perhaps we may learn it through Picasso's picture of that small Basque village, Guernica, which was destroyed in an unimaginably horrible way by the demonic powers of Fascism and Nazism. And perhaps we learn it through the disrupting sounds in music that does not bring us restful emotions, but the feeling of being torn and split. . . . It is noteworthy that today, in order to know the meaning of sin, we have to look outside our churches and their average preaching to the artists and writers and ask *them*. But perhaps there is still another place where we can learn what sin is, and that is our own hearts.

Paul seldom speaks of sins, but he often speaks of Sin—Sin in the singular with a capital "S," Sin as a power that controls world and mind, persons and nations.

Have you ever thought of Sin in this image? It is the Biblical image. But how many Christians or non-Christians have seen it? Most of us remember that at home, in school and at church, we were taught that there were many things that one would like to do that one should not. And if one did them, one committed a sin. We also remember that we were told of things we should do, although we disliked doing them. And if we did not do them, we committed a sin. We had lists of prohibitions and catalogues of commands; if we did not follow them, we committed sins. Naturally, we did commit one or more sins every day, although we tried to diminish their number seriously and with good will. This was, and perhaps still is, our image of sin—a poor, petty, distorted image, and the reason for the disrepute into which the word has fallen.

The first step to an understanding of the Christian message

that is called "good news" is to dispel the image of sin that implies a catalogue of sins. Those who are bound to this image are also those who find it most difficult to receive the message of acceptance of the unacceptable, the good news of Christianity. Their half-sinfulness and half-righteousness make them insensitive to a message that states the presence of total sinfulness and total righteousness in the same man at the same moment. They never find the courage to make a total judgment against themselves, and therefore, they can never find the courage to believe in a total acceptance of themselves.

Those, however, who have experienced in their hearts that sin is more than the trespassing of a list of rules know that all sins are manifestations of Sin, of a power of estrangement and inner conflict. Sin dwells in us, it controls us, and makes us do what we don't want to do. It produces a split in us that makes us lose identity with ourselves. Paul writes of this split twice: "If I do what I do not want, it is no longer I that do it, but sin which dwells within me." Those who have suffered this split know how unexpected and terrifying it can be. Thoughts entered our mind, words poured from our mouth, something was enacted by us suddenly and without warning. And if we look at what happened, we feel—"It could not have been *I* who acted like this. I cannot find myself in it. Something came upon me, something I hardly noticed. But there it was and here am I. It is *I* who did it, but a strange I. It is not my real, my innermost self. It is as though I were possessed by a power I scarcely knew. But now I know that it not only can reach me, but that it dwells in me."

Is this something we really know? Or do we, after a moment of shock, repress such knowledge? Do we still rely on our comparatively well ordered life, avoiding situations of moral danger, determined by the rules of family, school and society? For those who are satisfied with such a life, the words of Paul are written in vain. They refuse to face their human predicament.

. . . It is dangerous to preach about sin, because it may induce us to brood over our sinfulness. . . . I believe it is possible to conquer the dangers implied in the concentration on sin, if we look at it *indirectly*, in the light of that which enables us to resist it—reunion overcoming estrangement. Sin is our act of turning away from participation in the divine Ground from which we come and to which we go. Sin is turning toward ourselves, and making ourselves the center of our world and of ourselves. Sin is the drive in everyone, even those who exercise the most self-restraint, to draw as much as possible of the world into oneself. But we can be fully aware of this only if we have found a certain level of life above ourselves. Whoever has found himself after he has lost himself knows how deep his loss of self was. If we look at our estrangement from the point of reunion, we are no longer in danger of brooding over our estrangement. We can speak of Sin, because its power over us is broken.

It is certainly not broken by ourselves. . . . Only if we accept with our whole being the message that it *is* broken, is it also broken in us.[9]

Cherbonnier does not like the emphasis some theologians, including Tillich, place upon the inevitability of sin as the tragic state in which men find themselves. He therefore lays greater stress on man's freedom by defining sin as idolatry—that is, man's giving his final allegiance to something less than God.

E. La B. CHERBONNIER

According to the Bible, sin is properly defined as misplaced allegiance or, to use its technical word for it, idolatry. No man is without his "god," in the sense of a focal point around which his life takes its orbit and which imparts a distinctive complexion to his values, purposes, and actions. Christian thinking has tended historically to assimilate the notion of sin as intrinsic to human nature. In the popular mind this is precisely what the phrase

[9] Paul Tillich, *The Eternal Now* (New York, 1963), pp. 50–53, 55–56.

"original sin" connotes. This puts the theologian in the unenviable position of endorsing a view which the Bible itself repudiates. . . .

The awkwardness of the extreme orthodox position is nicely illustrated by its current disadvantage in discussions with thoughtful non-Christians, especially those of a broad humanitarian concern. Having absorbed indirectly the genuine biblical emphasis upon the dignity and worth of man, modern humanists are now obliged to repudiate Christianity in order to defend these principles! When men like John Dewey, Horace Kallen, and Erich Fromm accuse Christianity of devaluating worldly existence and the good things of life, one is embarrassed by how many theological citations they can muster in support of the charge. Little suspecting that the foundation for their own ideals is to be found in the Bible, they abhor the doctrine of sin as an affront to the dignity and creativity of man, a medieval superstition invented by the priesthood to block progress and keep the ignorant in subjection to sacerdotal privilege. . . .

If the tide of argument appears to be running with the humanist, however, his advantage is only temporary. When obliged to defend his position, he encounters formidable difficulties of his own. It is one thing simply to assert the dignity of man but quite another to establish it by argument. His case collapses the moment he is pressed for a rationale. This becomes evident when he confronts the catalogue of atrocities in the past and the present history of the race—that is, when the *fact* of sin stares him squarely in the face. Fearing that to admit the reality of sin would impugn the dignity of man, he searches for an alternative interpretation of the grim realities. His only recourse is to deny on principle that man is even *capable* of sin. But this expedient, by robbing man of his freedom, has the opposite of its intended effect. Instead of preserving human nobility it forfeits it. For, although to commit sin is certainly no compliment, the ability to do so *is*. Only if man *can* do evil is there any meaning in doing good. Only if he is free can creative action be distinguished from destructive.

A perfect illustration of the humanist's dilemma is provided by Erich Fromm's recent book, *Man for Himself*, whose explicit purpose is to construct a humanistic ethic. The author begins with a glorification of human freedom and the creative capacities of man. . . .

His reluctance to recognize the full implications of the human freedom which he sometimes exalts leads the humanist to contract an injudicious alliance. Having hailed science as the liberator of mankind, he credulously embraces a philosophy which purports to be based upon it: not simply science as a method, but the dogma that there is no other method. From the standpoint of this dogma human freedom is neither possible nor desirable. It is not possible, because of the assumption that human behavior can be exhaustively explained in causal terms. It is not desirable because it would introduce an element of incalculability into the scientist's field of study. Man is reduced either to the status of a cog in a machine, whose only distinguishing characteristic is a certain cog-consciousness; or he is submerged in an undertow of biological impulses which make a mockery of his fancied rational intentions. In either case the depersonalization of man is accomplished. . . .

When partisans to the two sides of debate must vindicate themselves by pointing to the other's weakness, then the argument has somewhere taken a wrong turn. It is time to begin again and inquire what false premise has insinuated itself into the thinking of both sides. If such a premise can be detected and replaced, then there is hope of a fresh start, a genuine third alternative which can combine the strength and avoid the pitfalls of the rival factions.

As the foregoing discussion suggests, the error common to both orthodoxy and humanism is the failure consistently to appreciate the fact of human freedom. While the one disregards it

83

in the name of science, the other accomplishes a similar effect by defining sin as a constitutional necessity of human nature, outside the realm of responsibility and freedom.

By contrast, the biblical version of sin as idolatry, or misplaced alligiance, is based squarely upon the fact of freedom. Indeed, it follows from it so inevitably that no one who grants the latter can consistently deny the former. . . . The implication for Christian thought is that there is a biblical wisdom which constitutes its strongest weapon; for the humanist, that the authentic doctrine of sin, far from being opposed to a true humanism, is in fact indispensable to it. . . .

In contrast to the rather optimistic belief that the individual can perfect himself by an effort of will, most of the world's philosophers and many of its artists have taken a radically different view. The majority subscribe to the melancholy doctrine that man's woes are due to the very "conditions of human existence" or to human nature as such.

. . . This sophisticated teaching sometimes succeeds in infiltrating the popular mind itself. Naive common sense is intimidated by the wholly arbitrary claim that any philosophy is superficial which lacks a "tragic sense of life"; in other words, that one must be pessimistic in order to be profound. . . .

Plato's yardstick is the same one which underlies the "determinist's creed": the ideal of perfect "knowability," in the sense of absolute certainty. Knowledge in man's present state is always partial, never certain. Even the wisest and oldest scientist knows only a fraction of what there is to know, and his surest knowledge attains no more than a high degree of probability. This is why the Oriental scoffs at the achievements of Western science as a chasing after wind. . . .

Whoever thus deifies knowledge will discover all manner of grounds on which to convict the everyday world of obstructionism. In addition to his primary target, human freedom, he trains his fire on the mere fact of time, matter in general, the flesh in particular, and all desire whatever. . . .

84

Man Against Himself: Sin and Evil

Philosophers and poets throughout the ages have been nearly unanimous in their lament over man's involvement in the temporal process. It automatically precludes perfect knowledge, for the future is at best only imperfectly anticipated and the past only fragmentarily remembered. The realm of time is the realm of change, whereas the truth is that which never changes. . . .

The man for whom complete knowledge is the ultimate goal resents "the flesh" on the ground that it is the seat of desire. For two reasons he finds desire "undesirable." First, it destroys his precious self-sufficiency. The thirst for knowledge for its own sake always goes hand in hand with the craving for self-sufficiency and indeed often turns out to be simply the means to this end. Desire, by relating a man to something outside himself, makes his happiness dependent upon circumstances beyond his control. Second, desire is incompatible with the idolization of knowledge as the supreme good. By preventing the knower from being completely "disinterested," it introduces a "subjective" factor to distort the clarity of intellectual apprehension. . . .

The field of art and literature is not the only one in which the modern temper reveals a certain animus against human existence. It is implied . . . by the undue exaltation of the scientific method. The scientist who applies it to areas beyond its competence, the description of fact and the explanation of unfree acts and occurrences, is continually frustrated. A personal factor inevitably intrudes upon every controlled experiment. In a value system which regards knowledge as the supreme good, this residual "subjective element" will be resented as the worm in the apple. . . .

For the Bible, creation is good because of who created it. The watershed which separates this view from pessimistic philosophies and religions reflects the difference between their respective gods. When knowledge, conceived in terms of immediate or demonstrable certainty, is deified, the derogation of the world follows. For the Bible, on the contrary, knowledge, though a very great good, is not an end in itself, and indeed is only made perfect when devoted to the right end, the service of agape. Without love, it runs amuck. In St. Paul's words, "If I understand all mysteries and all knowledge . . . but have not love, I am nothing." (1 Corinthians 12:2)

* * *

Two decisive turning points in the history of Christian thought were brought to a head over the question of whether or not sin could be exhaustively defined as the breaking of rules. These were the Protestant Reformation, in the sixteenth century, and the historic controversy between St. Augustine and the British monk Pelagius at the turn of the fourth century. The latter contended that sin was the failure to live up to moral laws. God had made perfectly clear through the Ten Commandments and the Sermon on the Mount what was required of man and how he ought to use his freedom. If he would, man could discipline himself to obey these rules and thereby earn God's favor and assistance in the perfection of his moral nature. It is at once evident that Pelagius's doctrines are still very much alive today. The man in the street, whether nominally a Christian or not, is apt to regard Christianity as essentially a kind of moralism. The difference between Christians and non-Christians appears to him to depend simply on whether one thinks that on the whole this system of "do's" and "don't's" benefits society or, with Dr. Kinsey, that its restrictions are irrelevant and harmful in the twentieth century.

Competition for virtue, even more than competition for money, dries up the springs of sympathy and compassion. The lovelessness of the moralist has become proverbial in much of the world's great literature. In Victor Hugo's *Les Miserables*, Javert's passion for legal justice drives him to the lifelong persecution of one whose nobility of character stands in ironic contrast to his technical guilt before the law.

Nathaniel Hawthorne's *The Scarlet Letter* exposes the way

in which the mask of virtue can provide the perfect disguise for unlovely motives. It discloses the secret gratification with which the Puritan denounces immorality and the vindictiveness with which he demands the miscreant's hide. Modern psychiatry reinforces biblical insights when it discovers the reason why the moralist takes such pleasure in pointing the guilty finger. The intensity of his gratification reflects either the measure of his own inner hostility or the strength of his secret desire for the forbidden fruit which he condemns, while his show of outrage serves to hide this embarrassing fact from both himself and the world.

In the same way any good work *may* be done from an ulterior motive. A financier's contribution to charity may be made simply for the sake of reputation; a diplomat's banquet may be intended to appease or ingratiate; a parent's self-denial may be exploited to induce in the child a hopeless sense of infinite indebtedness. These abuses are encouraged wherever good works are made into an end in themselves. The motives behind them being thereby exempt from criticism, they can operate without detection.[10]

The reason that pride is so destructive is that it corrupts and distorts the very things that make man creative—his ambition, his intellect, and his moral judgment. It transforms his natural ambition into the will to power and the desire for social prestige. He is no longer content simply to satisfy his needs. Just where this natural ambition becomes excessive and cruel is hard to detect. Others see where it is changing him before he does. The natural insecurity of a competitive world accentuates his desire for power to hold his place. But he wants more than this. He wants power over others; he wants to control and manipulate people. He readily assumes that he is good enough to make them subservient and use them to solve his problems without

[10] E. La B. Cherbonnier, *Hardness of Heart* (New York, 1955), pp. 13–17, 68–69, 71, 77–78, 83, 61, 63–65.

solving theirs. Thus pride drives natural ambition straight into injustice toward others. Injustice breeds discontent and generates a new fear—the fear of men.

Intellectual pride has always shown up in tyrannical regimes to bolster the power of the ruling group. Whenever human beings have acquired absolute power to bring in a new social order, they have been tempted to think that their wisdom is sufficient to bring all the issues of life in line with their program. History is rewritten with the bias of a new interpretation. Art and literature are fitted into a propaganda pattern. All teaching is redirected to glorify the state and villify all who oppose it. Book burning and censorship become the order of the day. Science in all its branches must submit its teaching to the criticism of the party. Thus knowledge, which is always incomplete and imperfect, is given a false universality and finality. The control of the press and radio makes it possible for a few limited minds with terrific power to shape the mental outlook of a whole people, Pride, in other words, tempts men to dissolve the mystery of life and get rid of its complexities. It leads them to say, "This is the answer, this is the solution, this is what it all means—nothing but this. What's more, you have to believe it."

REINHOLD NIEBUHR

The secularists and the faithful alike usually fail to see that religion as such is no cure for human pride and pretension. It is the final battleground between pride and humility. There is no form of the Christian faith, no matter how profound its insights about the finiteness and sinfulness of man and the majesty of God, which can prevent some devotees of that faith from using it to claim God too simply as the ally of this or that human enterprise and as the justification for this or that partial human judgment. But these terrible aberrations of faith also can not invalidate the truth of the final insight of Christian faith in which the God is recognized who stands above (and in some sense against) all human judgments; who judges us even while we judge our foe; who completes the drama of history which we always complete falsely because we make ourselves, our culture, and our nation, the premature center of its completion.[11]

Niebuhr's discussion of the Tower of Babel myth is a nice illustration of the way in which an ancient story can express profound truth about the human condition and provide us with a kind of mirror in which we see what we are and what we are doing. In this passage Niebuhr gives us a clear definition of sin. "Man is mortal. That is his fate. Man pretends not to be mortal. That is his sin." It is this kind of pretension that is meant when the word "pride" is used to describe man's sin.

We are deceivers, yet true, when we say that man fell into evil. The story of the fall of man in the Garden of Eden is a primitive myth which modern theology has been glad to disavow, for fear that modern culture might regard belief in it as a proof of the obscurantism of religion. In place of it we have substituted various accounts of the origin and the nature of evil in human life. Most of these accounts, reduced to their essentials, attribute sin to the inertia of nature, or to the defect of reason (ignorance) and thereby either explicitly or implicitly place their trust in developed reason as the guarantor of goodness. In all of these accounts the essential point in the nature of human evil is missed, namely, that it arises from the very freedom of reason with which man is endowed. Sin is not so much a consequence of natural impulses, which in animal life do not lead to sin, as of the freedom by which man is able to throw the harmonies of nature out of joint. He disturbs the harmony of nature when he centres his life about one particular impulse (sex or the possessive impulse, for instance) or when he tries to make himself, rather than God, the centre of existence. This egoism is sin in its quintessential form. It is not a defect of creation but a

[11] REINHOLD NIEBUHR, *op. cit.*, p. 16.

defect which becomes possible because man has been endowed with a freedom not known in the rest of creation.

The Tower of Babel myth belongs to the same category of mythical fancies as the Promethean myth, though the two are independent and not derived from each other. They both picture God as being jealous of man's ambitions, achievements and pretensions. The modern mind, which has exchanged the wooden-headed literalism of orthodoxy for a shallow rationalism, can find no validity in the idea of a jealous God. It either does not believe in God at all, or the God of its faith is so very kind and fatherly as to be really grandmotherly. . . . Yet the idea of a jealous God expresses a permanently valid sense of guilt in all human striving. Religion, declares the modern man, is consciousness of our highest social values. Nothing could be further from the truth. True religion is a profound uneasiness about our highest social values. Its uneasiness springs from the knowledge that the God whom it worships transcends the limits of finite man, while this same man is constantly tempted to forget the finiteness of his cultures and civilisations and to pretend a finality for them which they do not have. Every civilisation and every culture is thus a Tower of Babel.

The pretensions of human cultures and civilisations are the natural consequence of a profound and ineradicable difficulty in all human spirituality. Man is mortal. That is his fate. Man pretends not to be mortal. That is his sin. Man is a creature of time and place, whose perspectives and insights are invariably conditioned by his immediate circumstances. But man is not merely the prisoner of time and place. He touches the fringes of the eternal. He is not content to be merely American man, or Chinese man, or bourgeois man, or man of the twentieth century. He wants to be man. He is not content with his truth. He seeks *the* truth. His memory spans the ages in order that he may transcend his age. His restless mind seeks to comprehend the meaning of all cultures so that he may not be caught within the limitations of his own.

Thus man builds towers of the spirit from which he may survey larger horizons than those of his class, race and nation. This is a necessary human enterprise. Without it man could not come to his full estate. But it is also inevitable that these towers should be Towers of Babel, that they should pretend to reach higher than their real height; and should claim a finality which they cannot possess. The truth man finds and speaks is, for all of his efforts to transcend himself, still his truth. The "good" which he discovers is, for all of his efforts to disassociate it from his own interest and interests, still "his" good. The higher the tower is built to escape unnecessary limitations of the human imagination, the more certain it will be to defy necessary and inevitable limitations. Thus sin corrupts the highest as well as the lowest achievements of human life. Human pride is greatest when it is based upon solid achievements; but the achievements are never great enough to justify its pretensions. This pride is at least one aspect of what Christian orthodoxy means by "original sin." [12]

Man is born into a world that is already corrupted, and he must deal with evils which have been doing a lively business long before he came along. He must work in an imperfect nation with imperfect laws, leaders, political parties, social customs, businesses, and unions. He finds that if he is to live a normal life he cannot avoid sharing in this evil. In fact, he cannot help perpetuating it in some degree no matter how pure his motives or lofty his ideals. If he locks himself in his room and never comes out, he is guilty because he is failing in his obligation to do something about the evil that is bringing injustice upon innocent people. If he comes out of the room and tries to cope with social injustice, he finds he must work "through channels." He decides to vote a man into political office who will clean up the mess. He then discovers he has a choice between two imper-

[12] REINHOLD NIEBUHR, *Beyond Tragedy* (New York, 1937), pp. 11, 27–30.

fect candidates. Of course, he is free to register a protest vote, but he knows this does not really change anything, so he votes for the best man and that man wins. But this man belongs to a party and is not an absolutely free agent. Therefore the voter must share responsibility both for the good that party does and for the evil also.

There is no need to elaborate further. The point is that the individual cannot jump out of the problems of his society and leave responsibility to others, nor can he participate in that society without being involved either directly or indirectly in its evils.

Peter Berger is a Christian whose professional discipline is sociology. In this passage his term "bad faith" is similar in its implications to many of the notions of sin that we have been considering. Pride, self-deception, separation, idolatry are all here. Though his approach is satirical, he is profoundly aware of the evil that infects a society whenever men conspire to hide from their own moral responsibility for their actions. The last paragraph contains an interesting and provocative treatment of the God-man encounter. Consider what he says about the way we seek to establish ourselves in the world, about our reluctance to think of ourselves simply as men.

PETER BERGER

We understand a man to be in bad faith who excuses himself by pointing to his social role and to the ideologies in which the role is enveloped. . . . Bad faith means that society assists us in hiding our own actions from our awareness. . . . Modern bureaucratic procedures provide an excellent occasion for the denial of personal responsibility. However, it would be an error to put all the blame on bureaucracy or to regard bad faith as a peculiar modern invention. . . . Bad faith, in the sense here described, must have been an accompaniment of the earliest human societies. While the modern hangman has, as it were, a more streamlined model of the old thing, the most savage chieftain chopping off a head in the name of a demon of revenge possessing his body is practicing bad faith in just the same sense. We are dealing here with original sin indeed—that is, sin presumably dating from the origins of the human adventure.... Perhaps bad faith is one of the essential ingredients of being human....

It is not necessary to go to the extreme situations of human life in society to see in operation this mechanism of evading the moral questions. For example, the ideologies of occupations provide very much the kind of alibi in economic life that national and military creeds do in wartime, or that the law does in the administration of what is commonly called justice. "Business is business" sums this up fairly well. It means that little Johnny is putting on one of his magic hats and announcing: "I'm not speaking to you as your friend, your neighbor, and your prospective brother-in-law. I'm speaking to you as chairman of the board of this company. As such, I have no option but to say to you what I just said." At which point the Knife falls. The interesting problem, once more, is contained in the words "no option." Now it is perfectly true that there are economic necessities over which our man has no control. It may, for example, be true that he can only stay in business by dumping inferior products under threat of some kind of economic blackmail. That's the way this business is, there's nothing to be done about it, and the alternative is bankruptcy. True enough. This does not change the fact that the man has first of all chosen to go into this kind of business, probably knowing what its economic realities are. What is more important, it is he who accepts and assents to the so-called economic necessities over which our man has no control. If the alternative to blackmail is really bankruptcy, then it is he who chooses not to go bankrupt. Now it may quickly be said that the man could never make the other choice, that he has a family to support, stockholders to face, and so on. Again, true enough. But

93

then let him say honestly that he is performing blackmail for the sake of his family and his stockholders. In other words, between the possibilities of blackmail and bankruptcy, he is opting for the former. It need not be our concern at the moment what the moral implications of this choice are. It is enough to point out that the alibi "no option" will not withstand even a cursory examination. To put this in a different way, all our actions have a price. It is we who decide at what point we agree to be bought. . . .

Bad faith is so important because it is the other side of freedom. Bad faith is the denial of freedom, because it deludes men into thinking that they have no choice in a situation. In reality there are very few situations indeed where the words "no option" are literally true. At the very least, as the Stoics knew, there is the choice of death. If a man chooses not to die he is ipso facto opting to continue living under the particular circumstances of the situation. . . . Most of the situations in which men speak of necessity are actually cases of choice. If necessity means that I must do certain things to succeed, then it is I who choose not to fail. If necessity means doing this if I am not to become an object of ridicule, then it is I who choose to save my face. . . . Bad faith is the denial of this fact.

* * *

The confrontation with the living God of the Christian faith strips men of their alibis and disguises. . . . Every literate man knows that certain positions in society entail responsibilities, privileges, and immunities. There are many books written about this, such as text books of ethics, codes of law, constitutions, and statutes. We would suggest that God, regrettably, has not read any of them. . . . This denuding character of the encounter between God and man is understandable in terms of the Christian doctrine of creation. God created the heavens and the earth. And then He created man. He did not create society. That latter achievement belongs entirely to man's own ingenuity. . . . God addresses man as man and as nothing else. . . . Man enters into the world naked, without a name, without social roles, without involvement in the great institutions. For the remainder of his life he impresses upon others and upon himself the importance of his name, social roles and institutional positions. God remains unimpressed. . . . It goes without saying that the same argument applies to . . . racial, national, or ethnic identifications. Here too we have to do with the illiterate God. Everyone knows very well that we have no choice in certain situations but to act "as white Southerners," "as Americans," "as Europeans," "as Jews," and so on. After all, this is what the social libretto says—here is our name and next to it it says in clear writing "a Jew," "a German," or whatever the play has cast us as. Again it is a great pity that this libretto has not come to God's attention. He thus remains inconsiderately uninterested in our description in the *dramatis personae.* Indeed, it is in the etymologically literal sense of the word (persona=dramatic mask) that God is "no respecter of persons." [13]

For the humanist who finds the word "sin" either meaningless or related only to immorality, "alienation" has become a useful term to describe what the Bible would call the fallen state of man. Too many of us are diverted from the reality by worrying about the word or the beliefs of him who used the word. The image of the "package" is an interesting way of suggesting the loss of freedom that follows upon undue concern for the self's security.

ERICH FROMM

Alienation as we find it in modern society is almost total. . . . Man has created a world of man-made things as it never existed before. He has constructed a complicated social machine to administer the technical machine he built. Yet this whole

[13] Peter L. Berger, *The Precarious Vision* (Garden City, N.Y., 1961), pp. 89, 92–94, 192–194, 196.

creation of his stands over and above him. He does not feel himself as a creator and center, but as the servant of a Golem, which his hands have built. The more powerful and gigantic the forces are which he unleashed, the more powerless he feels himself as a human being. . . . He is owned by his own creation, and has lost ownership of himself.

. . . Each person is a "package" in which several aspects of his exchange value are blended into one: his "personality," by which is meant those qualities which make him a good salesman of himself; his looks, education, income, and chance for success—each person strives to exchange this package for the best value obtainable. Even the function of going to a party, and of social intercourse in general, is to a large extent that of exchange. One is eager to meet the slightly higher-priced packages, in order to make contact and possibly a profitable exchange. One wishes to exchange one's social position, and that is, one's own self, for a higher one, and in this process one exchanges one's old set of friends, set of habits and feelings for the new ones, just as one exchanges one's Ford for a Buick.

. . . Just as a sensitive and alive person cannot avoid being sad, he cannot avoid feeling insecure. The psychic task which a person can and must set for himself, *is not to feel secure, but to be able to tolerate insecurity, without panic and undue fear. . . . Free man is by necessity insecure; thinking man by necessity uncertain.*[14]

Roberts takes up the theme of the bondage of the will. This is a tricky problem that runs through a Christian view of man, particularly Protestant thought. On the one hand, man is exalted over the rest of creation, i.e., created in the image of God to have dominion over the earth; on the other hand, he is seen as creature of the dust, mortal, weak, utterly dependent, though this material, earthy limitation is not understood to be the

[14] ERICH FROMM, *The Sane Society* (New York, 1955), pp. 124–125, 148, 196.

source of evil. Rather, the sin of man is seen in his refusal to accept his creaturely status. To the degree that he uses his freedom to achieve a Godlike independence, security, and certainty, he ironically leads himself into an enslaving dependence, insecurity, and uncertainty. The reason this is hard to express rationally is that the Christian "solution" talks about a kind of dependence, uncertainty, and insecurity that is "perfect freedom."

DAVID E. ROBERTS

If man is caught, not merely by external circumstances beyond his control, but by internal bondage to a predisposition to evil, then how can he take responsibility for the latter? The Christian doctrine asserts that man becomes caught in bondage to his own nature, not because the nature he has received from God is evil, but because man makes it evil himself. . . . The most influential contemporary statements of the doctrine do not contemplate a chronology wherein man started, historically, as good, and then became evil through his own act. They conceive of every human being as finding himself in a setting, from birth to death, wherein he is continually violating his own good nature, not merely because he is ignorant of what he ought to do, or because social and physical influences prevent him from doing what he ought, but because he will not do it. Yet he is so enslaved to this evil will that he cannot unfetter himself by an act of will.

. . . The doctrine . . . has grown up because it has described accurately the situation in which spiritually sensitive men have found themselves; and the more insight they possessed, the more inescapable have such descriptions of their plight become.[15]

He who sees no fault within himself or who is confident that he can correct what faults he finds has not really probed the depths of self-knowledge. But if, like St. Paul, he finds himself

[15] ROBERTS, *op. cit.*, pp. 106–107.

caught in the vicious circle of self-contradiction from which he cannot release himself, he too may ask, "Who shall deliver me?" To have achieved the point where this question is seriously asked is to have gained the readiness to accept the help of resources beyond man. It is the first step that must be taken if one is to find the faith about which the Bible speaks.

PART III

Whence Cometh Our Salvation—
God, Man, or Natural Process?

INTRODUCTION

Part III will examine several ways in which men have be-lieved they could attain their true potentiality or fulfillment. Of course there are some people who reject the notion of salva-tion altogether and see nothing but meaninglessness and futility for man. But anyone who finds any sort of direction or purpose to human existence has a conception of salvation. Salvation means a saving from something, and therefore one's conception of salvation will largely depend on how one has defined the human predicament. For example, if one believes that moral evil is the product of man's social institutions, then one's conception of salvation will involve the abolition or change of those institu-tions. If ignorance is the cause of moral evil, then salvation is to be found through education and perfection of scientific under-standing and control. If cultural lag is to blame, then time alone can save us.

Another way of focusing the issue is to consider whether salvation is a matter of man's knowing and willing, or whether there is a saving power beyond man to which he can turn and from which he can receive help. Does man, in other words, save himself or does he need to be saved? This issue becomes particu-larly clear in those points of view that identify the power of salvation in some way with the power of love. The question to ask is whether man can love on his own initiative or whether he must first be loved. Is love an art to be practiced or a gift to be received which enables man to love?

This same problem arises in connection with overcoming sin and guilt. How does one overcome self-centered pride and achieve humility? How does one get rid of a guilty conscience and gain a sense of genuine self-acceptance? Can one simply forgive oneself? How does one turn what one ought to do into what one wants to do? Is knowing these things to be true and necessary sufficient to change one's motivation and empower one to accomplish them?

Some theological views make man totally dependent upon God for salvation. This is usually a reaction against the notion that man need worship nothing more than himself and the aims of his society. Or it arises as a criticism of moral legalism, which is an attempt to make oneself good by obeying the moral law. Critics of legalism believe it creates only the outward appearance of righteousness and fails to change the inner spirit. However, in avoiding the dangers of legalism and self-sufficiency, such theologies run the risk not only of denying man's freedom and responsibility but also of stifling the creative and healing resources within man himself. On the other hand, those theologies whose chief concern is with building a better world and bringing God's kingdom to earth generally give man a greater role in his own salvation and make him a kind of partner with God in the process of new creation. Such a view emphasizes man's moral responsibility and free choice and plays down the seriousness of man's bondage to sin.

As long as one tries to evaluate these various interpretations purely at the level of statements, it is easy to get totally confused. But if truth is more than a property of statements, if it is instead what is really so regardless of whether anyone has made a statement, then the critic of a statement must go behind the words to the event, the personal experience, the lived reality and see what particular words do justice to the real nature of his experience. For truth is reality, event, participated in by a person before it is a statement. This is why many writers speak of truth as something that is done, something one lives in, something that happens in personal experience and especially in the encounter of person with person. It is something that happens to the whole person and not just to his mind. True being, when it meets us in our lives, compels us to respond with either a serious "yes" or a serious "no." It does not allow us to remain indifferent or uncommitted, and we know that what we are going to become hangs upon our decision. It is this characteristic of our apprehension of truth that is pointed to in the theological concept of revelation which was discussed in Part I. It is also this concept of truth as revelatory event that is at the foundation of religious rituals and sacraments. They become for the participant an outward and visible symbol of an inner, spiritual event.

It is worth noting that a significant number of both religious and secular views of salvation can be adequately described by the word "atonement," which means quite literally "at-one-ment": man at one with himself (inner integrity and wholeness), at one with his neighbor (genuine community and communion), at one with God (living in the power of true being). This is something one experiences here and now in this world. Yet because such fulfillments are fragmentary and incomplete, many people look forward in faith to an ultimate or final fulfillment.

THE INESCAPABLE CHOICE:
GOD OR IDOL

To a remarkable degree the selection from The Brothers Karamazov illustrates directly or by implication all the major themes we deal with in this book. One can see the blindness and self-concern, the unconditional surrender to false values that divides men within themselves and from each other and prevents them from knowing what they are doing. One can see the anxiety that witnesses to the inner struggle of a man who senses the meaning of his life is threatened. And one can see how through a curious constellation of events truth floods in upon a man, making him literally a new being who sees a new world and who enters a new relationship with his fellow man. It is quite clear that as far as Zossima is concerned, he has moved from bondage to freedom, from fear to joy, from hate to love. The question is whether this radical change is something a person can achieve through his own reason and will or whether it is the result of some power beyond him, something that is given to him to which he responds. Both Fromm and the theologians would agree that Zossima has become what a man is created to be, yet they would differ in their analysis of how he arrived at that state. Of course there are those, like the seconds in the story, who would say he has made a fool of himself.

The Inescapable Choice: God or Idol

FYODOR DOSTOYEVSKY

[*The speaker here is Father Zossima, an old Russian monk, who recalls an incident that occurred when he was a young army officer. He had quarreled with a friend over a young lady and was about to fight a duel.*]

It was the end of June, and our meeting was to take place at seven o'clock the next day on the outskirts of the town—and then something happened that in very truth was the turning point of my life. In the evening, returning home in a savage and brutal humour, I flew into a rage with my orderly Afanasy, and gave him two blows in the face with all my might, so that it was covered with blood. He had not long been in my service and I had struck him before, but never with such ferocious cruelty. And, believe me, though it's forty years ago, I recall it now with shame and pain. I went to bed and slept for about three hours; when I waked up, the day was breaking. I got up—I did not want to sleep any more—I went to the window—opened it, it looked out upon the garden: I saw the sun rising; it was warm and beautiful, the birds were singing.

What's the meaning of it, I thought, I feel in my heart, as it were, something vile and shameful. Is it because I am going to shed blood? No, I thought, I feel it's not that. Can it be that I am afraid of death, afraid of being killed? No, that's not it, that's not it at all. . . . And all at once I knew what it was; it was because I had beaten Afanasy the evening before! It all rose before my mind, it all was as it were repeated over again; he stood before me and I was beating him straight on the face and he was holding his arms stiffly down, his head erect, his eyes fixed on me as though on parade. He staggered at every blow and did not even dare to raise his hands to protect himself. That is what a man has been brought to, and that was a man beating a fellow creature! What a crime! It was as though a sharp dagger had pierced me right through. I stood as if I were struck dumb, while the sun was shining, the leaves were rejoicing and the birds were trilling the praise of God. . . . I hid my face in my hands, fell on my bed and broke into a storm of tears. . . . Suddenly my second, the ensign, came in with the pistols to fetch me.

"Ah," said he, "it's a good thing you are up already. It's time we were off. Come along!"

I did not know what to do and hurried to and fro undecided; we went out to the carriage, however.

"Wait here a moment," I said to him. "I'll be back directly. I've forgotten my purse."

And I ran back alone, straight to Afanasy's little room.

"Afanasy," I said, "I gave you two blows on the face yesterday. Forgive me," I said.

He started as though he were frightened, and looked at me; and I saw that it was not enough, and on the spot, in my full officer's uniform, I dropped at his feet and bowed my head to the ground.

"Forgive me," I said.

Then he was completely aghast.

"Your honor . . . sir, what are you doing? Am I worth it?"

And he burst out crying as I had done before, hid his face in his hands, turned to the window and shook all over with his sobs. I flew out to my comrade and jumped into the carriage.

"Ready," I cried. "Have you ever seen a conqueror?" I asked him. "Here is one before you."

I was in ecstasy, laughing and talking all the way, I don't remember what about.

He looked at me. "Well, brother, you are a plucky fellow. You'll keep up the honor of the uniform, I can see."

So we reached the place and found them there waiting for us. We were placed twelve paces apart; he had the first shot. I stood gaily, looking him full in the face; I did not twitch an eyelash. I looked lovingly at him, for I knew what I would do. His shot just grazed my cheek and ear.

"Thank God!" I cried, "no man has been killed," and I

seized my pistol, turned back and flung it far away into the wood.

"That's the place for you," I cried.

I turned to my adversary.

"Forgive me, young fool that I am, sir," I said, "for my unprovoked insult to you and for forcing you to fire at me. I am ten times worse than you and maybe more. Tell that to the person whom you hold dearest in the world."

I had no sooner said this than they all three shouted at me.

"Upon my word," cried my adversary, annoyed, "if you did not want to fight, why didn't you let me alone?"

"Yesterday I was a fool. Today I know better," I answered him gaily.

"As to yesterday, I believe you, but as for today, it is difficult to agree with your opinion," said he.

"Bravo," I cried, clapping my hands. "I agree with you there too. I have deserved it."

"Will you shoot, sir, or not?"

"No, I won't," I said. "If you like, fire at me again, but it would be better for you not to fire."

The seconds, especially mine, were shouting too: "Can you disgrace the regiment like this, facing your antagonist and begging his forgiveness! If I'd only known this!"

I stood facing them all, not laughing now.

"Gentlemen," I said, "is it really so wonderful in these days to find a man who can repent of his stupidity and publicly repent of his wrongdoing?"

"But not in a duel," my second cried again.

"That's what's so strange," I said. "For I ought to have owned my fault as soon as I got here, before he had fired a shot, before leading him into a great and deadly sin; but we have made our life so grotesque that to act in that way would have been almost impossible, for only after I had faced his shot at the distance of twelve paces could my words have any significance for him, and if I had spoken before, he would have said, 'He is a coward. The sight of the pistols has frightened him. No use to listen to him.' Gentlemen," I cried suddenly, speaking straight from my heart, "look around you at the gifts of God, the clear sky, the pure air, the tender grass, the birds. Nature is beautiful and sinless, and we, only we, are sinful and foolish, and we don't understand that life is heaven, for we have only to understand that and it will all at once be fulfilled in all its beauty. We shall embrace one another and weep." [1]

The long selection from the work of Erich Fromm is particularly important as a statement of a humanistic point of view. We can see here how he defines the problem of man and what he believes must be done to overcome it. He says, "To me the concept of God is only a historically conditioned one. . . . But I believe also that the consequences of strict monotheism and a non-theistic ultimate concern with the spiritual reality are two views which, though different, need not fight each other." You may be struck by the many similarities between his point of view and a Christian one. The differences appear if you read with care his analysis of love. Notice how much he relies on man's reason and will power for accomplishing the salvation he describes. He is right in saying that the person who hates himself cannot love others and that our capacity to love others is related to our ability to accept our selves. The heart of the problem lies here. How does one reach self-acceptance? How does one deal with one's own guilt? How does one acquire the courage to be honest with oneself? Theology finds the basis for self-acceptance in the redemptive power of God which the Christian sees incarnate in Christ. To refer back to the Karamazov passage, does Zossima free himself from enslavement to a bad conscience with his own powers or is he delivered by a power that might be described as divine as well as human?

[1] FYODOR DOSTOYEVSKY, *The Brothers Karamazov* (New York, Modern Library edition), pp. 355–358.

The Inescapable Choice: God or Idol

ERICH FROMM

In the development of both Capitalism and Communism as we can visualize them in the next fifty or a hundred years, the process of automatization and alienation will proceed. Both systems are developing into managerial societies, their inhabitants well fed, well clad, having their wishes satisfied, and not having wishes which cannot be satisfied; automatons, who follow without force, who are guided without leaders, who make machines which act like men and produce men who act like machines; men, whose reason deteriorates while their intelligence rises, thus creating the dangerous situation of equipping man with the greatest material power without the wisdom to use it.

. . . No change must be brought about by force, it must be a simultaneous one in the economic, political and cultural spheres. Changes restricted to *one* sphere are destructive of every change.

. . . Man can protect himself from the consequences of his own madness only by creating a sane society which conforms with the needs of man, needs which are rooted in the very conditions of his existence.

. . . When things have truly become his servants rather than his idols, he will be confronted with the truly human conflicts and problems; he will have to be adventuresome, courageous, imaginative, capable of suffering and of joy, but his powers will be in the service of life, and not in the service of death. The new phase of human history, if it comes to pass, will be a new beginning, not an end.

. . . Mental health cannot be defined in terms of "the adjustment" of the individual to his society, but, on the contrary, . . . *it must be defined in terms of the adjustment of society to the needs of man.*

. . . Love is one aspect of what I have called the productive orientation: the active and creative relatedness of man to his fellow man, to himself and to nature. In the realm of *thought,* this productive orientation is expressed in the proper grasp of the world by reason. In the realm of *action*, the productive orientation is expressed in productive work, the prototype of which is art and craftsmanship. In the realm of *feeling*, the productive orientation is expressed in love, which is the experience of union with another person, with all men, and with nature, under the condition of retaining one's sense of integrity and independence.[2]

* * *

Love is an art, just as living is an art; if we want to learn how to love we must proceed in the same way we have to proceed if we want to learn any other art, say music, painting, carpentry, or the art of medicine or engineering.

The process of learning an art can be divided conveniently into two parts: one, the mastery of the theory; the other, the mastery of the practice. . . . there is a third factor necessary to becoming a master in any art—the mastery of the art must be a matter of ultimate concern; there must be nothing else in the world more important than the art. . . . And, maybe, here lies the answer to the question of why people in our culture try so rarely to learn this art, in spite of their obvious failures: in spite of the deep-seated craving for love, almost everything else is considered more important than love—success, prestige, money, power—almost all our energy is used for the learning of how to achieve these aims, and almost none to learn the art of loving.

. . . Man of all ages and cultures is confronted with the solution of one and the same question: the question of how to overcome separateness, how to achieve union, how to transcend one's own individual life and find at-onement. . . . the question is the same, for it springs from the same ground: the human situation, the conditions of human existence. . . .

One way of achieving this aim lies in all kinds of orgiastic states. These may have the form of an auto-induced trance,

[2] ERICH FROMM, *The Sane Society* (New York, 1955), pp. 359–362, 72, 32.

sometimes with the help of drugs. Many rituals of primitive tribes offer a vivid picture of this type of solution. In a transitory state of exaltation the world outside disappears and with it the feeling of separateness from it. Inasmuch as these rituals are practiced in common, an experience of fusion with the group is added which makes this solution all the more effective. . . . As long as these orgiastic states are a matter of common practice in a tribe, they do not produce anxiety or guilt. . . . It is quite different when the same solution is chosen by an individual in a culture which has left behind these common practices.

All forms of orgiastic union have three characteristics: they are intense, even violent; they occur in the total personality, mind and body; they are transitory and periodical. Exactly the opposite holds true for that form of union which is by far the most frequent solution chosen by man in the past and the present: the union based on conformity with the group, its customs, practices and beliefs. . . . One can only understand the power of the fear to be different, the fear to be only a few steps away from the herd, if one understands the depths of the need not to be separated. Sometimes this fear of non-conformity is rationalized as fear of practical dangers which could threaten the non-conformist. But actually, people *want* to conform to a much higher degree than they are *forced* to conform. . . . Most people are not even aware of their need to conform. They live under the illusion that they follow their own ideas and inclinations, that they are individualists, that they have arrived at their own opinions as the result of their own thinking—and that it just happens that their ideas are the same as those of the majority.

This increasing tendency for the elimination of differences is closely related to the concept and the experience of equality, as it is developing in the most advanced industrial societies. Equality had meant, in a religious context, that we are all God's children, that we all share the same human-divine substance, that we are all one. It meant also that the very differences between individuals must be respected, that while it is true that we

111

are all one, it is also true that each one of us is a unique entity.
... It meant that no man must be the means for the end of
another man, that all men are equal inasmuch as they are ends,
and only ends, and never means to each other. . . .

In contemporary capitalistic society the meaning of equality
has been transformed. By equality one refers to the equality
of automatons; of men who have lost their individuality. Equality today means "sameness" rather than "oneness." . . . Contemporary society preaches this ideal of unindividualized equality
because it needs human atoms, each one the same, to make
them function in a mass aggregation, smoothly, without friction;
all obeying the same commands, yet everybody being convinced
he is following his own desires.

. . . A third way of attaining union lies in creative activity, be
it that of the artist or the artisan. In any kind of creative work the
creating person unites himself with his material, which represents the world outside of himself. . . . This, however, holds true
only for productive work, for work in which I plan, produce, see
the result of my work. In the modern work process of a clerk, the
worker on the endless belt, little is left of this uniting quality of
work. The worker becomes an appendix to the machine or to the
bureaucratic organization. . . . The unity achieved in productive
work is not interpersonal; the unity achieved in orgiastic fusion is
transitory; the unity achieved by conformity is only pseudo-
unity. Hence they are only partial answers to the problem of
existence.

The full answer (to the problem of existence) lies in the
achievement of interpersonal union, of fusion with another person in *love*. . . . Mature love is union under the condition of
preserving one's integrity, one's individuality. Love is an active
power in man; a power which breaks through the walls which
separate man from his fellow men, which unites him with others; love makes him overcome the sense of isolation and separateness, yet it permits him to be himself, to retain his integrity. In

love the paradox occurs that two beings become one and yet remain two.

... In the most general way, the active character of love can be described by stating that love is primarily *giving*, not receiving. What is giving? Simple as the answer to this question seems to be, it is actually full of ambiguities and complexities. The most widespread misunderstanding is that which assumes that giving is "giving up" something, being deprived of, sacrificing. ... People whose main orientation is a non-productive one feel giving as an impoverishment. Most people of this type therefore refuse to give. Some make a virtue out of giving in the sense of sacrifice. They feel that just because it is painful to give, one *should* give. ...

For the productive character, giving has an entirely different meaning. Giving is the highest expression of potency. In the very act of giving, I experience my strength, my wealth, my power. This experience of heightened vitality and potency fills me with joy. I experience myself as overflowing, spending, alive, hence as joyous.

The most important sphere of giving, however, is not that of material things, but lies in the specifically human realm. What does one person give to another? He gives of himself ... he gives of his life. This does not necessarily mean that he sacrifices his life for the other—but that he gives him of that which is alive in him; he gives him of his joy, of his interest, of his understanding, of his knowledge, of his humor, of his sadness—of all expressions and manifestations of that which is alive in him. ... Giving implies to make the other person a giver also and they both share in the joy of what they have brought to life.

... Beyond the element of giving, the active character of love becomes evident in the fact that it always implies certain basic elements, common to all forms of love. These are *care, responsibility, respect,* and *knowledge.*

Love is the active concern for the life and the growth of

113

that which we love.... One loves that for which one labors, and one labors for that which one loves.

Care and concern imply another aspect of love: that of responsibility. Today responsibility is often meant to denote duty, something imposed upon one from the outside. But responsibility in its true sense is an entirely voluntary act; it is my response to the needs, expressed or unexpressed, of another human being.

Responsibility could easily deteriorate into domination and possessiveness were it not for a third component of love, respect. Respect means the concern that the other person should grow and unfold as he is. Respect thus implies the absence of exploitation. I want the loved person to grow and unfold for his own sake, in his own ways, and not for the purpose of serving me.... It is clear that respect is possible only if I have achieved independence.... Respect exists only on the basis of freedom.

To respect a person is not possible without knowing him; care and responsibility would be blind if they were not guided by knowledge. Knowledge would be empty if it were not motivated by concern ... the knowledge which is an aspect of love is one which does not stay at the periphery but penetrates to the core. ...I may know, for instance, that a person is angry even if he does not show it overtly; but I may know him more deeply than that ... then I know that his anger is only a manifestation of something deeper, and I see him as anxious and embarrassed, that is, as the suffering person rather than as the angry one.

The basic need to fuse with another person so as to transcend the prison of one's separateness is closely related to another specifically human desire, that to know the "secret of man" ... the innermost nucleus which is "he." ... There is one way, a desperate one, to know the secret: it is that of complete power over another person; the power that makes him do what we want, feel what we want, think what we want; which transforms him into a thing, our thing, our possession.

The other path to knowing the "secret" is love.... I know

in the only way knowledge of that which is alive is possible for man—by experience of union—not by any knowledge our thought can give. . . . In the act of loving, of giving myself, . . . I find myself, . . . I discover us both, I discover man. . . . This act transcends thought, it transcends words. It is the daring plunge into the experience of union. However, knowledge in thought, that is psychological knowledge, is a necessary condition for full knowledge in the act of love. I have to know the other person and myself objectively, in order to be able to see his reality, or rather, to overcome the illusions, the irrationally distorted picture I have of him. Only if I know a human being objectively, can I know him in his ultimate essence in the act of love.

Love is not primarily a relationship to a specific person; it is an attitude, an orientation of character which determines the relatedness of a person to the world as a whole, not toward one "object" of love. If a person loves only one other person and is indifferent to the rest of his fellow men, his love is nothing but an enlarged egotism. . . . The most fundamental kind of love which underlies all types of love is brotherly love. By this I mean the sense of responsibility, care, respect, knowledge of any other human being, the wish to further his life. . . . Brotherly love is love for all human beings; it is characterized by its very lack of exclusiveness. . . . [It] is based on the experience that we all are one. . . . If I perceive in another person mainly the surface, I perceive mainly the differences, that which separates us. If I penetrate to the core, I perceive our identity, the fact of our brotherhood. . . .

In contrast to [brotherly love] is erotic love. It is the craving for complete fusion, for union with one other person. It is by its very nature exclusive and not universal; it is also perhaps the most deceptive form of love there is. . . . Because sexual desire is in the minds of most people coupled with the idea of love, they are easily misled to conclude that they love each other when they want each other physically. . . . If the desire for physical union is not stimulated by love, if erotic love is not also brotherly love, it never leads to union in more than an orgiastic, transitory sense. Sexual attraction creates for the moment the illusion of union, yet without love this "union" leaves strangers as far apart as they were before—sometimes it makes them ashamed of each other, or even makes them hate each other, because when the illusion has gone they feel their estrangement even more markedly than before.

. . . It is a widespread belief that, while it is virtuous to love others, it is sinful to love oneself. . . . These questions arise: Is love for oneself the same phenomenon as selfishness, or are they opposites? Furthermore, is the selfishness of modern man really a concern *for himself* as an individual, with all his intellectual, emotional and sensual potentialities? . . . Is his selfishness identical with self-love or is it not caused by the very lack of it?

. . . If it is a virtue to love my neighbor as a human being, it must be a virtue and not a vice to love myself, since I am a human being too . . . love of others and love of ourselves are not alternatives. On the contrary, an attitude of love toward themselves will be found in all those who are capable of loving others. . . . The selfish person does not love himself too much but too little; in fact he hates himself. This lack of fondness and care for himself, which is only one expression of his lack of productiveness, leaves him empty and frustrated. He is necessarily unhappy and anxiously concerned to snatch from life the satisfactions which he blocks himself from attaining. . . . Actually he only makes an unsuccessful attempt to cover up and compensate for his failure to care for his real self.

Now I shall discuss those qualities which are of specific significance for the ability to love. According to what I have said about the nature of love, the main condition for the achievement of love is the overcoming of one's narcissism. The narcissistic orientation is one in which one experiences as real only that which exists within oneself, while the phenomena in the outside world have no reality in themselves, but are experienced only from the viewpoint of their being useful or dangerous to one. The opposite pole to narcissism is objectivity; it is the faculty to see people and things *as they are,* objectively, and to be able to separate this objective picture from a picture which is formed by one's desires and fears.

... The faculty to think objectively is *reason;* the emotional attitude behind reason is that of *humility.* To be objective, to use one's reason, is possible only if one has achieved an attitude of humility, if one has emerged from the dreams of omniscience and omnipotence which one has as a child.... If I want to learn the art of loving, I must strive for objectivity in every situation, and become sensitive to the situations where I am not objective. I must try to see the difference between *my* picture of a person and his behavior ... and the person's reality as it exists regardless of my interests, needs, and fears.... The ability to love depends ... on our capacity to grow, to develop a productive orientation toward the world and ourselves. This process of emergence, of birth, of waking up, requires one quality as a necessary condition: *faith....* What is faith? ... Is faith by necessity in contrast to, or divorced from, reason and rational thinking? ... Rational faith is a conviction which is rooted in one's own experience of thought or feeling. Rational faith is not primarily belief in something, but the quality of certainty and firmness which our convictions have. Faith is a character trait pervading the whole personality, rather than a specific belief.... How does the scientist, for instance, arrive at a new discovery? Does he start with making experiment after experiment, gathering fact after fact, without having a vision of what he expects to find? Rarely has a truly important discovery in any field been made in this way.... At every step from the conception of a rational vision to the formulation of a theory, faith is necessary: faith in the vision as a rationally valid aim to pursue, faith in the hypothesis as a likely and plausible proposition, and faith in the final theory, at least until the general consensus about its validity has been reached.... While irrational faith is the acceptance of something as true only *because* an authority or the majority says so, rational faith is rooted in an independent conviction based upon one's own productive observing and thinking, *in spite of* the majority's opinion.

In the sphere of human relations, faith is an indispensable quality of any significant friendship or love. "Having faith" in another person means to be certain of the reliability and unchangeability of his fundamental attitudes, of the core of his personality, of his love. . . . In the same sense we have faith in ourselves. We are aware of the existence of a self, of a core in our personality which is unchangeable and which persists throughout our life in spite of varying circumstances, and regardless of certain changes in opinions and feelings. . . . Another meaning of having faith in a person refers to the faith we have in the potentialities of others.

The faith in others has its culmination in faith in *mankind*. . . . Like faith in the child, it is based on the idea that the potentialities of man are such that given the proper conditions he will be capable of building a social order governed by the principles of equality, justice and love.

To have faith requires *courage*, the ability to take a risk, the readiness even to accept pain and disappointment. Whoever insists on safety and security as primary conditions of life cannot have faith; whoever shuts himself off in a system of defense, where distance and possession are his means of security, makes himself a prisoner. To be loved, and to love, need courage, the courage to judge certain values as of ultimate concern—and to take the jump and stake everything on these values. . . .

The practice of faith and courage begins with the small details of daily life. The first step is to notice where and when one loses faith, to look through the rationalizations which are used to cover up this loss of faith, to recognize where one acts in a cowardly way, and again how one rationalizes it. To recognize how every betrayal of faith weakens one, and how increased weakness leads to new betrayals, and so on, is a vicious circle. Then one will also recognize that while one is consciously afraid

118

of not being loved the real though usually unconscious fear is that of loving. To love means to commit oneself without guarantee, to give oneself completely in the hope that our love will produce love in the loved person. Love is an act of faith, and whoever is of little faith is also of little love. . . .

The art of loving cannot be restricted to the personal realm. . . . It is inseparably connected with the social realm. If to love means to have a loving attitude toward everybody . . . there is no "division of labor" between love for one's own and love for strangers. On the contrary, the condition for the existence of the former is the existence of the latter. . . . While a great deal of lip service is paid to the religious ideal of love of one's neighbor, our relations are actually determined at their best by the principle of *fairness*. Fairness meaning not to use fraud and trickery in the exchange of commodities and services, and in the exchange of feelings. "I give you as much as you give me" in material goods as well as in love, is the prevalent ethical maxim in capitalistic society. . . .

The Jewish-Christian norm of brotherly love is entirely different from fairness ethics. It means to love your neighbor, that is, to feel responsible for and one with him, while fairness ethics means *not* to feel responsible and one, but distant and separate; it means to respect the rights of your neighbor, but not to love him. . . .

Here, however, an important question arises. If our whole social and economic organization is based on each one seeking his own advantage, if it is governed by the principle of egotism tempered only by the ethical principle of fairness, how can one do business, how can one act within the framework of existing society and at the same time practice love?

I am of the conviction that the answer of the absolute incompatibility of love and "normal" life is correct only in an abstract sense. The *principle* underlying capitalistic society and the *principle* of love are incompatible, but modern society seen concretely is a complex phenomenon. A salesman of a useless com-

119

modity, for instance, cannot function economically without lying; a skilled worker, a chemist, or a physician can. . . . Love is by necessity a marginal phenomenon in present-day Western society, not so much because many occupations would not permit a loving attitude, but because the spirit of a production-centered, commodity-greedy society is such that only a non-conformist can defend himself successfully against it. Those who are seriously concerned with love as the only rational answer to the problem of human existence must then arrive at the conclusion that important and radical changes in our social structure are necessary, if love is to become a social and not a highly individualistic, marginal phenomenon. . . . If man is to be able to love, he must be put in his supreme place. The economic machine must serve him, rather than he serve it. . . . If it is true that love is the only sane and satisfactory answer to the problem of human existence, then any society which excludes, relatively, the development of love, must in the long run perish of its own contradiction with the basic necessities of human nature.[3]

In this short passage Niebuhr puts his finger on the central issue that bothers the theologian about the humanist's point of view. He criticizes the humanist for assuming too readily that if man knows what is wrong and learns what needs to be done, he will do it and will be able to get others to cooperate in the effort. Niebuhr would argue that actually men cling more stubbornly to evil and use their reason to rationalize their interest far more than the humanist likes to admit.

REINHOLD NIEBUHR

When the modern man speaks of mastering human nature, or ordering society, or manipulating historical destiny, he dis-

[3] ERICH FROMM, *The Art of Loving* (New York, 1956), pp. 5–6, 11–18, 20–31, 46–47, 52, 54, 57–61, 118, 120–123, 126–133.

misses the real self with its anxieties and fears, its hopes and ambitions both from the concept of the man who is to become master of historical destiny, and from the picture of the stuff of history which is to be mastered. This real self as a force to be mastered has unique powers of recalcitrance not known in nature; and as the instrument of mastery it is betrayed by confusions not known in pure mind.[4]

Loren Eiseley is a scientist and anthropologist. While he obviously believes that science has contributed enormously to man's understanding and well-being, he is profoundly aware of its limits and its dangers. "Science is not enough for man," he writes. "It is not the road back to the waiting Garden, for that road lies through the heart of man." In this passage he describes how modern man, by drawing false inferences from scientific discoveries, has been tempted to reject the very power that has made him what he is. When man denies this power, he seems to find himself victimized by powers that deny his humanity and threaten him ultimately with destruction. One might consider whether the meaning of destruction is limited solely to the physical existence of man. If being alive means something more than merely existing, then to speak of a creative power as theologians do would mean something more than a physical force that started the universe.

LOREN EISELEY

The educated public has come to accept the verdict of science that man along with the plant and animal world about us, is the product of endless evolutionary divergence and change. In accepting this verdict of science, however, men have frequently failed to inquire in what way human evolution may differ from that of other animals, or by what extra dangers and responsibili-

[4] Reinhold Niebuhr, *Faith and History* (New York, 1949), p. 91.

ties the human brain may be haunted. In the revolt from the fanatical religiosity of past centuries, we have too often welcomed with open arms a dogmatic naturalism which, like the devil with Faust, seemed to offer unlimited material power over nature, while at the same time assuring us that our moral responsibilities were limited and excusable since we were, after all, only the natural evolutionary culmination of a line of apes that chanced to descend upon the ground. . . . Each year the public grows more accustomed to this history, feels more at home in the natural world which it casually assumes to be dominated by struggle, by a dog-eat-dog interpretation of existence which descends to us from the Darwinian period.

[Eiseley quotes a remark by a school science teacher.]

"There are two kinds of people, the tough and the tender minded. The tough minded will survive."

This archaic remark shook me. I knew it was not the product of the great selfless masters of the field, but it betrayed an attitude which demanded an answer. In that answer is contained the whole uniqueness of man. Man has not really survived by toughness in a major sense. Instead he has survived through tenderness. Man in his arrogance may boast that the battle is to the strong, that pity and affection are signs of weakness. Nevertheless . . . the truth is that if man at heart were not a tender creature toward his kind, a loving creature in a peculiarly special way, he would long since have left his bones to the wild dogs that roved the African grasslands. . . .

Man, in the achievement of a unique gift—a thinking brain capable of weighing stars or atoms—cannot grow that brain in the nine months before birth. It is moreover a peculiarly plastic brain, intended to receive impressions from a social world around it. Instinct unlike the case in the world of animals, is here reduced to a minimum. This brain must grow and learn, be able to profit by experience. . . . The demands of learning thus placed upon the human offspring are greater than in any other animal. They have made necessary the existence of a continued family, rather than the casual sex life of many of the lower animals.

Man's first normal experience of life involves maternal and paternal care and affection. It continues over the years of childhood. Thus the creature who strives at times to deny the love within himself, to reject the responsibilities to which he owes his own existence, who grows vocal about "tough mindedness" and the "struggle for existence" is striving to reject his own human heritage. . . .

Family life is a fact that underlies everything else about man—his capacity for absorbing culture, his ability to learn—everything in short that enables us to call him human. He is born of love and he exists by reason of a love more continuous than in any other form of life.

A society has an image of itself, its way of life. This image is a wavering, composite picture reflected from millions of minds. If the image is largely compounded of the events of the present, if tradition is weak, the past forgotten, that image can alter by subtle degrees. A cold "war" such as we are fighting demands great tenacity in democratic institutions. Secrecy grows, technicians multiply . . . the humane tradition—arts, letters, philosophy, the social sciences—threatens to be ignored as unrealistic in what has become a technological race for survival.

Man, unlike the animal, is aware of the nature of his society. His conscious image of it is tremendously important in shaping what it will become. It is this that helps to build a human future, and why the future must be fought for day by day in the lives of innumerable and humble men.

Man, whether he engages in war or not is in a pyramiding technological society whose values are largely directed outward upon things. The important fact in such a material age is that we do not abandon or forget that man has always sought to transcend himself spiritually, and that this is part of his strange heritage. It is a heritage which must be preserved in our schools and churches, for in a society without deep historical memory, the future ceases to exist and the present becomes a meaningless cacophony.[5]

This selection of Cherbonnier's simply points up the inevitability of the choice that confronts all men. It might be of interest to those who think that cynicism is a way of avoiding this choice. It is worth noting his idea that thoroughgoing self-centeredness is impossible because every self has some center of value which the self relies on for meaning. Our hidden, unacknowledged gods are further illustration of the self's capacity for self-deception and confusion.

E. La B. CHERBONNIER

According to the Bible, life confronts every man and nation with a decisive either/or: choose the true God, and live; or choose a false god, and perish. There remains one final device by which men have sought to escape this choice. It is cynicism, the attempt to avoid entanglement with the fickle gods of idealism by espousing none at all. . . .

If the biblical analysis is correct, a thoroughgoing self-centeredness is impossible. Man cannot make himself the sole center of his own life. His freedom necessarily relates him to something beyond himself. The proper diagram of even the most selfish life is therefore not a closed circle but an ellipse with two centers, representing the false god around which the individual makes his orbit. . . .

If this were more widely recognized, Christianity would not make the mistake of championing "selflessness" as the highest good. It could only be so if self-centeredness were the worst evil.

[5] LOREN EISELEY, "An Evolutionist Looks at Modern Man," in *Adventures of the Mind*, Richard Thruelsen and John Kobler, editors (New York, 1959).

But since self-centeredness is not even possible for a free agent, ... the Christian conception of good is not the meaningless goal of "selflessness" but the abandonment of every false god for the true one.

An examination of cynicism reveals exactly what the biblical analysis would lead one to expect. Every cynic turns out to be a covert idealist, in the sense that he does gravitate toward some standard outside himself as the criterion of his decision. Moreover, no matter how different his particular standard is from those of other men, the cynic cannot consistently speak or think of it without calling it "good." In his heart of hearts he really believes that although not commonly recognized as such, or perhaps precisely *because* of this, it is a "better" good than the conventional standards of the average man. In fact, the real motive power behind his apparent lawlessness is generally some hidden virtue. Most often it is the virtue of honesty. Perceiving the hypocrisy of the idealist, he fancies his own disillusioned outlook to be truer to the facts of life. The Communist's self-righteous contempt for "bourgeois idealism" is a familiar illustration. The zeal behind his fanatical denunciations is derived from the hypnotic power of his own "higher" ideal. His counterpart in the history of philosophy is Friedrich Nietzsche. He named his heartless hero after Zoroaster because he stood for "the truth" against the deceit and pretension of the moralist. Another of the cynic's secret virtues may be kindness. Perceiving the vindictiveness with which the pharisee feeds upon the shortcomings of others, he often professes contempt for all morality whatever. Despite his effort at concealment, this kind of cynic turns out to be a sheep in wolf's clothing. In the moment of crisis it may be he who puts into practice what the moralist is content to preach. ...

Perhaps the hardiest garden variety of cynicism is the glorification of rebellion and iconoclasm for their own sake. Man's true greatness, it claims, lies in the consistent defiance of whatever law or custom happens to prevail at the moment. ...

The hidden ideal which pulls the strings of this sophisticated vandalism is not far to seek. It is the liberty and integrity of the individual. It is beneath the dignity of man, so runs the argument, to submit to any externally imposed pattern. Bakunin, for example, for all his revolutionary nihilism, was at the same time a transparent idealist. The destruction which he demanded was a prelude to the flowering of a "more perfect" society of liberty and equality.

Whenever an idol persuades its worshiper to advocate rebellion for its own sake, his betrayal is accomplished. He becomes the victim of an upside-down legalism. The rebel's bondage to the law of nonconformity is quite as real as the legalist's subservience to established norms.[6]

Does man make up the moral order or does he rather discover such an order built in to the structure of human existence? Is everything relative to the time and culture in which it appeared? If one admits the limited character of man's understanding of right and wrong, does this mean there are no absolutes? Perhaps this selection will shed some light on the biblical assertion that there is a reality independent of man and his societies which stands in judgment upon man and upon the answers he has given to the question of right and wrong, something like Amos' conception of the plumb line that God holds in the midst of the people.

C. S. LEWIS

. . . Quarrelling means trying to show that the other man is in the wrong. And there would be no sense in trying to do that unless you and he had some sort of agreement as to what Right and Wrong are; just as there would be no sense in saying that a footballer had committed a foul unless there was some agreement about the rules of football.

[6] E. La B. Cherbonnier, *Hardness of Heart* (New York, 1955), pp. 173–175.

Now this Law or Rule about Right and Wrong used to be called the Law of Nature. Nowadays, when we talk of the "laws of nature" we usually mean things like gravitation, or heredity, or the laws of chemistry. But when the older thinkers called the Law of Right and Wrong "the Law of Nature," they really meant the Law of *Human* Nature. The idea was that, just as all bodies are governed by the law of gravitation and organisms by biological laws, so the creature called man also had *his* law— with this great difference, that a body could not choose whether it obeyed the law of gravitation or not, but a man could choose either to obey the Law of Human Nature or to disobey it.

This law was called the Law of Nature because people thought that every one knew it by nature and did not need to be taught it. They did not mean, of course, that you might not find an odd individual here and there who did not know it, just as you find a few people who are colour-blind or have no ear for a tune. But taking the race as a whole, they thought that the human idea of decent behaviour was obvious to every one.

I know that some people say the idea of a Law of Nature or decent behaviour known to all men is unsound, because different civilisations and different ages have had quite different moralities.

But this is not true. There have been differences between their moralities, but these have never amounted to anything like a total difference. If anyone will take the trouble to compare the moral teaching of, say, the ancient Egyptians, Babylonians, Hindus, Chinese, Greeks and Romans, what will really strike him will be how very like they are to each other and to our own.

... People may be sometimes mistaken about them, just as people sometimes get their sums wrong; but they are not a matter of mere taste and opinion any more than the multiplication table. Now if we are agreed about that, I go on to my next point, which is this. None of us are really keeping the Law of Nature. If there are any exceptions among you, I apologise to them.

Whence Cometh Our Salvation?

... If we do not believe in decent behaviour, why should we be so anxious to make excuses for not having behaved decently? The truth is, we believe in decency so much—we feel the Rule or Law pressing on us so—that we cannot bear to face the fact that we are breaking it, and consequently we try to shift the responsibility. For you notice that it is only for our bad behaviour that we find all these explanations. It is only our bad temper that we put down to being tired or worried or hungry; we put our good temper down to ourselves.

... Isn't what you call the Moral Law just a social convention, something that is put into us by education? I think there is a misunderstanding here. The people who ask that question are usually taking it for granted that if we have learned a thing from parents and teachers, then that thing must be merely a human invention. But, of course, that is not so. We all learned the multiplication table at school. A child who grew up alone on a desert island would not know it. But surely it does not follow that the multiplication table is simply a human convention, something human beings have made up for themselves and might have made different if they had liked?

... When you think about these differences between the morality of one people and another, do you think that the morality of one people is ever better or worse than that of another? Have any of the changes been improvements? If not, then of course there could never be any moral progress. Progress means not just changing, but changing for the better. If no set of moral ideas were truer or better than any other, there would be no sense in preferring civilised morality to savage morality, or Christian morality to Nazi morality. . . . The moment you say that one set of moral ideas can be better than another, you are, in fact, measuring them both by a standard, saying that one of them conforms to that standard more nearly than the other. But the standard that measures two things is something different from either. You are, in fact, comparing them both with some Real Morality, admitting that there is such a thing as a real

Right, independent of what people think, and that some people's ideas get nearer to that real Right than others.

... The law of gravity tells you what stones do if you drop them; but the Law of Human Nature tells you what human beings ought to do and do not. In other words, when you are dealing with humans, something else comes in above and beyond the actual facts. You have the facts (how men do behave) and you also have something else (how they ought to behave). In the rest of the universe there need not be anything but the facts. Electrons and molecules behave in a certain way, and certain results follow, and that may be the whole story. But men behave in a certain way and that is not the whole story, for all the time you know that they ought to behave differently.

Some people say that though decent conduct does not mean what pays each particular person at a particular moment, still, it means what pays the human race as a whole; and that consequently there is no mystery about it. Human beings, after all, have some sense; they see that you cannot have real safety or happiness except in a society where every one plays fair, and it is because they see this that they try to behave decently. ... But as an explanation of why we feel as we do about Right and Wrong it just misses the point. If we ask: "Why ought I to be unselfish?" and you reply "Because it is good for society," we may then ask, "Why should I care what's good for society except when it happens to pay me personally?" and then you will have to say, "Because you ought to be unselfish"—which simply brings us back to where we started.

... It begins to look as if we shall have to admit that there is more than one kind of reality; that, in this particular case, there is something above and beyond the ordinary facts of men's behaviour, and yet quite definitely real—a real law, which none of us made, but which we find pressing on us.[7]

[7] C. S. Lewis, *Mere Christianity* (New York, 1956), pp. 3–7, 10–11, 14–16.

Whence Cometh Our Salvation?

Erich Frank, a Roman Catholic philosopher, suggests that man gains his true freedom only when he recognizes this superior necessity that stands over against man and submits to its law. This is the other side of the notion that idolatry enslaves man.

ERICH FRANK

True freedom is not gained where man, liberated from reality and necessity, finds himself in a vacuum. Truly free is only he who in his subjective freedom can find a true, that is, an essential, content.... Freedom, in so far as it is truly creative and effective, must consist solely in the recognition of a superior necessity and in obedience to its law.[8]

If one is to appreciate what Christians say about the redemptive power of love, it is important that one understand the distinctions that Pike draws here as to the several types of love. There are crucial differences in motivation involved, and unless one sees this, it is difficult to see how anyone could possibly love his enemy.

JAMES A. PIKE

In the Greek there are three words for love: *eros, philia,* and *agapé. Eros* is the hardest to encompass within a definition, because it, of the three, is the least rational in nature. *Eros* is the love of the other because of the other's lovableness (real or apparent). It seeks to possess the other, to have and to hold. While its richest and most ecstatic fulfillment is in the sexual relationship, it is actually much broader, both in its scope and its means of expression. It is not, in fact, limited to persons of the opposite sex or to persons as to whom there might be any

[8] ERICH FRANK, *Philosophical Understanding and Religious Truth* (New York, 1952), p. 131.

130

thought of sexual relationship. We have a degree of *eros* love for many people—parents, friends, and even casual acquaintances—as we respond in respect, enthusiasm, and interest to various aspects of their make-up and personality; we express this love erotically (in a measure at least) in the natural warmth of a handshake or a slap on the back or in the mere desire to be with the other person. Many rational factors affect our responsive decision as to whom we wish to be with, but essentially the response itself is trans-ethical; as we have seen, it cannot be commanded. We like people or we don't, and we like some people much better than we like others.

Normally, of course, *eros* love has its most intense emotional implications in the case of the love of persons of the opposite sex. . . . *Eros* alone is not a dependable basis for marriage or any other sustaining relationship—though, except in unusual circumstances, no marriage should be undertaken without it and no one in a marriage should be content with a situation in which it is not present.

Philia is love for the other because of some third person, object, cause, or interest to which the two are mutually devoted. It too has a broader scope than two persons of opposite sex. It can exist between any two people who are mutually attracted by the same things. It may be that the two are fond of tennis, are wrapped up in some movement, or even share the same hatreds (though the latter is an undesirable, and in the long run destructive, basis for liaison). While this kind of love does have a broad scope, it exists most strongly where there is a basis of permanent tie, and it is especially evident in marriage where almost every event or important interest in the life of one is or can be a concern of the other. But it too is unreliable as a basis of lifelong marriage. Interest can fade; ennui can destroy former enthusiasms; causes can fail or lose their significance. . . .

Agapé is difficult to define, but it can readily enough be described. It can operate all along in a situation, but its character may not be evident when *eros* or *philia* are also in the picture, because they supply sufficient explanation for the love bestowed. But the operation of *agapé* is evident when the other does not appear to be lovable and when mutual interests do not seem to inspire. *Agapé* is a love of the other not because of the other's lovableness, or because of some outside source, but because of the other's *need* of love. It is a concern for the other's best interest when no benefit accrues to the lover and no response is counted on. . . .

This points to what the nature and source of this love really is. All things have a cause, including love. What is the true cause of *agapé* love? It is not what the philosophers call a "final" cause, i.e., it is not something done because of the anticipated result. Nor is there any apparent "effective" cause; there is present neither the lovableness of the object nor the interest in some third person or thing.

We are closer to discerning the true cause of *agapé* when we recognize that this love found its way into Western civilization only through the Judaeo-Christian tradition. The Greek language had no word for it: the word *agapé* was actually an archaic synonym for *eros* which St. Paul and the author (or authors) of the Fourth Gospel and the Johannine epistles "dusted off" (as it were) and used for this new kind of love. In fact, the famous passage in I Corinthians 13 is an elaborate definition of it for a culture that knew nothing of it heretofore. It is this love (translated somewhat quaintly as "charity" in the King James version) that "suffereth long, and is kind . . . envieth not . . . vaunteth not itself, is not puffed up, does not behave itself unseemly, seeketh not her own, is not easily provoked, thinketh no evil; rejoiceth not in iniquity, but rejoiceth in the truth; beareth all things, believeth all things, hopeth all things, and endureth all things." It is this love that "never faileth."

We get a strong hint of its import in the Old Testament book of Hosea. . . . But it is in the New Testament—especially in the central mighty act which it records, the saving passion and death of Jesus Christ—that we see demonstrated most vividly what the source of *agapé* is. Not only in this supreme moment but through His entire life we see God, who in Christ translated Himself into the language of a human life, showing forth *agapé* love toward us: "God so loved the world . . ."

As we have seen, God here takes up the hurt of our situation, takes up the slack between Himself and us, loves us though unlovable, accepts us though unacceptable. Thus the source of *agapé* love is gratitude for the fact that we have already been loved this way. This is why it needs no reward; this is why it does not depend upon the response from the one so loved; this is how it can be based upon the other's need of love and not upon the other's lovableness.[9]

Martin Buber is a Jewish religious philosopher who has had enormous influence on contemporary Christian theology. Here he makes an interesting observation of a change in his own thinking about "religious experience." In his earlier years he had equated the "religious" with the exceptional, the ecstatic, the mountaintop experience in which one is taken out of the ordinary context of life and plunged unexpectedly "into the lightning-pierced darkness of the mystery itself." He held this view until an everyday event proved to him its inadequacy.

MARTIN BUBER

What happened was no more than that one forenoon, after a morning of "religious" enthusiasm, I had a visit from an unknown young man, without being there in spirit. . . . I conversed attentively and openly with him—only I omitted to guess the questions which he did not put. Later, not long after, I learned from one of his friends—he himself was no longer alive—the essential content of these questions; I learned that he had come to me not casually, but borne by destiny, not for a chat but for a

[9] JAMES A. PIKE, *Doing the Truth* (New York, 1955), pp. 147–150.

decision. He had come to me, he had come in this hour. What do we expect when we are in despair and yet go to a man? Surely a presence by means of which we are told that nevertheless there is meaning.

Since then I have given up the "religious" which is nothing but the exception, extraction, exaltation, ecstasy; or it has given me up. I possess nothing but the everyday out of which I am never taken. The mystery is no longer disclosed. . . . I know no fulness but each mortal hour's fulness of claim and responsibility. Though far from being equal to it, yet I know that in the claim I am claimed and may respond in responsibility, and know who speaks and demands a response.

I do not know much more. If that is religion then it is just *everything*, simply all that is lived in its possibility of dialogue. Here is space also for religion's highest forms. As when you pray you do not thereby remove yourself from this life of yours but in your praying refer your thought to it, even though it may be in order to yield it. . . .

In the signs of life which happens to us we are addressed. Who speaks?

It would not avail us to give for reply the word "God," if we do not give it out of that decisive hour of personal existence when we had to forget everything we imagined we knew of God. . . . When we . . . begin to receive the signs, what can we know of that which—of him who gives them to us? Only what we experience from time to time from the signs themselves. If we name the speaker of this speech God, then it is always the God of a moment, a moment God.

I will now use a gauche comparison, since I know no right one.

When we really understand a poem, all we know of the poet is what we learn of him in the poem—no biographical wisdom is of value for the pure understanding of what is to be understood: the *I* which approaches us is the subject of this single poem. But when we read other poems by the poet in the same way their subjects combine in all their multiplicity, completing and confirming one another, to form the one polyphony of the person's existence. In such a way, out of the givers of the signs, the speakers of the words in lived life, out of the moment-Gods there arises for us with a single identity the Lord of the voice, the one.[10]

Dietrich Bonhoeffer was a young theologian in Nazi Germany. For his involvement with the resistance movement he was arrested by the Gestapo, spent two years in jail, and finally was hanged. The various selections from his work that appear here are taken from letters he wrote when he was in prison.

In this passage Bonhoeffer attacks religion from two directions. On the one hand, he feels that "religious" man tends to become preoccupied with his own individual needs, fears, sins, moral character, etc., to the neglect of his fellow man. Religion then becomes a bargain by which the believer manipulates God in an effort to get himself into heaven. On the other hand, he sees in the metaphysical systems that "religious" man creates, the anxious attempt to explain life and give it meaning so that we can feel secure. What Bonhoeffer is rejecting, among other things, is "fox-hole" religion, God as the "stop-gap" answer to all unsolved problems, and the approach of some Christian apologists who seek to persuade the healthy they are really sick, the happy they are really miserable, so that they will despair and turn to God for deliverance.

He feels that it is essentially unbiblical for man to seek escape from God's creation, a world for which Jesus lived, and from which not even death could take him. Like Buber, and many of the other writers who have seen a side of religion that would fit Peter Berger's term "bad faith," he is highly suspicious of the otherworldly interpretations of Christianity.

[10] MARTIN BUBER, *Between Man and Man* (New York, 1947), pp. 13-15.

DIETRICH BONHOEFFER

What do I mean by "interpret in a religious sense"? In my view, that means to speak on the one hand metaphysically, and on the other individualistically. Neither of these is relevant to the Bible message or to the man of today. Is it not true to say that individualistic concern for personal salvation has almost completely left us all? Are we not really under the impression that there are more important things than bothering about such a matter? (Perhaps not more important than the matter itself, but more important than bothering about it.) I know it sounds pretty monstrous to say that. But is it not, at bottom, even biblical? Is there any concern in the Old Testament about saving one's soul at all? Is not righteousness and the kingdom of God on earth the focus of everything, and is not Romans 3:14 ff., too, the culmination of the view that in God alone is righteousness, and not in an individualistic doctrine of salvation? It is not with the next world that we are concerned, but with this world as created and preserved and set subject to laws and atoned for and made new. What is above the world is, in the Gospel, intended to exist *for* this world . . . in the Bible sense of the creation and of the incarnation, crucifixion, and resurrection of Jesus Christ.[11]

This passage of H. Richard Niebuhr's is taken from a chapter entitled "Faith in Gods and in God" and in it he discusses the question of God's nature and existence, beginning with the assumption that we have dealt with in many sections of the book, namely, the universal human experience of faith, of reliance or trust in something which the individual believes gives worth and meaning to life. He points out that in this experience of faith we do not begin by arguing about the abstract question of the "existence" of our "god." For example, we have faith in democracy not insofar as we believe in the existence of such a

[11] DIETRICH BONHOEFFER, *Letters and Papers from Prison* (New York, 1953), p. 168.

reality as "democracy," but insofar as we count on the spirit of democracy to maintain itself and continuously influence the lives of people. In this way he shows that we must always go beyond what we actually know, and act on faith.

Notice how, near the end of his article, he handles the problem: which is the true God of all the gods men worship?

H. RICHARD NIEBUHR

There is nothing distinctive or peculiar about a Protestant's interest in the ultimate theological problem. We are concerned with the questions of God's nature and existence not as Protestants or Catholics, Christians or Jews, theologians or philosophers, laymen or clergy, but simply as human beings. Yet each of us raises these problems in a specific form, each asks his question in that special way which he has not only learned from his tradition, but which has been made necessary by his own personal wrestling with the question of life's meaning. Hence we often quarrel about the answers we get to our questions without realizing that they are answers to different questions. . . . So the philosopher of religion may begin with a certain definition of the term "God" and then ask, "Does a being having this nature exist?" This is a perfectly legitimate question. But it is wrong to think of it as the only proper way of raising the problem. Many different definitions of the nature of God may be framed, and hence many problems of existence may be raised. . . .

How, then, does Protestantism raise the question of God and how does it seek and find its answers to its problems? How does the problem of God present itself to us who work in this living tradition? It comes to us as an eminently practical problem, a problem of human existence and destiny, of the meaning of human life in general and of the life of self and its community in particular. It does not arise for us in the speculative form of such questions as "Does God exist?" or "What is the first cause, what the ultimate substance?" Our first question is, "How is faith in God possible?" In other words, the problem of God arises for us in its subjective rather than objective, or, better, in personal rather than impersonal form. . . . The point at which such Protestants begin their analysis of the problem of God is that of practical human faith in deity. . . . Faith is an active thing, a committing of self to something, an anticipation. It is directed toward something that is also active, that has power or is power. . . .

When we inquire into this element of faith or confidence in our life as human beings, we become aware of one aspect of it which may above all else be called religious, because it is related to our existence as worshipping beings. . . . This is the faith that life is worth living, or better, the reliance on certain centers of value as able to bestow significance and worth on our existence. . . . Now to have faith and to have a god is one and the same thing, as it is one and the same thing to have knowledge and an object of knowledge. When we believe that life is worth living, by the same act we refer to some being which makes our life worth living. We never merely believe that life is worth living, but always think of it as made worth living by something on which we rely. And this being, whatever it be, is properly termed our god. . . .

We note that these centers of value, these objects of adoration, have many different forms of existence. Some are visible and tangible objects of whose reality our senses give us assurance. Some are essences, ideas, concepts, or images which are accessible only to abstract thought, but which exercise a certain compulsion over the mind. Some are movements known only by a kind of empathy or by an intuition that outruns sense; some have the peculiar and hard-to-define reality of selves or persons. But in some sense they all exist.

Yet this is true—and this constitutes the tragedy of our religious life—that none of these values or centers of value exists universally, or can be the object of a universal faith. . . . They are all finite in time as in space and make finite claims upon us, hence we become aware of two characteristics of our faith and its gods: that we are divided within ourselves and socially by our religion, and that our gods are unable to save us from the ultimate frustration of meaningless existence. . . . there is a greater tragedy—the twilight of the gods. None of these beings on which we rely to give content and meaning to our lives is able to supply continuous meaning and value. . . . All our causes, all our ideas, all the beings on which we relied to save us from worthlessness are doomed to pass.

What is it that is responsible for this passing, that dooms our human faith to frustration? We may call it the nature of things, we may call it fate, we may call it reality. But by whatever name we call it, this law of things, this reality, this way things are, is something with which we all must reckon. We may not be able to give a name to it, calling it only the "void" out of which everything comes and to which everything returns, though that is also a name. But it is there—the last shadowy and vague reality, the secret of existence by virtue of which things come into being, are what they are, and pass away. Against it there is no defense. This reality, this nature of things, abides when all else passes. It is the source of all things and the end of all. . . . What it is we do not know save that it is and that it is the supreme reality with which we must reckon.

Now a strange thing has happened in our history and in our personal life; our faith has been attached to that great void, to that enemy of all our causes, to that opponent of all our gods. The strange thing has happened that we have been enabled to say of this reality, this last power in which we live and move and have our being, "Though it slay us yet will we trust it." We have been allowed to attach our confidence to it, and put our reliance in it which is the one reality beyond all the many, which is the last power, the infinite source of all particular beings as well as their end. And insofar as our faith, our reliance for meaning and worth, has been attached to this source and enemy of all our gods, we have been enabled to call this reality God.

To have faith in this reality means that having been driven away from our reliance on all lesser causes, we have learned to conceive of and to rely upon this last power, this nature of things, as itself the greatest of all causes, the undefeatable cause. ... And to have faith is also to live in hope, in constant anticipation of new unfoldings of worth and meaning. ... To attach faith, hope, and love to this last being, this source of all things and this slayer of all, is to have confidence which is not subject to time, for this is the eternal reality. ... When we say that we conceive faith in the great void and the great enemy, we mean that we have learned to count on it as friend ... as that which will make all our lives and the lives of all things valuable even though it bring them to death.

How is such faith possible? How does it happen that this void, this enemy, is recognized as friend, that faith attaches itself to the last power, to the great hidden mystery, and calls it God? ... It does not happen without the struggle of his reason. For by reason he discovers the inadequacy of all his gods and is driven to despair in life's meaning. It does not happen without experience, without the experience of frustration, of noting the death of all things, the experience of the internal division in which his various worship involves him, the experience of the great social catastrophes which show the weakness of the great causes and beings in which he trusted as saviors of life. It does not happen without the operation of something we must call spiritual, something which is like the intuition of the thinker, like the creative insight of the artist, like the flash of recognition of truth. All these elements are involved. Furthermore, this transfer of faith to the ultimate being does not take place without moral struggle, without recognition of the unworthiness both of our transgressions and our obediences to our moral laws.

But for most men another element is involved—the concrete meeting with other men who have received this faith, and the concrete meeting with Jesus Christ. There may be other ways, but this is the usual way for us, that we confront in the event of

Jesus Christ the presence of that last power which brings to apparent nothingness the life of the most loyal man. Here we confront the slayer, and here we become aware that this slayer is the life-giver. He does not put to shame those who trust in him. . . .

We do not say that this faith in the last power is something men ought to have. We say only this, that it is the end of the road of faith, that it is unassailable, and that when men receive it they receive a great gift.[12]

[12] H. Richard Niebuhr, *Radical Monotheism and Western Culture* (New York, 1960), pp. 114–125.

THE CONCEPT OF GOD:
THE INFINITE POWER OF BEING,
JUDGE, SAVIOR, CREATOR, SOVEREIGN

In trying to describe the power or spirit that drives the human spirit above itself and lays claim to one's unqualified loyalty, one becomes most conscious of the limitations of language. We can see a concrete example of this if we consider the problem Father Zossima has in trying to communicate the meaning of his experience to his fellow officers. They simply cannot understand him. Yet to them the "honor code" of dueling and the aristocratic notion of a social "elite" has a sanctity and ultimacy which completely shapes their attitude toward themselves and their fellow man and which therefore takes on for them the role of God. Their picture of the "last power" enables them to say in effect, "We are the lords of creation. We decide who shall live and who shall die. This world belongs to us, and the Afanasys and their kind are our things, objects we are free to use or abuse as we choose." This view seems arrogant and pretentious to us only because we have been influenced by a totally different picture of the ultimate frame of reference in which we believe all men stand.

We may be bothered by what might appear to be a self-contradiction in some of the religious writers, who on the one hand emphasize the mystery of God and the symbolic character of the language of faith and who on the other hand seem to describe God as if there were no mystery and seem to use words in a literal rather than symbolic fashion. This is most evident in selections from books that seek to instruct Christians in their own faith rather than from books directed to a wider audience. Every particular group uses a language and a set of symbols peculiarly its own and tends to be unaware of the fact that it is doing so. They may use the same words as the larger community, yet these words will carry meanings unrecognizable to those outside the circle. The jazz musician playing to "cats" or "chicks," the schoolboy who "gets on the back" of some "meatball" feels no need to explain to his friends the special meaning of these words; yet to a foreigner or to the uninitiated his words are nonsense. This is just as true for the scientist, the mathematician, and the lawyer. But unlike these groups, the religious man generally feels under an obligation to convert those outside his circle to his way of thinking and this necessarily involves him in the difficulties of communication and explanation.

To talk about God, to attempt to define or describe God is really a contradiction in terms. In order to do so one has to make God the object of one's thought, one has to stand apart from God and look at him. But this is precisely what God is not. God is not an object, a being among other beings, for if the word "God" means anything, it means the infinite, unconditional, unlimited source or ground of all being "in whom," as St. Paul quotes, "we live and move and have our being." Most responsible theologians have always known this and have insisted that man cannot comprehend God, cannot encompass God in his thinking, but that he can apprehend God and respond to Him. Unfortunately, popularizers of religion write and talk with such apparent familiarity and confidence about God that they dissolve the sense of mystery, awe, and wonder which characterizes all profound attempts to express the ultimate dimension of human experience. It is this Magic Helper in the sky of popular religion that is probably responsible for most of the skepticism and atheism among educated people today.

Yet to go beyond the simple picture of the old man in the

sky is not a simple matter. In fact, the most sophisticated philosophers and theologians have discovered that this picture of the old man as conceived by a Michelangelo, a Blake, a Job, or an Isaiah is a more adequate expression of the God of personal faith than the abstract conceptual terms like "depth," "Ground of Being," "Being-Itself," etc., even though these terms may be descriptively more accurate. Therefore in dealing with the following selections, it is important to recognize that all of these writers are attempting to put into words what they would be the first to admit is beyond words. As Reinhold Niebuhr suggests, they are telling a kind of lie in order to point to the truth.

We might point out in general that man's life has always been a combination of what he does with his resources and what is added from resources that are not his own. Here common sense prepares us for the biblical view. Every day we accept as a gift what we did not create ourselves. This "givenness" is what makes living possible. We cannot preserve our bodies without relying on the natural elements and forces which give us "our daily bread." Our scientific progress has been achieved through harnessing powers which are given before we use them. Life itself is a gift we did not manufacture. It is not unreasonable therefore to expect that resources which we do not possess ourselves might be available to "deliver us from evil" and fulfill the meaning of our life, which always seems to be in the making.

We not only accept what is given, but we always wait for results which we ourselves can never wholly account for. Tolstoy emerged from a period of youthful doubt when he realized that more is done with what we do than we can foresee. Some decisions which we considered good at the time, turn out to be against our best interests; and some bad decisions are often transformed into a benefit which we never suspected. This fact is the basis for a saying attributed to Kierkegaard: "We live life forward, we understand it backward." Only as we take a long look across the past, can we observe the emergence of unexpected meaning.

In an age when man's self-sufficiency has been overemphasized, it is important to recover this broader truth of common sense that man's power is forever in a partnership with some source of power, always present but always hidden.

Turning now to the personalities of the Bible, we find their initial contact with a living God was always associated in their minds with a moral shock. From Moses, down the line of the great prophets of Israel, and over into the New Testament history, this shock is always the first sign of man's confronting God. Even Plato recognized that the highest good, which was so different from calculated goodness, first met men as a kind of "check" on their self-esteem. But in the biblical examples we will notice that the shock not only convicts men of shortcoming and guilt, but also creates a kind of revolution at the very center of life, convincing them that the guilt is but the intimation of a call to some higher mission than their own desires. This whole experience was taken as a merciful acceptance of a faulty life, as though all were forgiven when all was offered for the utmost usefulness.

We will select three examples of this revolutionary conversion from Bible history.

(a) First there was the experience of Moses, with whom the religion of the Hebrews began. (Exodus 2:11–3:22) He was a member of a race of slaves in Egypt. By a strange chance he received special privileges in the King's household, and became a leader of his oppressed people. Accused as a dangerous agitator, he fled into the wilderness, where he brooded over the fate of the people he had deserted. Then in the startling incident of the burning bush, the shock came. "God called unto him out of the burning bush and said, 'Moses, Moses.' And he said, 'Here am I.'" Note the intensely personal nature of this call, and its humbling effect: "Put off thy shoes from off thy feet, for the place whereon thou standest is holy ground." And the Lord said: "I have seen the affliction of my people. . . . And I am come down to deliver them. . . . Come now and I will send thee to Pharaoh." A profound sense of weakness and unworthiness grasped Moses, and he said: "Who am I that I should go unto Pharaoh?" Then came the conviction of being accepted in the service of One who was greater than himself: "Certainly I will be with thee... when thou has brought forth the people... ye shall serve God upon this mountain."

Here the world was introduced to the unique idea that God works in and through the events of history, calling men not to meditation and withdrawal, but to participation in a purpose that concerned all men. This original idea was often misunderstood and misrepresented, and required a long time to be clarified, but it constantly emerges through the Old Testament.

(b) Next we will take the experience of the prophet Isaiah in the eighth century B.C. (Isaiah 6) In the days of King Uzziah, when the Hebrew nation was just tottering to its doom, Isaiah had a vision of God "high and lifted up." Here the word "holy" is applied to God to suggest the utter distinction between him and all our human powers. The next step in the vision was a feeling of profound humility and contrition. Isaiah felt like a man of unclean lips living among a people of unclean lips. There was no presumption of personal superiority in him, for he shared the sins of his people. Following this came a purging experience which brought to him a call like a moral obligation laid upon him: "Whom shall I send?" This appeal came to his conscience as it came to the conscience of Moses, like the call to a mission; and he answered, "Here am I, send me."

With this familiar personal experience as a key, Isaiah sought to understand all human sinfulness which was constantly being met by some disturbing and unexpected consequences through which the Creator was recalling men to the true mission of their life. To the Hebrew people this relation of man's will to the will of his Creator was known as a "covenant with God," a "testament" or agreement. The "Old Testament" of the Bible is a record of how this "covenant" came to be understood.

(c) In the New Testament we find the same pattern of experience in the conversion of the Apostle Paul. (Acts 9) He had been a persecutor of the Christian sect because he felt they were traitors to the old Jewish laws which came down from Moses. Ever since he watched the stoning of Stephen, the first Christian martyr, his conscience had been troubling him, and he had tried to kick against it as an ox kicks against a goad. Suddenly the shock came to him on the road to Damascus. "Saul, Saul, why persecutest thou me?" All his self-righteous life was convicted as a great mistake, and out of his feeling of guilt came the inner change which made him ready to accept some new mission for his life, and he said: "What wilst thou have me to do?"

The similarity of the moral shock and its effect in these three instances throws light on the experience of all of us.

Men know this shock by their own inside information. A student once said that up to his sophomore year in college he had thoughtlessly done whatever was good for his own happiness. Then it dawned on him that his selfish happiness meant nothing to anyone else, and if his life did not mean anything it was not worth living. Suddenly, through a chance remark in a chapel address, he realized there was "something good to be anyway," whether it was profitable or not. And it would still be good if he had to die for it. It is hard to reduce this inner experience to any kind of explanation because it meets us as a living effect through unselfish people, and we either reject or accept it without any argument.

From the viewpoint of this moral shock and its effect, the men of the Bible looked out upon the world they lived in. What kind of a world was it? Where did it come from? What was the meaning of their relation to nature and to other people everywhere? What power was working in and through the whole creation? Following these questions they were made to see that the power that worked within men to judge and transform was the power of creation that brought everything into being.

The judging, the transforming, and the creating were all
united in one irreducible mystery called God.

The biblical approach to God leads to a right understanding
of the central importance of humility in human life. It is the attitude which admits that no person or group can ever possess final
and absolute knowledge about anything. It is the basis of an open
mind and an open life prepared to keep growing to the end. Read
the 38th Chapter of Job, where out of the whirlwind comes a voice
saying: "Where wast thou when I laid the foundations of the
earth?" and it will be forever difficult to make final assertions about
any human opinion. Paul said, "We all fall short," so that there can
be no perfect economic systems or political methods; no final solutions of any human problem. Fénelon once said, the only perfect
person is the one who is perfectly ready to be corrected. Paul steadily told himself: "I count not myself to have attained." On the
human level there can be no absolute.

To accept this fact with readiness to be corrected and to learn
from each other's point of view, instead of sticking to our opinion
as though it were the absolute truth, is the only hope that something creative and new can be done with us. Such an attitude is
essential to a free world. Democracy is based on the fundamental
belief that all men are imperfect. The totalitarian states want perfection but they never reach it. Democracy expects imperfection
and has plenty of it. Its hope rests on people who are willing to
differ and listen to each other. The danger of democracy is the political claptrap which talks in terms of black and white as though
all evil lay with the party that is in power and all hope of peace
and prosperity lay with that party which wants to take its place.

Paul was repeatedly reminding his followers not to think
more highly of themselves than they ought to think. And Jesus
said the last word on the subject in his famous epigram: "He that
humbleth himself shall be exalted; and he that exalteth himself
shall be abased." To him, false humility was to be humble and
cringing before men, while true humility came from final loyalty
to God alone which made him afraid of no man.

The Concept of God

Kim Malthe-Bruun wrote this letter when he was twenty-two; he wrote it to his girl; he wrote it the day before he was shot by a German firing squad. Perhaps it conveys more effectively than theological language can what is meant by the love of God and the victory over death.

KIM MALTHE-BRUUN

Vestre Prison [Copenhagen]
German Section, cell 411
4 April 1945

My own little darling,

Today I was taken before the military tribunal and condemned to death. What a terrible blow this is for a little girl of twenty! I've been given permission to write this farewell letter, but what shall I write? . . . What is the final and most precious thing I can give you? What do I possess that I can leave you as a parting gift so that in spite of your loss you will smile and go on living and developing?

We sailed on a stormy sea, we met in the trusting way of playing children and we loved each other. We still love each other and always will, but one day a storm separated us. I went aground while you were washed up on shore, and you are going to continue living in a new world. I don't expect you to forget me. Why should you forget something so beautiful as that which existed between us? But you mustn't become a slave to this memory. You must keep on going with the same easy and graceful approach to life as before and twice as happy because on your way Life gave you one of its greatest gifts. Free yourself— let this greatest of joys be everything to you, let it shine brighter and clearer than anything else, but let it be only one of your treasured memories. Don't let it blind you and keep you from seeing all the wonderful things life has in store for you. . . . You will live on and you will have other beautiful adventures, but promise me—this you owe to everything I have lived for—that never will the thought of me come between you and Life. Remember, I will continue to live in your heart, but the part of me which remains there should be sound and natural and mustn't take up too much room. Gradually as bigger and more important things appear, I shall glide into the background and be a tiny speck of the soil out of which your happiness and your development will keep on growing.

Now you are heartbroken and this is what is known as sorrow, but Hanne, look beyond this. All of us are going to die and it isn't for us to judge whether my going a little early is good or bad. . . .

There is something inside me alive and growing—an inspiration, a love—call it what you like; something which I still haven't been able to define. Now I'm going to die and I still don't know if I have started a little flame in another being, a flame which will survive me. But still, my mind is at rest because I've seen the richness and abundance of nature. No one takes notice if a few seeds are trampled under and die. When I see all the riches that still live on, why should I despair?

Lift up your head, my precious love, and look! The sea is still blue, the sea which I loved and which has enveloped us both. Now you will live for the two of us. . . . Remember—and I swear this is true—that all sorrow gradually turns into happiness. But few are those who admit it when the time comes. They cloak themselves in mourning; habit makes them think it is sorrow, and so they continue to cloak themselves in it. The truth is that after suffering comes maturity and after this maturity the fruits are gathered.

You see, Hanne, one day you will meet the man who will be your husband. The thought of me will flash through you, and you will perhaps deep down have a vague, uneasy feeling that you are betraying me or something in you which is pure and sacred. Lift up your head once more, Hanne, look straight into my eyes which are smiling at you and you will understand that the only way to betray me is by not completely following your natural instincts. When you see him, let your heart go out to meet him—not to drown your sorrow but because you truly love him. . . . I would like to breathe into you all the life that is in me, so that it can go on and as little as possible of it go to waste. This is the way I was made.

Yours, but not for always.[13]

Niebuhr in this selection asserts that a genuine faith begins with a recognition of the mystery of life. He criticizes those who claim to be able to explain everything in terms of cause and effect and see nothing more to life than nature and also those who claim to know with a kind of absolute certainty the ulti- mate meaning and purpose of life. He says that a genuine faith is more humble. It recognizes that life is not self-explanatory, but it claims no more than a clue to the ultimate mystery. The believer lives in the tension between mystery and meaning.

REINHOLD NIEBUHR

A genuine Christian faith must move between those who claim to know so much about the natural world that it ceases to point to any mystery beyond itself and those who claim to know so much about the mystery of the "unseen" world that all rever- ence for its secret and hidden character is dissipated. A genuine faith must recognize the fact that it is through a dark glass that we see; though by faith we do penetrate sufficiently to the heart of the mystery not to be overwhelmed by it. A genuine faith resolves the mystery of life by the mystery of God. It recognizes that no aspect of life or existence explains itself, even after all known causes and consequences have been traced. All known existence points beyond itself. To realize that it points beyond

[13] KIM MALTHE-BRUUN, *Heroic Heart* (New York, 1955), pp. 164–167.

itself to God is to assert that the mystery of life does not dissolve life into meaninglessness. Faith in God is faith in some ultimate unity of life, in some final comprehensive purpose which holds all the various, and frequently contradictory, realms of coherence and meaning together. A genuine faith does not mark this mysterious source and end of existence as merely an X, or as an unknown quantity. The Christian faith, at least, is a faith in revelation. It believes that God has made Himself known. It believes that He has spoken through the prophets and finally in His Son. It accepts the revelation in Christ as the ultimate clue to the mystery of God's nature and purpose in the world.[14]

To understand what Tillich is talking about here we must rid our mind of the picture of God as an invisible being in the sky and think rather of the power or powers that make us what we are and that are shaping what we will become. We will then begin to realize that some of these powers are demonic and some are healing and creative. Most of the time we are simply driven by them without being conscious of the fact. But once aware of them, we then become responsible for our relation to them. It is for this reason that he denies the possibility of atheism.

PAUL TILLICH

God is close to each one of us; it is in Him that we live and move and exist.... Even the atheists stand in God—namely, that power out of which they live, the truth for which they grope, and the ultimate meaning of life in which they believe. It is bad theology and religious cowardice ever to think that there may be a place where we could look *at* God, as though He were something outside of us to be argued for or against. Genuine atheism is not humanly possible, for God is nearer to a man than that man is to himself. A God can only be denied in the name of

[14] Reinhold Niebuhr, *Discerning the Signs of the Times* (New York, 1946), pp. 154–155.

another god; and God appearing in *one* form can be denied only by God appearing in another form. . . .

God is nearer to us than we ourselves. We cannot find a place outside of Him; but we can try to find such a place. . . . We can be in the condition of continuous flight from God. We can imagine one way of escape after another; we can replace God by the products of our imagination; and we do. Although mankind is not strange to God, it is estranged from Him. Although mankind is never without God, it perverts the picture of God, it is ignorant of God. Mankind is separated from its origin; it lives under a law of wrath and frustration, of tragedy and self-destruction, because it produces one distorted image of God after another, and adores those images. The . . . theologian must discover the false gods in the individual soul and in society. He must probe into their most secret hiding-places. He must challenge them through the power of the Divine Logos, which makes him a theologian. Theological polemic is not merely a theoretical discussion but rather a spiritual judgement against the gods which are not God, against those structures of evil, those distortions of God in thought and action.[15]

Tillich is a theologian who has spent much time trying to find a new way of speaking about God in an age that has by and large ceased to find the word meaningful. In this selection he elaborates on the notion of God as the "depth" of our individual and social being. Perhaps then we can understand him when he says, "God is nearer to us than we ourselves," or the biblical notion that we live and move and have our being in God. Perhaps too, it will make understandable the notion of sin as separation from God, from self, from neighbor.

All visible things have a surface. Surface is that side of things which first appears to us. If we look at it, we know what

---

[15] PAUL TILLICH, *The Shaking of the Foundations* (New York, 1948), pp. 127–129.

things *seem* to be. Yet if we act according to what things and persons *seem* to be, we are disappointed. ... And so we try to penetrate below the surfaces in order to learn what things really are. ...

Most of our life continues on the surface. We are enslaved by the routine of our daily lives, in work and pleasure, in business and recreation. We are conquered by innumerable hazards, both good and evil. We are more driven than driving. We do not stop to look at the height above us, or the depth below us. We are always moving forward, although usually in a circle, which finally brings us back to the place from which we first moved. We are in constant motion and never stop to plunge into the depth. We talk and talk and never listen to the voices speaking to our depth and from our depth. We accept ourselves as we appear to ourselves, and do not care what we really are. ... We miss, therefore, our depth and our true life. And it is only when the picture that we have of ourselves breaks down completely, only when we find ourselves acting against all the expectations we had derived from that picture ... that we are willing to look into a deeper level of our being.

The wisdom of all ages and of all continents speaks about the road to our depth. It has been described in innumerably different ways. But all those who have been concerned ... have found that they were not what they believed themselves to be, even after a deeper level had appeared to them below the vanishing surface. That deeper level itself became surface, when a still deeper level was discovered, this happening again and again, as long as their very lives, as long as they kept on the road to their depth. ...

The name of this infinite and inexhaustible depth and ground of all being is *God*. That depth is what the word *God* means. And if that word has not much meaning for you, translate it, and speak of the depths of your life, of the source of your being, of your ultimate concern, of what you take seriously without any reservation. Perhaps, in order to do so, you must forget ev-

erything traditional that you have learned about God, perhaps
even that word itself. For if you know that God means depth,
you know much about Him. You cannot then call yourself an
atheist or unbeliever. For you cannot think or say: Life has no
depth! Life itself is shallow. Being itself is surface only. If you
could say this in complete seriousness, you would be an atheist;
but otherwise you are not. He who knows about depth knows
about God. . . .

We are only in a world through a community of men. And
we can discover our souls only through the mirror of those who
look at us. There is no depth of life without the depth of the
common life. We usually live in history as much on the surface
as we live our individual lives. We understand our historical
existence as it appears to us, and not as it really is. The stream of
daily news, the waves of daily propaganda, and the tides of con-
ventions and sensationalism keep our minds occupied. The noise
of these shallow waters prevents us from listening to the sounds
out of the depth, to the sounds of what really happens in the
ground of our social structure, in the longing hearts of the
masses, in the struggling minds of those who are sensitive to
historical change. Our ears are as deaf to the cries out of the
social depth as they are to the cries out of the depth of our
souls. . . .

It is only now, in the decade in which the most horrible
social earthquake of all times has grasped the whole of mankind,
that the eyes of the nations have been opened to the depth
below them and to the truth about their historical existence. Yet
still there are people, even in high places, who turn their eyes
from this depth, and who wish to return to the disrupted surface
as though nothing had happened. . . .

The name of this infinite and inexhaustible ground of history is *God*. That is what the word means, and it is that to which
the words *Kingdom of God* and *Divine Providence* point. And
if those words do not have much meaning for you, translate
them and speak of the depth of history, of the ground and aim

of our social life, and of what you take seriously without reservation in your moral and political activities. Perhaps you should call this depth *hope,* simply hope. For if you find hope in the ground of history, you are united with the great prophets who were able to look into the depth of their times, who tried to escape it, because they could not stand the horror of their visions, and who yet had the strength to look to an even deeper level and there to discover hope.[16]

This selection from Erich Frank, a Catholic, is very like the one from H. Richard Niebuhr in Section 1 of this part. Where Niebuhr speaks of the "last power" that is the "enemy" of man's powers, Frank talks of the "impassable boundaries" or limit to which our whole existence is related, an objective power by which our whole existence is determined. If you remember the various discussions of sin, you will recall that one of the definitions of sin was man's denial of his limits, his pretension of being unlimited, his usurping of the place of God.

ERICH FRANK

In all these situations, in the inevitablitiy of death, of failure and suffering, of history, and of conflict, man finds himself at the ultimate limits of his sovereignty. In becoming aware of the limitations even of his purely theoretical and intellectual understanding, he recognizes the true nature of his existence, which everywhere impinges upon impassable boundaries. . . . If he accepts these limitations as part of his own existence—in constantly contending with them he grows and matures, and thus becomes a true personality. In this way he understands the full import of the fact that we are dependent on an objective power by which our whole existence is determined.

. . . Of this power we become aware only in practical life,

[16] *Ibid.,* pp. 53, 55–59.

where we experience it as the limit to which our whole existence is related, and through which we are what we are.

This spontaneous feeling, however, that our existence has its center not in itself, is precisely what in religion is called faith. ... Even faith is experience, not the experience of an external object, but the experience that in his own existence, in his own consciousness and truth, man is dependent upon an objective force. "Faith is the evidence of things not seen." It is only in the experience of faith that God is felt to be present as the power which determines our being and thinking.

At the bottom of faith, there is doubt, fear lest it be our own arbitrariness from which God ensues. This doubt is far from being the comparatively harmless distrust of the sceptic; it is absolute doubt, it is despair which shakes man in his entirety. This is not only denial of God; this is defiance against Him. However, it is precisely in this desperate struggle against God that man experiences what God really is. He finds he cannot escape Him. In his frustration he recognizes God as a "gigantic massif with threatening precipices and heights." He discovers that God is terrifying, that He is a hidden God, that "what can be comprehended is not yet God."

Thus it may be permissible to make the paradoxical statement that the real proof of God is the agonized attempt to deny God. It has often been remarked that atheism is but a kind of negative theology. The atheist may feel the inadequacy of all human concepts of God compared with that which God would really be, the author of all things, even of the atheist. ...

What does it really mean: God exists? Existence is a category much too inferior to be applied to the greatness of God. For this reason some Christian philosophers, following Plato, even defined God as non-existence or super-existence. For as the source of all reality, He is so far above the sphere of any determinate being that He cannot be called existent in a sense similar to the existence of all other beings. In their intention these philosophers were right: like all other categories, that of existence, if applied to God, can be used only in an analogical sense. Existence of God can be only an analogy of existence. For the existence of God infinitely transcends our thought, our will, and even our belief. And it is precisely in this transcendence that God and His existence can be grasped by us.[17]

The word "holy" should remind us that religion is not God. Religion is what man thinks about God. It is everything man does to preserve and deepen his relation to God. It is the Bible, prayers, doctrines, creeds, church and the modes of behavior that become accepted. At their best these resources have nourished the greatest lives we know; at their worst they have produced division, bigotry, formalism, persecution and fanaticisms of all kinds. But, whether good or bad, religion is never God. This distinction has great importance because criticism of what is going on, or of what has been done, in the name of religion often turns honest people away from God. The cure for bad religion is better religion, but even the best religion should point beyond itself to God "whose ways are higher than our ways."

In the remaining passages in this section you will find a fairly detailed analysis of the basic vocabulary connected with the biblical conception of God. When the Bible speaks of God as Judge, Savior, Creator, Sovereign, it seeks to characterize the nature of the ultimately determinative power that faith sees operating in personal life and history. In contrast to Fromm's emphasis on man's activity, you will notice that biblical thought emphasizes the activity of a power other than man's that judges man inwardly through his conscience and outwardly through the consequences that follow from the exercise of his freedom. If man accepts this judgment, it becomes the basis for an inner change (repentance, conversion) and a new life (redemption and salvation). It is against the background of this experience that the idea of creation as a continual process makes sense. Man, in other words, is not alone in an indifferent universe

[17] FRANK, *op. cit.*, pp. 15–17, 43–44.

moved by chance. Biblical faith makes the affirmation that this is a purposive, meaningful creation and that a creative power works through people and the events of history in a definable direction, namely, toward the establishment of the dominion of love and the overcoming of the divisions between men and within man.

JUDGE

In the Bible, God's corrective judgments are taken as opening the way for his saving activity.

In the first place the shock of moral judgment was described in the Bible as a searching experience, exposing the hidden depths of the individual soul. Brother Lawrence, in his little book on the Practice of the Presence of God, says that as he systematically exposed himself to this searching, he became aware of faults in himself about which he had become complacent, and at the same time was made aware of more opportunities of service which had before been overlooked. The Book of Common Prayer expresses this familiar experience in the words: "Almighty God unto whom all hearts are open, all desires known, and from whom no secrets are hid," as though such acknowledgment was the first step toward "newness of life." In Psalm 139 we have the classic description of God's searching of man, which illuminates the depths of human life in all religions and all ages. This passage should be read here, noting that it concludes on the positive note—"see if there be any wicked way in me . . . and lead me in the way everlasting."

It is a great and terrible thing to live under such judgment from God. It is great because it starts us toward a new beginning; it is terrifying because it destroys the security of our self-satisfaction. This means that whatever we say or do or think is recognized, as though each of us made a difference in the vast scheme of things. Jesus was always emphasizing the importance of "one sinner" being recovered.

In the second place the judgment of God operates not only by this inner searching, but also in the working out of the consequences of action in our lives and through all human relations. Every decision made by men or nations leaves a conclusion to be drawn, but the drawing of the conclusion is always beyond human calculation.

God's correction of our free moral choices affects us like a challenge that demands a response, for better or for worse. We make a free decision. Then consequences beyond our control work out a new situation that in turn challenges a new decision. If we continue to respond in the wrong way, more consequences follow to pile up into crises that bring us to a halt. If we respond in the right way, new possibilities for fulfillment are opened up. We never escape from this combination of challenge and response where creative activity that is not our own confronts us with inescapable situations.

Unfortunately the Bible itself has led to misunderstanding because its figures of speech have been often taken too literally. For instance, in the earlier stages of Hebrew history the symbol of God as an absolute monarch was quite natural because absolute monarchs were all that men were acquainted with at the time. His will had to be obeyed or the offender suffered the wrath of his ruler, and punishment was purely arbitrary. Here the relation was a legal relation. The monarch's will is expressed in rules laid down and every infringement of the rule is followed by some inevitable punishment. Every infraction brings a man under the wrath of his lord. There is no room in this legalism for forgiveness, because where a law is broken it must be punished or men would lose respect for the law. Because of this autocratic picture of God it became a problem for religion to know how a God of law could forgive those who broke his law. All through the Bible there appears this difficulty of holding together the justice and the mercy of God; and the problem has pestered theology down through the ages. Much of the hell-fire preaching that we have heard about, which threatened sinners with the tortures of Hell to bring them to repentance, was inspired by a legal system of rewards for the good and punishments for the bad. It has often produced a selfish type of religion in which people selfishly wish to save their souls for Heaven in order to escape the punishments of Hell. All these symbols of Hell and damnation have a profound truth in them because they emphasize the sternness and the reality of the corrective power of the Creator. But alone they may not get beyond the legal idea of moral life.

Another biblical way of describing the divine correction is much more natural and fitted to our modern mind. The prophet Amos speaks of God holding up a "plumb line" to all the constructions of man. Whatever is out of plumb will bring on its own natural consequences of destruction. Christ utilized this same notion in his famous parable about the house that was built on the sand instead of on the rock where it ought to be. When the flood and the winds beat on the house the natural consequence was that it fell and brought down in its ruin all who were within the house. These expressions enable us to see more readily that correction is not so much punishment as a way of bringing men to their senses for the purpose of recovery and reform. One of our ablest New Testament scholars points out that where Paul used these words, "the wrath of God," he never says that God is angry. He speaks of "the wrath" as though it were some kind of impersonal process, like the regular working out of consequences which men bring on themselves. Augustine said that it was never necessary for God to break in on this system of consequences and do something extra and arbitrary in the way of correction.

This experience of divine correction stands in contrast to some familiar substitutes. It grows deeper than any mere comparison of ourselves with others who are better. For even when we equal others, or perhaps surpass them, we still are made to feel our shortcomings. In fact the "saints" are the very ones who are made to feel most deeply this difference between their goodness and the goodness that confronts them. The shock cuts across all men's preferences and patterns of behavior

Again, it is more than the influence of our social environment, no matter how much our environment may affect us. For it is the source of that discontent which makes men challenge their environment and change it at any cost. In fact this inner wrestling with some higher goodness than our own is common everywhere in the world in all religions. Our self-will is in a perpetual contest with some will or purpose, greater and better than our purposes. If we stick to our self-will we lose much that might be a part of us; if we yield our will to the higher one, we find more of what we were meant to be, even when we suffer for it.

The corrective activity is also considered in the Bible as something more than our conscience. Our conscience might be described as our sensitivity to the source of all that is good and true which forever remains out of man's reach. Our conscience itself therefore needs to be confronted by a check from beyond itself. It can often become less sensitive by self-indulgence. Complacency can make it feel easy when it ought to be uneasy. Wherever men have identified their conscience absolutely with the will of God, we have been cursed by all the persecutions, inquisitions and tyrannies of the world; and in private life the person who is too sure he is right may be the hindering factor in mutual understanding. Furthermore, our conscience is often divided between different loyalties and becomes confused. This last problem was humorously illustrated in the words Mark Twain put into the mouth of Huckleberry Finn, when he wanted to lie to save his friend Jim from being returned to slavery, and at the same time was worried about not telling the truth: "It don't make no difference whether you do right or wrong, a person's conscience ain't got no sense and goes for him anyway. If I had a yaller dog and he had no more sense than my conscience, I would poison him."

From these qualifications of the idea of conscience we may realize that we can be safely guided by it only when we recognize that conscience must always be kept sensitive to a correction higher than itself—the divine correction is not simply a personal matter. We are created to be together so that we must take the consequences of each other's lives. When we allow an evil act to enter into this interrelationship, in time we reap the consequences of the worst that men do. In such a situation the innocent cannot possibly be rewarded according to their worth and the wicked made to pay for their evil in a clean-cut manner. For this reason it is never possible for human beings to decide exactly just where the judgment of God is falling or to be too sure as to what judgment is. All we can know is that the creative activity is at work in every situation to bring men to see that all the sins of the world must be borne by somebody. It is through this social solidarity that we are brought to a sense of shame that makes forgiveness and new beginnings possible.

In the Old Testament, the prophets pointed out that when the Hebrew people were unfaithful, God sometimes used a nation like Assyria with all its wickedness and cruelty to bring judgment on the Chosen People. The prophets also saw that those nations that were used as instruments of judgment were themselves subject to the same kind of judgment when they became too proud and cruel in their own right. In an interrelated world there is no possibility that divine justice can always be administered without human instruments that are imperfect, and at the same time there is no possibility that the sufferings of good men are entirely lost where God the Creator uses all men in his larger purpose. It will never be as plain to us perhaps as it was to the prophets of old that God is working in history, but it is very significant that our so much longer view of history justifies their interpretation of the inevitable corrective action of the Creator. The Communists in our day, however mistaken their theories may be, have been used to show up the shortcomings of our free world; and at the same time their shortcomings are now being judged in reactions occurring all over the world.

SAVIOR

Christ's way of explaining the saving power of God was to illustrate it in action, in the familiar relations of everyday life. We shall take three illustrations from the record of his life. One is an incident from his own career, and the others are parables in his teaching.

(1) This saving power comes as a surprise before we have earned or deserved it.

Read the story of Zaccheus. (Luke 19:1–10) This man was a Jew, collecting taxes from his own people for the hated Roman conqueror, and taking a fat profit for himself on the side. Naturally he was despised and treated like a dog. Jesus, in the crowd, noticed this little man who had climbed a tree for a chance to see. The people were shocked when Jesus asked him to come down that they might dine together in the outcast's house. At that meeting Zaccheus felt himself accepted while he was yet unworthy. And that experience worked a strange, inner change in his life. As the two parted, he said that he would give half of his goods to the poor, and if he had wrongfully exacted anything from anyone, he would restore it fourfold. And Jesus said, "This day is salvation come to this house." In that act of undeserved acceptance, there was released a power that created a disposition that was entirely new in the inner nature of this despised man.

We all know in ourselves the change which has come over our attitude when we have been accepted and trusted before we deserved it. Any one of us looking back over his family life can see just what influence really changed his disposition from time to time. It was never where we had been given advice, no matter how good the advice may have been. But something new hap-

164

pened where, after our behavior had caused some suffering to those who loved us, we were still accepted and trusted with a faithfulness that we had not deserved.

Modern practice of psychiatric treatment has rediscovered this same experience. Where patients have become sick of themselves and could not stand themselves, the cure comes where they are accepted and understood without criticism. There they learn to accept themselves again, and some healing power secretly begins to release them from their own mistrust, and a new tide of life enters into them to possess and recreate them. Something is done that their will alone could not do.

Our friendships have bound us to people who, knowing all our faults and often suffering from them, have still stuck to us and trusted us. Through them we have learned the kind of love that Paul described in his first letter to the Corinthians: "Love suffereth long and is kind; love vaunteth not itself, is not puffed up; seeketh not her own, is not easily provoked, thinketh no evil; knoweth all things, believeth all things, hopeth all things, endureth all things. Love never faileth."

(2) *Saving power creates an inner willingness that needs no rule.*

Read the parable of the Good Samaritan. (Luke 10:25–37) The point of this story lies in the fact that it was an answer to the question of a lawyer who thought of life in terms of obedience to laws. He asked Jesus to define the law about loving your neighbor, for he wanted a rule that would give him an explicit enumeration of the sort of people who should be considered as neighbors. The story tells of two religious men—the priest and the Levite—passing a wounded man who had been attacked by robbers. They had no rule that applied to this particular case of a man who was not a Jew, so they passed by on the other side. But the Samaritan, who had a neighborly disposition that responded to a need, required no rule. He did something that the other two men would not think of doing. Originality in creative action always comes out of such inner willingness which goes beyond what the rules require. Nothing is said here about the origin of this willingness, but we all know that none of us can make ourselves willing, any more than Zaccheus could work that change in himself.

This conversion to willingness has a very intimate relation to all the problems of authority in our social life, from the family up to the school and on to all public relations. Thorton Wilder, the novelist, has made a splendid statement of this truth: "If you have to do a thing you have lost your freedom; if you have to say a thing, you have lost your sincerity; if you have to love your parent, wife, child or cousin, you begin to be estranged from them already. Life is full of things one has to do, and if you have a passion for spontaneity, how do you convert what you have to do into the things you choose to do? That is one of the most exciting things about being an American—how an American will succeed in converting necessity into volition. It is a very beautiful thing and it is new, and it is closely related to our problem of authority." When anyone wonders why our religious faith has something vital to do with democracy, here is at least one answer: The power that can create willingness is the very foundation of a free life.

(3) Saving power creates the disposition to treat other people as persons for their own sakes instead of things which we use for our interest.

Read the parable of the Prodigal Son. (Luke 15:10–32) The significance of this story is in the contrast between a father and an older brother in relation to the younger son who had left home and wasted his substance in riotous living and who had sunk to the position of a herder of swine. When the boy reached the end of his rope and started home with deep misgivings, his father saw him while he was a long way off and ran out to meet him and treated him like a person who needed understanding and sympathy. The older brother showed an entirely different attitude. He had stayed home and been a very good boy and had attended to his father's business. Yet, with all his goodness, he looked on his brother, not as a person, but as an object of disgust and a possible obstacle to his own ambitions in the family. Thus Jesus pointed up the flaw in his "goodness" when he lacked the inner disposition to treat people as persons rather than as things. Little do we realize in the difficulties of our social relations how much we must depend today upon this free disposition to see a person where others see only "factory hands," "overhead labor expense," "lambs in a bear market," "clerks" in a store. Our modern life has grown so interdependent in a machine age that it is necessary to use other people as conveniences and to take advantage of their abilities. They become our substitutes in work that we cannot do, which makes it easy to forget that such lives have purposes of their own. The attitude which values persons is essential in every problem that we face.

It is particularly important in that difficult area of doing good to others. Sometimes when people want to do others good, they unconsciously deal out the benevolence in their own way and to suit their own convenience, without really understanding how it is going to affect the person to whom they dispense it.

Also, the disposition to understand people instead of using them enters into all our experiments to change outward control into partnership. Throughout the industrial world the experiments in partnership between management and labor are teaching us every day that the conversion of necessity into willingness through partnership is the secret of making a community out of parties who have been at strife. Wherever this inner willingness is generated anywhere in life it creates something that is entirely new. Thornton Wilder was right: "It is a very beautiful thing and it is new."

CREATOR

The word "creation" in the biblical sense refers to the miracle of all miracles: the activity which brings everything into being. This miracle was summed up in the first sentence of Genesis: "In the beginning God. . . ." This is a way of saying that nothing in the world, including man, can be self-sufficient. Nothing can have its origin and meaning in itself.

We have time in these discussions to point out only a few of the conclusions that can be drawn from this religious truth of creation.

First, it means that God is not nature of which man is a part. His power is not identical with all that has been created. In some modern thought, the natural world is just a series of causes and effects which have no meaning or purpose. In some oriental religions God includes everything. But both nature and man have been set apart from God, the way a table or a machine is set apart from the man who created them. Man is given a will of his own, his nature has laws of its own, and the natural world has been given an order of its own which scientists may study. But the biblical view of creation stresses the fact that both man and his world have limits. They are dependent on a power which made them possible and which has purposes of its own. In other words the world and all of us who are in it border on something that is not human or temporary but eternal, "from everlasting to everlasting."

Second, the idea of "creation" means that something new keeps happening in human history. This is in contrast to a view that has been held in various religions and philosophies, that all events are mere repetitions of similar events that preceded them in time. Of course many experiences seem to be repeated on the human stage, and man seems to repeat his follies age after age. But according to the religious view of the Bible everything that happens is created into something new that never before was quite the same and will never recur. In the New Testament, Jesus and and Paul speak of the "new creation" that is forever occuring in our lives when our selfish life is made over, again and again, into a life of a different kind. All these new things that are constantly brought forth give meaning to the course of events—whether or not we can always see it. Life is so endless in its development that we cannot at any time know more than part; but we can be sure that at every point some new thing can be created that was never there before.

In a continuous creation a continuous revolution of the mind is our standard. By that standard we recognize two classes of people in the world. One lives under the power of what he has been used to in the past, and the other lives under the power of what might be expected in the future. In the former group are many people who are not entirely opposed to what is new, but who do not encourage it when it disturbs anything that they happen to like. There are many constructive conservative people who do not want to move too fast and they are of great value in the world; but there is another type of person who, to save what he likes, refuses to favor any change anywhere. Dante pictures a crowd of such people just outside of Hell because no one wanted them in Heaven and nobody wanted them in Hell. They were neither for God nor for the Devil, but for themselves. The whole progress of the world is held up by this class of people who want to hold things as they have always been. Since they favor no change until they must, society has to be changed from the bottom, not because the best minds are there, but because contented minds prove too slow and the Creator has to use what minds he can get. For this reason someone has said that good often comes into the world on the back of evil. It is a very easy thing for people with a comfortable income to settle down, perform their community duties, support the church and develop a charming personality and at the same time stand as a block in the way of creation. Communist ideology points to a utopia after one revolution; but Christianity envisions continuous revolution, with something new to be made out of everything and everybody. In order to be open for that kind of new activity a man must be always ready to be corrected and made over. This is the essence of a free man.

Finally the work of creation indicates that no line can be drawn between what God does and what man does because all creative activity of God is "hidden." Every time we make a garden we must prepare the ground and fertilize it and cultivate it and plant the seed, but we cannot manage the growth of what we plant for that is an invisible operation. It happens when we are not giving it a thought, and yet our action was entirely necessary; so also with the development of our mind and personality. We read and study and practice and expose ourselves to other people, and our development occurs while we are not thinking of it. The two kinds of activity merge into each other so that there is no invasion of human freedom and no substitute for human responsibility. It might be likened to a man swimming in a strong tide. When he goes with the tide it reinforces his own efforts but he still must swim or he will drown. There is no way to distinguish between the strength of the man and the strength of the tide—the two forces act constantly together.

THE SOVEREIGNTY OF GOD

The idea of the sovereignty of God has been expressed in many different ways, from the naked power of the One who consumes his enemies like stubble, to the God who empties himself and takes the form of a servant—images which modern man has found somewhat less than helpful. He is likely to argue that if God does rule the world, then he is a tyrant because he tolerates suffering and cruelty. If he is loving and just, then he is surely not the ruler of the world, for he cannot prevent evil. No one has ever found a totally satisfying answer to this dilemma, and if they have, they have not observed the side of life described by Ivan Karamazov. When Ivan himself tries to eliminate the problem by saying no one is guilty, for everything is simply a chain of cause and effect, he recognizes that while it may be a sound theory it does not account for his own sense of outrage, his incapacity to accept the suffering of children, his longing for a human world in which people love one another. This is what Niebuhr means when he says that the kingdom or rule of God "which is not of this world is always in this world in man's uneasy conscience." One might well ask why we do not despair of life when we see the innocent killed. Why do we not find it in us to settle for the claw and fang of the jungle when a man like John Kennedy is gunned down? What do we make of the few weeks in which the world was almost healed; almost all men, brothers; almost all humbled and given a new spirit, a "new being"? Could it be true, as the Cross suggests, that enmity and hatred are only defeated by their victims, that a love that suffers evil is finally the victor over evil? This is far from an explanation of the mystery of iniquity. Rather it should remind us of a dimension of evil beyond our comprehension as well as a depth of goodness that has divinity within it. Life confronts us as a mystery in and through which we dimly but confidently discern a pattern whereby even the worst that men do to each other is turned into the service of healing and new life, so that we may say with St. Paul: "For I am persuaded, that neither death, nor life, nor angels, nor principalities, nor powers, nor things present, nor things to come, nor height, nor depth, nor any other creature, shall be able to separate us from the love of God, which is in Christ Jesus our Lord." (Romans 8:38–39)

REINHOLD NIEBUHR

The kingdom which is not of this world is in this world, through man and in man, who is in this world and yet not altogether of this world. Man is not of this world in the sense that he can never rest complacently in the sinful standards which are normative in the world. He may be selfish but he cannot accept selfishness as the standard of conduct. He may be greedy but he knows that greed is wrong. Even when his actions do not conform to his ideals he cannot dismiss his ideals as irrelevant.

The kingdom which is not of this world is always in this world in man's uneasy conscience.[18]

[18] REINHOLD NIEBUHR, *Beyond Tragedy* (New York, 1937), pp. 278–279.

In this passage Frank shows how the doctrine of creation becomes for the believer a way of expressing his meaningful relationship to a world which does not explain itself to man's unanchored reason.

ERICH FRANK

The individual wakes up to the fact that he has been thrown into this alien world as an utterly dependent being. He does not know when he came or where he is going. Our origin and our destiny remain inscrutable to reason. That is the fundamental fact from which all philosophy has to start. If in spite of this, man wants to believe that his own existence, his volition, his thoughts have a meaning and a truth, he can do so only by relating himself to an absolute truth through which his existence and his thought are determined. It is this absolute dependence which is meant by the idea of creation. This concept, although it cannot rationally explain the riddle of human existence, serves to point to it and to make man aware of it. The greatness of the religious idea of creation consists in this: that amidst this finite and dependent world it keeps alive in man a sense of his own mysterious place within creation.

. . . It is in Christianity that man in his own heart, in his soul, discovers the true nature of God. In the sphere of religion, the most human, the most deeply felt expression is the most truthful.

As man himself, as his conscience is, so is his God. But this does not mean that man venerates as his God nothing but his own ideal projected into the Absolute. For the religious person the true idea of himself is not that one which he holds, but that one which God has of him.[19]

The basic doctrine that permeates the Bible from beginning to end is that man's life is a dialogue between heaven and earth,

[19] FRANK, *op. cit.*, pp. 73, 98.

an encounter with God who addresses man and is addressed by him. It speaks of God approaching man in the concrete, particular events of history. The prophets are those who read "the signs of the times," who hear the voice out of the depths, and proclaim the real to those whose concern is with the surface of things.

MARTIN BUBER

The idea of responsibility is to be brought back from the province of specialized ethics, of an "ought" that swings free in the air, into that of lived life. Genuine responsibility exists only where there is real responding.

Responding to what?

To what happens to one, to what is to be seen and heard and felt. Each concrete hour allotted to the person, with its content drawn from the world and from destiny, is speech for the man who is attentive. Attentive, for no more than that is needed in order to make a beginning with the reading of the signs that are given to you. . . . It will, then, be expected of the attentive man that he faces creation as it happens. It happens as speech, and not as speech rushing out over his head but as speech directed precisely at him. . . . But the sounds of which the speech consists—I repeat it in order to remove the misunderstanding, which is perhaps still possible, that I referred to something extraordinary and larger than life—are the events of the personal everyday life. In them, as they now are, "great" or "small," we are addressed.

[Buber gives here a detailed example of what this address means.]

In a receptive hour of my personal life a man meets me about whom there is something, which I cannot grasp in any objective way at all, that "says something" to me. That does not mean, says to me what manner of man this is, what is going on in him, and the like. But it means, says something *to me*, addresses something to me, speaks something that enters my own life. It can be something about this man, for instance that he needs me. But it can also be something about myself. The man himself in his relation to me has nothing to do with what is said. He has no relation to me, he has indeed not noticed me at all. It is not he who says it to me, as that solitary man silently confessed his secret to his neighbor on the seat; but *it* says it.

. . . The effect of having this said to me is completely different from that of looking on and observing. I cannot depict or denote or describe the man in whom, through whom, something has been said to me. Were I to attempt it, that would be the end of saying. This man is not my object; I have got to do with him. Perhaps I have to accomplish something about him; but perhaps I have only to learn something, and it is only a matter of my "accepting." It may be that I have to answer at once, to this very man before me; it may be that the saying has a long and manifold transmission before it, and that I am to answer some other person at some other time and place, in who knows what kind of speech, and that it is now only a matter of taking the answering on myself. But in each instance a word demanding an answer has happened to me. We may term this way of perception *becoming aware*.

It by no means needs to be a man of whom I become aware. It can be an animal, a plant, a stone. No kind of appearance or event is fundamentally excluded from the series of things through which from time to time something is said to me. Nothing can refuse to be the vessel for the Word. The limits of the possibility of dialogue are the limits of awareness.[20]

In many of his letters Bonhoeffer speaks of "the world come of age" in which man no longer needs God as a working hypothesis. He therefore attacks the deus ex machina, the god

[20] BUBER, *op. cit.*, pp. 16, 9–10.

who is lowered from the sky in a basket to extricate man from disaster. He speaks of the God who "makes us live in the world without using him," the paradoxical notion of a weakness that is more powerful than power. It might be fair to say that whenever the Church has sought to establish the rule of God by power, miracle, or bread it has won a battle but lost a war.

DIETRICH BONHOEFFER

God is teaching us that we must live as men who can get along very well without him. The God who is with us is the God who forsakes us. (Mark 15:34) The God who makes us live in this world without using him as a working hypothesis is the God before whom we are ever standing. Before God and with him we live without God. God allows himself to be edged out of the world and on to the cross. God is weak and powerless in the world, and that is exactly the way, the only way, in which he can be with us and help us. Matthew 8:17 makes it crystal clear that it is not by his omnipotence that Christ helps us, but by his weakness and suffering.

This is the decisive difference between Christianity and all religions. Man's religiosity makes him look in his distress to the power of God in the world; he uses God as a *Deus ex machina.* The Bible, however, directs him to the powerlessness and suffering of God; only a suffering God can help. To this extent we may say that the process we have described by which the world came of age was an abandonment of a false conception of God, and a clearing of the decks for the God of the Bible, who conquers power and space in the world by his weakness. This must be the starting point for our "worldly" interpretation.[21]

Will Herberg gives here a subtle and suggestive defense of the traditional way of speaking about God. He refuses to abandon the category of the personal, "Living God," but he clearly

[21] BONHOEFFER, *op. cit.*, pp. 219–220.

rejects the literalistic meaning of the term. Note also the connection he establishes between man's conception of God and man's conception of himself. Compare this to Frank's statement that for "the religious person the true idea of himself is not that one which he holds, but that one which God has of him." Herberg makes an important distinction between a creative relativity that is fostered by the biblical faith in God as the only absolute and the relativistic emphasis in modern thought which he says leads inevitably to nihilism.

WILL HERBERG

The God of Hebraic religion is not a philosophical principle, an ethical ideal or a cosmic process. The God of Hebraic religion, the God of the Bible, is a *Living God.* In this tremendous phrase—the Living God—which has become so strange to our ears but which occurs repeatedly in the Bible and continues right through rabbinic tradition, is concentrated the full potency of the Hebraic "God-idea." Only it is no longer a mere "God-idea." . . . When Judaism speaks of the Living God, it means to affirm that the transcendent Absolute which is the ultimate reality is not an abstract idea or an intellectual principle but a *dynamic power* in life and history—and a dynamic power that is *personal.* The God of Israel is thus best understood as a transcendent Person whose very "essence" is activity, activity not in some superworld of disembodied souls but in the actual world of men and things.

Attribution of personality to God is a scandal to modern minds. The religiously inclined man of today can understand and "appreciate" a God who—or rather, which—is some impersonal process or metaphysical concept. But a God who is personal, a person: that seems to be the grossest "anthropomorphism" and therefore the grossest superstition. Who can believe any such thing?

The embarrassment of modern man when confronted with

a personal God casts a revealing light on his entire outlook. In a certain sense, of course, every statement we make about God is bound to be misleading and paradoxical. . . . In whatever way we speak of God, whether we speak of him as a cosmic force or as a transcendent Person, we are making use of religious symbols. Everything depends upon the kind of symbols we use, for the symbols we use indicate not only the kind of God we affirm but also—what is very much the same thing in the end—our entire outlook on the universe. What do we mean when we speak of God as a Person? We mean that we meet God in life and history, not as an object, not as a thing, not as an *It*—to use Buber's pregnant distinction—but as a *Thou*. . . .

It seems to me this [modern reluctance to think of God as personal] is to be traced to the pervasive antipersonalistic bias of our culture. The whole tendency of mechanistic science and technology in the past two centuries has been to "dehumanize" our thinking and to imbue us with the conviction that personality is "merely subjective" and therefore unreal, since *real* reality, the reality presented to us by science, is impersonal. . . . To deny personality to God . . . is thus, at bottom, to deny the reality and worth of personality in man. On the other hand, the affirmation of God as personal is not only dictated by the reality of the divine-human encounter but is also a vindication of the pre-eminence of personal being as we find it in human existence over the nonpersonal categories of science and philosophy. . . . The denial of God leads inexorably to the devaluation and destruction of man. . . .

The traditional doctrine of creation *out of nothing* expresses the conviction that there is no ultimate principle in the universe aside from God. . . . Because God created the universe, existence as such must be good. . . .

The affirmation of the divine sovereignty taken seriously means, of course, that only God is absolute. . . . It implies that . . . nothing but God possesses any value in its own right. Whatever is not God—and that means everything in the world, every society, institution, belief or movement—is infected with relativity and can at best claim only a passing and partial validity. This God-centered relativism does justice to whatever is valid in the relativistic emphasis of modern thought without falling into the self-destructive nihilism to which the latter invariably leads.[22]

[22] WILL HERBERG, *Judaism and Modern Man* (New York, 1951), pp. 58–65.

THE SIGNIFICANCE OF CHRIST:
THE WORD MADE FLESH, THE NEW BEING

This is perhaps the most difficult area of faith to deal with in a non-partisan way, and consensus on the precise meaning of this doctrine is not easy to find, as the numerous divisions within Christianity would indicate. Yet the history of Christianity is the history of a community of people whose existence has been shaped and directed by their encounter with this person, their memories of him, their struggles to understand him and their reflections upon the meanings that radiate like light from his life and death and on-going spirit. The following selections are the merest taste of a vast and varied body of literature on the subject of the meaning of Christ. Some of them may disturb, some may enlighten, but this certainly is to be expected when one deals with the man who divides the dates of history and about whom such overwhelming assertions are made. Again in this section, notice that Christian thought lays stress on the idea of something that is done for us that we cannot do for ourselves, something that is given to us that we cannot achieve for ourselves.

Homer has just found out that his older brother has been killed in the war. We might contrast the attitude of Homer and Mr. Spangler to that of Ivan Karamazov. Perhaps we could say that if we read one set of signs we despair; if we read another, we find hope. In either case there has to be the element of what Tillich calls, "in spite of."

WILLIAM SAROYAN

They left the telegraph office and walked two blocks in silence. At last Homer began to speak. "What's a man supposed to do?" he said very calmly, almost gently. "I don't know who to hate. I keep trying to find out who it is, but I can't find out who it is. I just don't know. What's a man going to do? What can I do about it? What can I say? How does a man go on living? Who does he love?"

Now, coming down the street toward them, Homer and Spangler saw Auggie, Enoch, Shag, and Nickie. The boys greeted Homer and he greeted each of them by name. It was almost evening now. The sun was going down, the sky was red, and the city was darkening.

"Who can you hate?" Homer said. "I don't know anybody to hate. Byfield knocked me down while I was running the low hurdles, but I can't hate him, even. That's just the way he happens to be. I don't know what it is. I don't know who does it. I can't figure it out at all. The only thing I want to know is, What about my brother? That's all I want to know. Nothing like this has ever happened to me before. When my father died it was different. He had lived a good life. He had raised a good family. We were sad because he was dead, but we weren't sore. Now I'm sore and I haven't got anybody to be sore at. Who's the enemy? Do you know, Mr. Spangler?"

It was some time before the manager of the telegraph office could answer the messenger. "I know the enemy isn't people," he said. "If it were, then I would be my own enemy. The people of the world are like one man. If they hate one another, it is themselves they hate. A man cannot hate others—it is always himself. And if a man hates himself, there is only one thing for him to do—and that's leave—leave his body, leave the world, leave the people of the world. Your brother didn't want to leave, he wanted to stay. He will stay."

"How?" Homer said. "How will he stay?"

"I don't know how," Spangler said, "but I have to believe that he will stay. Maybe he will stay in you, in your little brother Ulysses. Maybe he will stay in the love you have for him."

"No," Homer said. "No, that isn't enough. I want to see him. I can't help it, but I want to see him the same way Ulysses wants to see him. I want to see him walking and standing. I want to smell him. I want to talk to him. I want to hear his voice. I want to hear him laughing. I want to have fights with him even—the way we used to. Now, where will I find him? If I look everywhere I won't find him. The whole world is different now. All the people in the world are different now. Something good has gone out of them. Everything in Ithaca is changed because now my brother is not going to look at any thing any more."

Now they were walking through the courthouse park, past the city jail, over to the games.

"I'm not going to try to comfort you," Spangler said. "I know I couldn't. But try to remember that a good man can never die. You will see him many times. You will see him in the streets. You will see him in the houses, in all the places of the town. In the vineyards and orchards, in the rivers and clouds, in all the things here that make this a world for us to live in. You will feel him in all things that are here out of love, and for love—all the things that are abundant, all the things that grow. The person of a man may leave—or be taken away—but the best part of a good man stays. It stays forever. Love is immortal and makes all things immortal. But hate dies every minute. Are you any good at pitching horseshoes?"

"No, sir," Homer said. "Not very."

"Neither am I," Spangler said. "Would you care to pitch a game of horseshoes before it's too dark?"

"Yes, sir," Homer said.[23]

[23] WILLIAM SAROYAN, *The Human Comedy* (New York, 1943), pp. 282 ff.

All of these writers have as a background for their remarks **a** particular assumption about man. The religious writers feel that something is wrong with man's will and that his reason cannot command his will. Therefore, they concern themselves with an analysis of a power they believe can change man's will. Knowledge, law, logic, force do not, in their opinion, produce this inner change. In most of these selections much is said about the suffering of the innocent and the willingness of some people to bear the consequences of evil for the sake of others. It is the Christian claim that the true meaning and purpose of life is revealed in such suffering, that it has the power to create in us the right will and take us out of ourselves to involve us in the lives of others. When this happens to a person, the traditional language is quite accurate. The old self that lives by a false power dies and is resurrected into a new life by the power of God which is none other than the power of love.

H. Richard Niebuhr speaks of using the life and death of Christ as a parable and an analogy, a kind of mirror in which we see ourselves and our world. In other words, as the Christian reads the story, he is compelled to confess that he too is a crucifier, he too is responsible for innocent victims in his world; yet at the same time he is made to see that people have died and are dying for his sake, that he has his life at the price of other life. In this picture we see what we are created to be and also how far we have departed from the pattern. It is this picture of ourselves that can create in us not only the proper degree of humility but also a genuine sense of our own worth. We are given a status we can never earn or make for ourselves. We are accepted just as we are. Therefore we do not have to pretend to be something other than what we are. Out of this can come repentance and the will to be what we ought to be. It has much to do with our capacity to accept others for what they are. Think how much our criticism and rejection of others is really a cover for our own guilt and an attempt to create a sense of our own worth. Consider what different implications emerge when one uses the jungle as the basic analogy for human existence. As Reinhold Niebuhr points out, there is no way to arrive at an understanding of the meaning of life and history without such a revelation. There is no necessity or logic that compels the inquiring mind to choose the Christian story over the jungle analogy or visa versa as the ultimate criterion of meaning.

H. RICHARD NIEBUHR

In interpreting our present, we use the life and death of Christ as a parable and an analogy. The scribes and Pharisees now sit in Peter's seat and in the churches of St. Paul priests plot defense against the disturber of the people; disciples are corrupted by thirty pieces of silver; money-changers and those who sell human victims for vain sacrifices conspire with Pilates who wash their bloody hands in public; poor unreasoning soldiers commit sins which are not their own; betrayals and denials take place in every capital; and so, out of cumulative self-deceit and treachery, out of great ignorance, out of false fears and all the evil imaginations of the heart, crosses are constructed not only for thieves but for the sons of God. We see, through the use of the great parable, how bodies are now being broken for our sake and how for the remission of our sins the blood of innocents is being shed. Not with complete clarity, to be sure, yet as in a glass darkly, we can discern in the contemporary confusion of our lives the evidence of a pattern in which, by great travail of men and God, a work of redemption goes on which is like the work of Christ. We learn to know what we are doing and what is being done to us—how by an infinite suffering of the eternal victim we are condemned and forgiven at the same time; how an infinite loyalty refuses to abandon us either to evil or to nothingness, but works at our salvation with a tenacity we are tempted to deplore. The story of Jesus and particularly of his passion, is the great illustration that enables us to say, "What we are now doing and suffering is like this." [24]

THE INCARNATION

"God was in Christ, reconciling the world unto Himself, not imputing their trespasses unto them; and hath committed unto us the word of reconciliation." (2 Corinthians 5:19)

Christ thought of God as a life-giver rather than a law-giver. An earthly father might discipline his child for violating the rule of honesty, but his real intention would be to give his child his own spirit of truthfulness. The fulfillment of the child's life required it, and the father was seeking to give what the child's nature required.

In some such way Christ represented God. He went about, mixing with sinners, identifying himself with men "while yet in their sin" and not waiting for them to become worthy. He went more than half way to win them away from self to give them his spirit. A great Jewish scholar once wrote that Christ's uniqueness lay in the fact that the love he showed did not wait for men to deserve forgiveness, but sought them out "while they were yet afar off." In our everyday life we all know self-giving love, that is not thinking about itself, is never acquired by will power or conscious reasoning. We are confronted by it, and either reject it or receive its power into our life like a gift. This is why Jesus met such opposition in his day from those who felt he was destroying the whole fabric of religion inherited from Moses.

According to this revolutionary view of God as a life-giver, the requirement is in our own nature which needs love for deliverance from self, and love is the spirit of God himself freely given whenever man's self stands out of the way. As the Bible said, man was "made in the image of God" expressly to this end that he might be invaded and subdued by the spirit of his Creator. Christians believe that the mystery of the union of human

[24] RICHARD NIEBUHR, *The Meaning of Revelation* (New York, 1941), pp. 124–125.

184

nature and the divine nature was once and for all perfectly revealed in this man. Nothing more could be done to reveal God's
love in relation to man. For this one person, in whom all claims
of self were forgone, became transparent to the divine love which
could appear in a single individual and yet be universal for
human nature in all places and in all ages.

It is important to recognize that when a Christian claims
that Christ mediates the saving encounter between man
and God he does not thereby limit salvation to Christians.
Hopefully, he remembers Jesus' warning, "Not everyone who
calls me 'Lord, Lord' enters into the kingdom." Reinhold
Niebuhr states that Christians "must guard against the assumption that only those who know Christ 'after the flesh,' that is, in
the actual historical revelation, are capable of such a conversion.
A 'hidden Christ' operates in history. And there is always the
possibility that those who do not know the historical revelation
may achieve a more genuine repentance and humility than those
who do. If this is not kept in mind the Christian faith easily
becomes a new vehicle of pride." *

REINHOLD NIEBUHR

The truth that the Word was made flesh outrages all the
canons by which truth is usually judged. Yet it is the truth. The
whole character of the Christian religion is involved in that
affirmation. It asserts that God's word is relevant to human life.
It declares that an event in history can be of such a character as
to reveal the character of history itself; that without such a revelation the character of history cannot be known. It is not possible
to arrive at an understanding of the meaning of life and history
without such a revelation. No induction from empirical facts
can yield a conclusion about ultimate meaning because every
process of induction presupposes some canon and criterion of
meaning.

* *The Nature and Destiny of Man*, Vol. II, p. 109, note 6.

In Christian thought Christ is both the perfect man, "the second Adam" who has restored the perfection of what man was and ought to be; and the Son of God, who transcends all possibilities of human life. It is this idea which theology sought to rationalise in the doctrines of the two natures of Christ. It cannot be rationalised and yet it is a true idea. Human life stands in infinity. Everything it touches turns to infinity. Every moral standard, rigorously analysed, proves to be no permanently valid standard at all short of perfect and infinite love. The only adequate norm of human conduct is love of God and of man, through which all men are perfectly related to each other, because they are all related in terms of perfect obedience and love to the centre and source of their existence.[25]

In making the point about what he calls the "paradoxical Christian secret," Baillie is seeking to describe the subtle difference between the kind of goodness that is a response to the spirit of Christ and the kind that is mere obedience to moral law. In the former, the person loves because he has been loved—he has forgotten himself in his concern for the other. He therefore is not thinking about himself doing a good deed, earning moral points, etc. This emphasis in Christian thought derives from the idea that the new life is a gift of God which is either received or rejected. It is not something the person fashions for himself out of moral effort or earns after some self-improvement.

D. M. BAILLIE

We may begin with the familiar words of St. Paul: "By the grace of God I am what I am: and his grace which was bestowed upon me was not found vain; but I laboured more abundantly than they all: yet not I, but the grace of God which was with me." (1 Corinthians 15:10)

[25] REINHOLD NIEBUHR, *Beyond Tragedy* (New York, 1937), pp. 13–14, 16.

186

Thus the paradoxical Christian secret, while it transcends the moralistic attitude by ascribing all to God, does not make us morally irresponsible. That is part of the paradox. No one knows better than the Christian that he is free to choose and that in a sense everything depends upon his choice. . . . My actions are my very own, expressions of my own will, my own choice. No one else can choose for me or relieve me of the responsibility. When I make the wrong choice, I am entirely responsible, and my conscience condemns me. And yet (here is the paradox) when I make the right choice, my conscience does not applaud or congratulate me. I do not feel meritorious or glow with self-esteem—if and in so far as I am a Christian. Instead of that I say: "Not I, but the grace of God." Thus while there is a human side to every good action, so that it is genuinely the free choice of a person with a will, yet somehow the Christian feels that the other side of it, the divine side, is logically prior. . . . It is not as if we could divide the honours between God and ourselves, God doing His part, and we doing ours. It cannot even be adequately expressed in terms of divine initiative and human co-operation. It is false to this paradox to think of the area of God's action and the area of our action being delimited, each by the other, and distinguished from each other by a boundary, so that the more of God's grace there is in an action, the less is it my own personal action. . . . We are not marionettes, but responsible persons, and never more truly and fully personal in our actions than in those moments when we are most dependent on God and He lives and acts in us. And yet the divine side is somehow prior to the human.

What I wish to suggest is that this paradox of grace points the way more clearly and makes a better approach than anything else in our experience to the mystery of the Incarnation itself; that this paradox in its fragmentary form in our own Christian lives is a reflection of that perfect union of God and man in the Incarnation on which our whole Christian life depends, and may therefore be our best clue to the understanding of it. In the New

Testament we see the man in whom God was incarnate surpassing all other men in refusing to claim anything for Himself independently and ascribing all the goodness to God. We see Him also desiring to take up other men into His own close union with God, that they might be as He was. And if these men, entering in some small measure through Him into that union, experience the paradox of grace for themselves in fragmentary ways, and are constrained to say, "It was not I but God," may not this be a clue to the understanding of that perfect life in which the paradox is complete and absolute, that life of Jesus which, being the perfection of humanity, is also, and even in a deeper and prior sense, the very life of God Himself? If the paradox is a reality in our poor imperfect lives at all, so far as there is any good in them, does not the same or a similar paradox, taken at the perfect and absolute pitch, appear as the mystery of the Incarnation?

. . . This is the Creator-God who made us to be free personalities, and we know that we are most free and personal when He is most in possession of us. This is the God of the moral order who calls us every moment to exercise our full and responsible choice; but He also comes to dwell in us in such a way that we are raised altogether above the moral order into the liberty of the sons of God. That is what Christians mean by "God." It is highly paradoxical, but it is bound up with the whole message of Christianity and the whole structure of the Christian life; and it follows inevitably if we take seriously the fundamental paradox: "Not I, but the grace of God." It is God's very nature to give Himself in that way: to dwell in man in such a manner that man, by his own will choosing to do God's will (and in a sense it must depend on man's own choice) nevertheless is constrained to confess that it was "all of God." [26]

If it is fair to say that a man's god molds him in its image, then Pike is saying that the three ways in which the Christian

[26] D. M. Baillie, *God Was in Christ* (New York, 1948), pp. 114, 116–118, 121–122.

experiences God become the formative power in shaping himself. Thus he sees himself as called in all his work to be like God—creative, redemptive, and a builder of community.

JAMES A. PIKE

What is God's nature in so far as His relation to the world is concerned?

First of all, He is Creator. He not only created the world, He creates it. God operates in and through the evolving order (assuming here the evolutionary hypothesis), expressing Himself in manifold and wondrous ways. . . . At one point along the line there are evolved creatures which, as Le Compte De Nouy has reminded us, are henceforth in on the evolving.

. . . Second, God is Redeemer. In His relationship to us He is not only a source of norms; He seeks to save those who have not kept the norms, who have come to moral shipwreck, who have to any degree missed the way. Supremely He reveals this character in Jesus Christ, through whom He has translated Himself into the language of human life. What we see in Jesus Christ of God's redemptive activity is a supreme image of how God always has been and always will be toward the sons of men.

Third, God is Holy Spirit. . . . God as Holy Spirit works through the life of the group, in the esprit de corps of "the blessed company of all faithful people," which is the Church, and beyond this He is the genuine inspiration of all wholesome group life. We too are meant to be carriers of the spark of corporate activity. We are meant to be involved in and build up an increasing web of human inter-relationship. . . . The Kingdom of God is a community of creative and redemptive persons whose lives have become increasingly interlaced and whose talents have received expression in such purposeful ways that all members of the Kingdom have a maximum relationship to each other, up to the limit of each one's capacities.

. . . God has related Himself to us in three ways corresponding to His very nature, yet He is one God. When God creates, the whole of God is acting. In Jesus Christ we are in touch with the whole God. When we are reached with the life of the Christian community we are reached by the whole God. This doctrine of the Trinity, which is really the proclamation of God's unity in the face of our threefold experience of God, is the model for us. The ideal view of personality is that man is to be integrated in all of his activity and that primarily in his creative efforts, in his service to others and in his life in community, he is to be pulling in the same direction, with the whole man totally involved withal.[27]

CRUCIFIXION AND RESURRECTION

"I am crucified with Christ; nevertheless I live; yet not I but Christ that liveth in me." (Galatians 2:20)

We would not even have the New Testament record if Jesus had been no more than a good example who died, like a martyr, for his ideals. These writings and the movement they set going in the world originated in men who discovered the climax of Jesus' story and mission in a crucifixion and a resurrection.

The meaning they found in these events, that turned defeated men into undefeatable apostles, cannot be gained by looking back as mere spectators of events which happened two thousand years ago. We have to stand inside of some experience, however small, of the new life which is created out of an old life of self-concern; for that is the point of view from which the early Christians were looking when they wrote the documents we have inherited.

First of all the Crucifixion can be seen as a judgment of God upon what men consider good enough. In some small way we know that the judgment we dread most in our selfishness is not in the consequences we have to take ourselves. It is in the suffering of those who had loved and trusted us, and who were

[27] JAMES A. PIKE, *Doing the Truth* (New York, 1955), pp. 34–38.

not to blame for what we did. In some such way the Crucifixion of one who revealed perfect love demonstrated how all the human goodness which society accepts as passable has enough badness in it to resist that love which appeared in Christ. He died at the hands of Roman justice which boasted of being fair to all; he died by the decisions of the pious leaders of religion in his day, who took their piety to be the measure for judging all men's virtues. The crowd that yelled, "Crucify him!" had listened uncritically to the lying innuendoes and slurs which biased witnesses gave forth as truth—just as today plenty of unthinking Americans have condemned innocent men because of unfounded accusations uttered in public hearings. Any one of us who dares honestly to submit his respectability to be measured by Christ's life, knows that his actual self, which he has accepted, is an enemy of the self he might be.

Second, the Crucifixion can mean, not only the judgment of God, but the supreme demonstration of saving power. It seemed a helpless power in protecting itself, but it is the only power in the universe which can effect a real change in a selfish heart. Other kinds of power can restrain, control, and force us, but they do not touch the heart. We know it is a tragic injustice when those who love us suffer for what we do. Such love has no power to force us to love in return, but if it cannot work a change in our spirit nothing else can.

The Bible treats the Crucifixion and the Resurrection as though they were inseparably united in one revealing story, containing a point of view that makes most sense out of our earthly existence that comes to an end in death. Often the Resurrection raises more questions than it answers to anyone looking back critically over twenty centuries as he would look back at the death of Caesar. The earliest accounts speak of some sort of communion between the risen man and his disciples; the later accounts add details of a more extraordinary nature. If there were some scientific way of piecing the stories together, testing

191

every historical detail, to gain a proof of immortality, the result would make little difference to anybody, for it would apply only to this very ancient personality.

A more fruitful way to view the story is to stand, as it were, in the shoes of the Apostle Paul and see what he says it revealed to him about the meaning of our earthly life. Paul, after his conversion, experienced within him the living power of the new life which Christ had embodied in the flesh. He had also, and this is important, watched the stoning of the Christian martyr Stephen and heard him say of his enemies: "Forgive them for they know not what they do," just as Christ had done before him. What Paul saw outside in these disciples he found coming alive inside himself, driving him as it had driven Christ and his followers. What the Roman authorities had tried to stop with a crucifixion, was still a living power in a new community of people who were bound together by this new Spirit, without regard to national traditions. And ever since, this new community which was called the Church, has persisted all over the world, as though it were an extension of the body of Christ, often betraying its source again and again, yet continuing as a channel for a living spirit inside the visible organization and outside of it wherever its influence spread.

In the following passage of Tillich's, and in the next two by Reinhold Niebuhr, the themes of death and resurrection, judgment and renewal, victory of God over the "princes of this world," are variously dealt with. Several questions deserve attention. Why does man push away true reality when he encounters it? Why can he not afford to see how far he has deviated from the true pattern of his nature?

If a man's worth is to be determined by what he accomplishes "out there" in the world, then he lives in "fear of death" and is "subject to bondage." If his worth is affirmed in spite of what he has or has not done, then he does not need time to create his worth, he is delivered from fear of death. However you want to formulate the truth that the Christian sees in Christ, it is basically involved with the proclamation that we have been died for, just as we are, with all our sins upon us. We are not worthy of this sacrifice but we are accounted worthy. Using this clue to the meaning of history, the Christian sees that everything he has, including his very life, is a gift, a gift he has at the expense of others' suffering and death. He is forced to see himself as the future that all past generations struggled to bring into being. Such a vision of reality, the Christian claims, has the power to break him down in judgment and renewal, and break out of him in new creation. This cannot be forced on anyone; it accepts our refusal to see; which is why it takes a Crucifixion, a bombing of Negro children, the assassination of a president, even to ask the right questions, let alone receive a healing answer.

PAUL TILLICH

The Christ had to suffer and die, because whenever the Divine appears in all its depth, It cannot be endured by men. It must be pushed away by the political powers, the religious authorities, and the bearers of cultural tradition. In the picture of the Crucified, we look at the rejection of the Divine by humanity. We see that, in this rejection, not the lowest, but the highest representatives of mankind are judged. Whenever the Divine appears, It is a radical attack on everything that is good in man, and therefore man must repel It, must push It away, must crucify It. Whenever the Divine manifests Itself as the new reality, It must be rejected by the representatives of the old reality. For the Divine does not complete the human; it revolts against the human. Because of that, the human must defend itself against It, must reject It, and must try to destroy It.

Yet when the Divine is rejected, It takes the rejection upon

Itself. It accepts our crucifixion, our pushing away, the defence of ourselves against It. It accepts our refusal to accept, and thus conquers us. That is the centre of the mystery of the Christ.[28]

REINHOLD NIEBUHR

The suffering of the guiltless, which is the primary problem of life for those who look at history from the standpoint of their own virtues, is made into the ultimate answer of history for those who look at it from the standpoint of the problematic character of all human virtue. This suffering of the guiltless one was to become in Christian faith a revelation of God's own suffering. It alone was seen to have the power to overcome the recalcitrance of man at the very center of man's personality, . . . it alone was also the final dimension of the divine sovereignty over human history. To make suffering love rather than power the final expression of sovereignty was to embody the perplexity of history into the solution.

. . . Suffering love, the same Agape of Christ which reveals the divine mercy is also the norm of a new life. Men may have this new life if they discern what they are and what God is in this focal point of God's self-disclosure. Such a point in human history can be regarded both as the beginning of a new age for all mankind and as a new beginning for every individual man who is "called" by it, because both the individual and the collective realities of human existence are fully disclosed in it. If apprehended at all, they are so apprehended that the old self, which makes itself its own end, is destroyed and a new self is born. That is why a true revelation of the divine is never merely wisdom but also power.

The climax of the crucifixion and resurrection thus becomes not merely the culmination of the whole series of revelations but the pattern of all subsequent confrontations between God and man. They must contain the crucifixion of self-abandonment

[28] TILLICH, *op. cit.*, p. 147.

194

and the resurrection of self-recovery. Men must die to sin with Christ and arise with Him to newness of Life.... This-worldly religions try to make sense out of life in the dimension of nature-history which man transcends. Other-worldly religions try to make sense out of life by abstracting some eternal essence of man from the fragments of history. Christianity insists upon the potential meaningfulness of man's fragmentary life in history and its final completion by a power and love not his own.... New Testament faith ends in the pinnacle of the hope of the resurrection ... for it is persuaded that a divine power and love have been disclosed in Christ, which will complete what man can not complete; and which will overcome the evil introduced into human life and history by man's abortive effort to complete his life by his own wisdom and power.

In the Epistle to the Hebrews Christ is portrayed as emancipating those "who through the fear of death were all their lifetime subject to bondage" (Hebrews 2:15). Thus the root of sin (excessive concern for the self) is found in the self's concern for its contingent existence. The release from this bondage involves emancipation from anxiety about death. Thus the resurrection of Christ is always portrayed as a triumph over both sin and death.[29]

* * *

The suffering servant does not impose goodness upon the world by his power. Rather he suffers, being powerless, from the injustices of the powerful. He suffers most particularly from the sins of the righteous who do not understand how full of unrighteousness is all human righteousness. The Saviour of the world is not crucified by criminals or obviously evil people; he is crucified with criminals by the "princes of this world," to use the Pauline phrase. Love is the law of life; but when it enters the world of relative justice and balanced egotism it is destroyed in it. The

[29] REINHOLD NIEBUHR, *Faith and History* (New York, 1949), pp. 144, 149–150, 176.

suffering servant dies on the cross. This paradox is perfectly expressed in the Johannine gospel: "He was in the world and the world was made through him . . . he came unto his own and his own received him not." The implication is that human nature has deviated from the law of its existence, that man is estranged from his essential nature. Christ is the essential nature of man, or as St. Paul expresses it, the "second Adam." . . . Thus when the Kingdom of God enters the world it is judged by the world and found to be dangerous to all of its tentative harmonies and relative justice. But it also judges the world in the very moment in which the world is condemning it. The commandment of love which Christ introduces in the world was "from the beginning," the life which he manifests is the very pattern of life. The world does not know how far it has strayed from that pattern until the original is revealed. . . . The Kingdom of God must still enter the world by way of the crucifixion. Goodness, armed with power, is corrupted; and pure love without power is destroyed. If it succeeds occasionally, as it does, it gives us vital and creative symbols of the fact that the Kingdom of God is a reality as well as a possibility.[30]

THE NEW BEING

"If any man be in Christ, he is a new creature." (2 Corinthians 5:5)

Once this new creation appeared in Christ it has put everything else in second place. All religions, with their rites and creeds, secular religions that avoid God, all of them are secondary to this fact of a new creation that can take place inside human beings. Paul Tillich in his book, The New Being, follows Paul in saying that nothing else really matters: "No particular religion matters. . . . But I want to tell you that something has happened that matters, something that judges you and me, your

[30] REINHOLD NIEBUHR, *Beyond Tragedy* (New York, 1937), pp. 181–185.

*religion and my religion. A New Creation has occurred ... and
we are all asked to participate in it. ... And so we should say:
Don't compare your religion and our religion ... the pious
amongst you and the pious amongst us. All this is of no avail. ...
We want only to show you something we have heard: that in
the midst of the old creation there is a New Creation, and that
this New Creation is manifest in Jesus who is called Christ."
This does not mean that our form of religion is to be repudiated
as false; it means that every form of religion is to be tested and
judged by this change of our self-love into a new kind of love
altogether, for this is what really matters. Jesus said, "Not everyone that calleth me Lord, Lord, shall enter into the Kingdom of
Heaven; but he that doeth the will of my father."*

*Tillich emphasizes here that the truth a Christian is con-
cerned with is not a matter of statements and propositions but a
life, a state of being. In what way is a person who seriously asks
about being in the truth already in it, already on his way to
liberation from untruth?*

PAUL TILLICH

The truth of which Jesus speaks is not a doctrine but a
reality, namely, He Himself: "I *am* the truth." ... If Jesus says,
"I am the truth," he indicates that in Him the true, the genuine,
the ultimate reality is present; or, in other words, that God is
present, unveiled, undistorted, in His infinite depth, in His un-
approachable mystery. Jesus is not the truth because His teachings are true. But His teachings are true because they express the
truth which He Himself is. He is more than His words. And He
is more than any word said about Him.

How do we reach this truth? "By doing it," is the answer of
the Fourth Gospel. This does not mean being obedient to the
commandments, accepting them and fulfilling them. Doing the

truth means living out of the reality which is *He* who is the truth, making His being the being of ourselves and of our world. ... The truth which liberates is the truth in which we participate, which is a part of us and we a part of it.

... We ask, "How can this happen?" There is an answer to this question in our Gospel which may deeply shock us: "Every one who is of the truth hears my voice." ... If we have part in it, we recognize it wherever it appears; we recognize it as it appears in its fullness in the Christ. But, some may ask in despair: "If we have *no* part in it, if we are *not* of the truth, are we then forever excluded from it? Must we accept a life without truth, a life in error and meaninglessness? Who tells me that I am of the truth, that *I* have a chance to reach it?" Nobody can tell you; but there is one criterion: If you *seriously* ask the question, "Am I of the truth?" you *are* of the truth. If you do not ask it seriously, you do not really want, and you do not deserve, and you cannot get, an answer! He who asks seriously the question of the truth that liberates, is already on his way to liberation. ...

On this road you will meet the liberating truth in many forms except in one form: you never will meet it in the form of propositions which you can learn or write down and take home. ... The truth which liberates is the power of love, for God is love.... Therefore, distrust every claim for truth where you do not see truth united with love; and be certain that you are of the truth and that the truth has taken hold of you only when love has taken hold of you and has started to make you free from yourselves.[31]

According to Berger, what is involved in affirming the Christian faith is not a retreat from reality but a move toward a man in whom reality is seen in a new way.

[31] PAUL TILLICH, *The New Being* (New York, 1955), pp. 69–72, 74.

PETER BERGER

There may well be people who have had a mystical or even miraculous experience of metaphysical reality, an experience of such conviction that thereafter doubt is possible only as an intellectual exercise. . . . Unfortunately the writer has not been thus privileged. He suspects strongly that he shares this underprivileged condition with the overwhelming majority of people. . . .

When one says "I believe" rather than "I know" one is expressing a view of which one is not completely certain. That this view is much more than a mere opinion or theoretical hypothesis, that it is the result of passionate commitment and may lead to the most far-reaching existential consequences, is beside the point here. If one says "I believe," in this sense, one faces the fact that one is essentially in the same boat as the unbeliever. . . . The message of redemption in Jesus Christ comes to believer and unbeliever alike from the outside, refraining from coercion, asking an act of faith. Speaking theologically, this means that the Christian remains a sinner (that is, one separated from God) also intellectually. Speaking humanly, it means that what is called for is a decision made on less than overwhelming evidence. . . .

There can be no basis for Christian faith except in the encounter with the figure of Jesus Christ, as it becomes manifest in the testimony of the Bible and the living proclamation in the church. Faith is the decision to stake one's existence on this figure. This is not a negative choice, because of any number of alternatives, because one cannot face finitude, meaninglessness, guilt, or death. It is a free and positive choice, not *away* from the realities of the human condition but *toward* this figure in whom the human condition is transfigured. To be human means to live with inconclusive information on the ultimate meaning of things. To have faith in Christ means to say that if there is any meaning at all, it is here that one must find it.[32]

In this passage you get a clear sense of the kind of intellectual struggle that goes on at the frontier of Christian thinking. Though it may sound to the skeptic like someone trying to have his cake and eat it too, it is important to recognize the degree of honesty that is here, especially when it comes from a man in prison. This seems scarcely the time for a Christian to pull the "linchpin" out from his own religion. Notice that he distinguishes between "religion" and faith in Christ as Lord. Whatever we think of his notion of a "secular" Christianity, it is necessary to hear his criticism of the usual ways in which men speak and think about God.

DIETRICH BONHOEFFER

What *is* Christianity, and indeed what *is* Christ, for us today? The time when men could be told everything by means of words, whether theological or simply pious, is over, and so is the time of inwardness and conscience, which is to say the time of religion as such. We are proceeding towards a time of no religion at all: men as they are now simply cannot be religious any more. Even those who honestly describe themselves as "religious" do not in the least act up to it, and so when they say "religious" they evidently mean something quite different. Our whole nineteen-hundred-year-old Christian preaching and theology rests upon the "religious premise" of man. What we call Christianity has always been a pattern—perhaps a true pattern—of religion. But if one day it becomes apparent that this *a priori* "premise" simply does not exist, but was an historical and temporary form of human self-expression, i.e. if we reach the stage of being radi-

[32] Peter L. Berger, *The Precarious Vision* (Garden City, N.Y., 1961), pp. 188–190.

cally without religion—and I think this is more or less the case already— . . . what does that mean for "Christianity"?

It means that the linchpin is removed from the whole structure of our Christianity to date, and the only people left for us to light on in the way of "religion" are the few "last survivals of the age of chivalry," or else one or two who are intellectually dishonest. . . . How can Christ become the Lord even of those with no religion? If religion is no more than the garment of Christianity . . . then what is a religionless Christianity? . . . How do we speak of God without religion, i.e. without the temporally-influenced presuppositions of metaphysics, inwardness, and so on? . . . (perhaps we are no longer capable of speaking of such things as we used to). In what way are we in a religionless and secular sense Christians, in what way are we the Ekklesia, "those who are called forth," not conceiving of ourselves religiously as specially favored, but as wholly belonging to the world? Then Christ is no longer an object of religion, but . . . indeed and in truth the Lord of the world. Yet what does that signify? What is the place of worship and prayer in an entire absence of religion? . . . . The Pauline question (Galatians 6:15) whether circumcision is a condition of justification is today, I consider, the question whether religion is a condition of salvation. Freedom from circumcision is at the same time freedom from religion. I often ask myself why a Christian instinct frequently draws me more to the religionless than to the religious, by which I mean not with any intention of evangelizing them, but rather . . . in "brotherhood." While I often shrink with religious people from speaking of God by name—because that Name somehow seems to me here not to ring true, and I strike myself as rather dishonest (it is especially bad when others start talking in religious jargon: then I dry up completely and feel somehow oppressed and ill at ease) —with people who have no religion I am able on occasion to speak of God quite openly and as it were naturally. Religious people speak of God when human perception is (often just from laziness) at an end, or human resources fail: it is really the *Deus ex machina* they call to their aid, either for the so-called solving of insoluble problems or as support in human failure—always, that is to say, helping out human weakness or on the borders of human existence. Of necessity that can only go on until men can, by their own strength, push those borders a little further, so that God becomes superfluous as a *Deus ex machina*. I have come to be doubtful even about talking of "borders of human existence." Is even death today, since men are scarcely afraid of it any more, and sin, which they scarcely understand any more, still a genuine borderline? It always seems to me that in talking thus we are only seeking frantically to make room for God. I should like to speak of God not on the borders of life but at its center, not in weakness but in strength, not, therefore, in man's suffering and death but in his life and prosperity. On the borders it seems to me better to hold our peace and leave the problem unsolved. Belief in the Resurrection is not the solution of the problem of death. The "beyond" of God is not the beyond of our perceptive faculties. . . . God is the "beyond" in the midst of our life. The Church stands not where human powers give out, on the borders, but in the center of the village.

* * *

We should find God in what we do know, not in what we don't; not in outstanding problems, but in those we have already solved. This is true not only for the relation between Christianity and science but also for wider human problems such as guilt, suffering and death. It is possible nowadays to find answers to these problems which leave God right out of the picture. It just isn't true to say that Christianity alone has the answers. In fact the Christian answers are no more conclusive or compelling than any of the others. Once more, God cannot be used as a stopgap. . . . he must be found at the center of life. . . . The ground for this lies in the revelation of God in Christ. Christ is the center of life, and in no sense did he come to answer our unsolved problems. From the center of life certain questions are seen to be wholly irrelevant.[33]

PAUL TILLICH

Nothing greater can happen to a human being than that he is forgiven. For forgiveness means reconciliation in spite of estrangement; it means reunion in spite of hostility; it means acceptance of those who are unacceptable, and it means reception of those who are rejected.

Forgiveness is unconditional or it is not forgiveness at all. Forgiveness has the character of "in spite of," but the righteous ones give it the character of "because." [34]

Pike is dealing here with one of the fundamentals of human healing and growth which he describes in terms of having the maximum of both self-criticism and self-acceptance. The only way a person acquires the courage to look honestly at himself is if he knows for sure that he is accepted regardless of what horrors he turns up in himself. This is why Tillich in the short passage above says that forgiveness is unconditional or it is not forgiveness at all. The righteous ones, he says, give it the character of "because." By this he means that those who divide people into the good guys and the bad guys will only accept the bad guys if they turn out to be good guys. But this condition is precisely what tempts the bad guy (which is each of us) into hiding from the one whose approval he seeks and therefore hiding from himself.

JAMES A. PIKE

Perhaps the central problem of human personality is how to reconcile self-criticism and self-acceptance. Both are essential,

[33] BONHOEFFER, *op. cit.*, pp. 162–166, 190–191.
[34] TILLICH, *op. cit.*, pp. 7–8.

yet they seem to contradict each other. The simple fact is that if a man judges himself rigorously by the whole law of love he will find himself unacceptable and yet it is essential that he find himself acceptable. This is basic both to his well-being and to his effectiveness in fulfilling his vocation. Some men achieve a high degree of self-criticism at the expense of self-acceptance; others achieve a high degree of self-acceptance at the expense of self-criticism. How can a man have a maximum of both at the same time? Since this is obviously the *desideratum* we should say at the outset that Christianity unequivocally has the answer to this problem, and, as we shall see, the answer is its unique message. . . .

It is commonly thought that psychoanalysis is a remedy for trouble with suppressed guilt feelings. If the accumulation of covered-up guilt feelings is considerable such anxiety may have resulted that analysis may well be the only way of bringing all the demons out into the open; then some of the guilt feelings when examined consciously may dissolve away when it is discovered that there was no guilt there in the first place, but only a baseless inhibition. But as to a sense of guilt which was founded on actual guilt, the problem remains. There are two alternatives, and these sum up the whole problem. Either the patient will muster new rationalizations and cover up the guilt feelings again, forcing them back into the unconscious, or else he will suffer loss of self-respect by retention of the sense of guilt on the conscious level. . . . If he feels "no good," and knows no way to relieve himself of the weight of his past, his incentive to change his negative ways is reduced and his drive to do positive good is impeded.

. . . What is needed is a way to be honest about the past—and yet break with it. It is precisely this that the Christian Gospel offers. It is a two-sided process, involving both God and man. On God's side it is called the Atonement. On man's side, justification.

As to God's side, we lose much of the dynamic of what can operate on man's side if we oversimplify things and simply say that God forgives sin. It cannot be *simply* this on God's part if there is preserved the full force of God's justice and God's unyielding claim to our full allegiance. This is why St. Paul in the Epistle to the Romans turns first to the problem of the justification of God before he turns to justification of man: assuming that God forgives, the problem is how is His righteousness maintained? If 100 percent is expected of us—and all our lives long—how can we be acceptable to Him (and thus to ourselves) if we have broken the law—once or repeatedly. It is important for the whole ethical structure that God not lower His standards, even for the ease of our consciences. With His righteousness is at stake our dignity and meaning. And at stake too is the high seriousness of our relationship with God. If I have been insulting to an acquaintance and his reply to my protestations of regret is, "Skip it, it didn't matter to me in the least," and if I think he means it, then I know that *I* don't matter to him and that my actions, one way or the other, have no meaning for him. This one thing is anchored down in Christian theology: God doesn't "skip it." To alter the analogy, when I have offended a friend who *does* care what I do, and I say that I am sorry, I know that as he forgives me he absorbs the hurt. The Christian faith proclaims that God absorbs the hurt in forgiving us, thus maintaining His justice and absolute expectancy as to our behavior and at the same time accepting us into full standing with Him. How He does this, particularly in the supreme manifestation of it in the saving passion and death of Our Lord, is more properly the subject of theology— and a difficult part of it it is; but the *fact* that He does so is one of the three great theological premises about the nature of God on which the system of Christian ethics rests. He takes up the slack between His righteousness and our actual behavior, if we repent. He takes the burden and hurt of our sins unto Himself. He closes up the gap of separation which is our sin. . . . Thus He accepts us over and over again. And on this acceptance rests our own self-acceptance. If God accepts me, who am I not to accept myself? [35]

John Wren-Lewis is a young industrial scientist and lay theologian who gained considerable attention in England for his criticism of the subtle deception the Church has tolerated for so long in its understanding of religion. Here again we see the dissatisfaction of an intelligent Christian with traditional language, especially that which suggests a hidden world somewhere behind the scenes. He has some useful remarks on problems generated by looking at the world as primarily a material system. His argument here is similar to Richard Niebuhr's idea of external and internal history. Also he has a good way of expressing the idea of "creation" as well as helpful interpretation of the doctrine of the fall.

JOHN WREN-LEWIS

Can we seriously go on thinking [of the universe as a place] when the astronomers calmly tell us that our sun, 90 million miles away, is only one amongst many millions of stars spread out in a galaxy which light itself takes 80 million years to get across? and that this galaxy itself is only one of the countless other galaxies, some even bigger, which disappear into the infinite distances. . . .

Can we really take seriously the idea that the universe is a place when these terms have to be used to describe it? On the contrary, I think what modern science has done here is to explode almost literally the notion of the world as a place, a material space-time system, and it forces us to recognize that when we are talking about space and time, we are talking about abstractions, we are talking about mathematical, technological abstractions, and not about real things.

[35] PIKE, *op. cit.*, pp. 79–80, 85–87.

... So long as you believe that this world is primarily a material system, a place spread out in space and time, then if you believe in spiritual reality at all, *you must believe that it lies behind the scenes*, in *another* world. If you believe in a creator, he inevitably becomes a vast manager "up there" who is working it all somehow. In fact the perversion of religion into superstition represents precisely *the attempt to fit religious notions into a picture of the world as a material system.*

... When you say the world is a material system, you are expressing an attitude. You are not simply expressing a belief about what the world is like. The principle of Karl Marx that theory and practice are always united is a very valuable one. ... For in fact this view, that the world is essentially a material system, springs from the generalization of the attitude of use, of manipulation. It is when you are concerned with the manipulation of things that you regard what you are dealing with as essentially material, for then they are precisely material for your use. The categories of distance and measured time are just the categories that you need when you are concerned with using things, with manipulating things, rather than with responding to the aesthetic quality of things or responding to their personal import. Of course, we all have for a large part of our lives to do just that. There is nothing wrong with using things. ... The error comes in generalizing that view of things, in believing that is what reality itself is like; for what you are then doing is to *generalize your attitude*, saying in effect *that life is essentially a matter of manipulation, that essentially we are concerned (either as individuals or as collective groups) with the manipulation of the world, and that is what life is really about.* Other things, the response to beauty and the meeting of persons, are mere frills on the surface of life.

Modern physics recognizes that you get into mathematical difficulties when you try to assume that the concepts with which science itself deals, matter, space, and time, are absolutes. You get into far fewer difficulties if you assume that they are derived from the communication of scientists (or "observers" to use the correct term) in their relation to one another—that is the significance of the theory of relativity. It drives us back to recognizing that science is a business of the communication between human beings who happen to be scientists.

. . . The tendency in the whole of modern science is towards recognizing that what we really know in experience is the *world of people, the universe of persons in communication with one another*. Space and time and matter are things which we know in our communication with one another, and the laws which "govern" the material world as we observe it are the laws which govern our communications with one another as persons.

In other words, modern science is recognizing exactly what every great religion in its inception recognized: that the real world is the world of persons and that all matter and space and time, whether it be the molecules of air that carry our speech from one to another or the galaxies in the nebulae, are all *contained within* the relation of persons to one another. We need no more be overwhelmed by the size of the vast universe "out there" than we need be overwhelmed by the vast numbers of atoms in the everyday objects of life, for both sets of numbers are only the abstractions of analysis.

Now once we have recognized that the real world is the world of persons in communication with one another, the science of psychology takes us even further towards the rediscovery of true religion by making us recognize that in this communication we ourselves are not the ultimate beings, that in fact in the relation between persons something happens which can only be described by the term "creation." In personal relationships persons do not merely learn from one another; what modern psychology and existentialist philosophy alike force us to acknowledge is that each person *only becomes a person by virtue of his being open in relation to another person*. In other words, A is created by his relation to B, and B is created by his relation to A. Now this can only happen if what is between A and B is the real creative agent, and this, I believe, is exactly what genuine religion has always meant by the affirmation that being is grounded in the activity of a Creator. For did not the Jews say that God "dwells in our togetherness"? and did not St. John say "God is love"? Such a statement might seem "merely psychological" only so long as we forget that the universe is the universe of persons. If, however, we learn this truth from modern physics, then we may learn from modern psychology that this universe of persons is always and all the time being created by the love between persons, which is known in human experience to be the same Love between every particular pair of persons who live in love.

So I believe science drives us to discover in immediate practical terms the truths of which the great religions of the world have always spoken.

. . . When the truth of religion is discovered in the core of experience, as I have tried to outline, I believe we can discover the meaning of the doctrine of the Trinity very clearly as something immediately practicable, a truth, which, quite literally, to refuse is to die. . . .

Love creates us as persons. We are what we are only because love creates us. We have no being of ourselves. Yet we continually deny love in this world. . . . The doctrine of the Trinity . . . warns us of when we are in this way cutting ourselves off from the source of life by telling us something of what true Love is like. . . . There must be a general attitude of giving, an attitude for which the word "fatherhood" is the best human analogy that we can find. Unless there is this general attitude of giving, there is no love.

. . . The fatherhood of God, the fatherhood of love, is the only true fatherhood in the universe, from which all human fatherhood takes its name, as St. Paul said. . . .

And in the doctrine of the Trinity it is said that this fatherhood is embodied in man's own action insofar as he dwells in

God. Insofar as God's creative activity makes him into a person, he has a general attitude of giving which does not change with circumstances: it is *eternal.* . . .

Yet giving itself is not enough. There must be, alongside giving and combined with giving, acceptance . . . —the acceptance of the other person himself *as* the other person, the acceptance of the other person for what he or she is in himself, never counting the cost, the acceptance which is "letting be," which is *suffering* that other person to be himself. If there is to be love, it is something that goes on all the time. It is a general attitude of acceptance, of suffering, for which the word Sonship is an appropriate term. Love is fatherhood and is sonship at the time.

. . . If love is merely a relation of give and take between two persons it is a wonderful start, but if it stops there, it is not love, it is obsession. . . . When love becomes self-enclosed it becomes something other than love and people do not quite understand why. Yet the truth is there in the doctrine of the Trinity that the essence of love is that it must always go out beyond itself, that true love is only known when the giving and the acceptance issue in the eternal procession beyond themselves of the interpretive Spirit. . . . the same thing must happen to every pair of lovers and every pair of friends and every family if that group is not to become enclosed, obsessive, a new power group, if it is to be the vehicle of that love which makes persons.

. . . The doctrine of the fall states that this world, though made by God, denies God and thereby denies itself. And this I believe is an existential truth about all human experience which modern psychology confirms again and again. Man from childhood upwards becomes a true person precisely insofar as he is created by love, yet our world is so organized that at every point it denies love. It denies all the three persons of the Trinity; it denies giving and tells you to grab what you can while you can; it denies acceptance and says that you must force other people into your way of doing things because to accept them as they are is really weakness; and it denies the ever growing inclusiveness of the Third Person of the Trinity and says that on the contrary you must stick to your own and do your duty by them first. It denies the eternity of love and says that if a relationship is strained beyond a certain point it should break. It denies the infinitude of love and says that you should only go on giving up to a certain point and if more demands are made upon you, you have the right to contract out. The world by its whole formation denies *the very thing that makes denial possible.* Psychology shows us that the ability of the human being to make choices, to be other than an animal who responds to his environment, to have what might be described as "the freedom of images" in the mind, is linked with the encounter of one person with another in love. It is out of this encounter that freedom of choice comes. Yet this freedom is always in our experience used to deny love and therefore to deny its own source. The effect of this is that we have before us a world of persons who are not living in their own true manner, who are living a life which is thoroughly unnatural to them.[36]

Karl Adam gives a picture of the way the community of faith, the living Body of Christ, becomes for the faithful a constant source of new life. It is in the Church, understood as this continual fount of the spirit, originating in Christ and flowing through the life of this community, that the Catholic feels himself grasped and renewed by the spirit of God Himself. Notice what he says about the certainty of faith. It obviously is not something established by decree or argument. This whole notion of the Church is not too different from what Berger means by the Church as the "place of truth."

[36] JOHN WREN-LEWIS, "Science, the World, and God," in *The Christian Scholar*, Vol. XLII, No. 3, September, 1959, pp. 174 ff.

KARL ADAM

The more closely the Catholic . . . gets into touch with his Church, not merely externally, but internally, with her prayer and sacrifice, with her word and sacrament, the more sensitive and attentive will he be to the inspiration of the divine Spirit in the community, the more vitally will he grasp the divine life that flows through the organism of the Church. . . . And when he thinks and prays, suffers and strives with the living Church, then he experiences a broadening, deepening and fulfilling of his whole being. And so the logical certitude of his faith becomes progressively a psychological, living experience that it is the very Life of all life by which he is sustained, that verily, as St. Paul expresses this experience, "the Lord is a Spirit" (2 Cor. 3:17). This certitude is a personal experience, the most personal experience that he has. He may delineate and describe it in rational language, though very crudely and imperfectly, but he cannot impart it to any other. For it is derived from that complete personal contact of his soul with the Spirit of Jesus that inspires the Christian community. But because it is certitude that he has tested for himself, no man, no doubt, no ridicule can deprive him of it. Therefore to be absolutely exact, I do not believe the Church, but the living God, who attests Himself to me in the Church. Nor is it I that believe, but the Holy Spirit that is in me. The Catholic grasps and affirms Jesus ultimately and decisively in the flowing life of His Church, in the Church as the mystical Body of Christ. . . .

It is quite wrong to estimate a religion solely according to its conceptual content, or even according to this or that dominant idea alone, and not rather to regard the totality of the vital forms that spring from it in past, present, and future. If this be true of religion in general, it is far more true of the life of Christ and of Christianity. As the history of Christianity shows, it is a life, which manifesting its power first in the Person of Jesus delivered the souls of men from an earth-bound existence, created a new, supernatural community, and through it for all time by word and sacrament provides humanity with streams of truth and grace. It is a life which not merely laid hold of the restricted group of His disciples, but in an incredibly short space of time gripped the whole ancient world and brought into being new civilizations, new peoples, new men, and which, still alive and effectual among us, attests itself to our own day as a perennial source of spiritual life.[37]

We have suggested that a person finds his identity only in relation to others. In a way he is told or shown who he is. Yet it seems fair to say that some types of relationships are likely to produce deeper, more authentic selfhood than others, i.e. trust and friendship as opposed to suspicion and conformity. We depend on each other's view of ourselves more than we like to admit, and are made anxious by the disapproval or rejection by the group we are in. Moreover, our picture of ourselves often changes radically as our situation changes or as we move into a different group. So the question of our real self, our true identity is never easily answered because there seem to be no convincing criteria for determining the real and the true.

Fromm offers the idea of a law of human nature, Tillich speaks of the depth of our individual and social existence, Reinhold Niebuhr points to Christ as "the essential nature of man," Buber talks about the life of dialogue in which the attentive self is "addressed" by the eternal "Thou." All of them seem to suggest that there is a definitive measure of man that judges his limited and partial judgments of himself and his neighbor. Man, in other words, finds himself when he finds or is found by the power of true being. It is in connection with precisely this problem that many discover the relevance of the church. The following comments by Peter Berger may explain this role of the church. Of those who might question his idea, one might well

[37] KARL ADAM, *The Spirit of Catholicism* (Doubleday Image Book), pp. 60–62.

ask what other structured relationships there are that could serve a similar purpose.

PETER BERGER

Quite apart from what the church may or may not do in the way of social action, the church, if it is faithful to its mission, can play a vital role in society and its clash of ideologies. *The church is the place of truth.* When we say this, of course, we are fully aware that this is pretty much the opposite of what the empirical church normally is. But the church can be the place of truth when it stands on the ground of Jesus Christ and no other—that is when it liberates itself from its social and psychological functionality. The church can then be not only the proclaiming church but the listening church, providing those rare opportunities in society where men can look truthfully at themselves and their roles. . . . We would suggest that one of the most urgent tasks of the church in our present situation is the providing of such places of truth (be it local congregation or in other locales), places where men can think through in freedom the moral and human dilemmas of their social roles.[38]

[38] BERGER, *op. cit.*, p. 207.

ULTIMATE FULFILLMENT: THE KINGDOM
OF GOD

This phrase contained the doctrine which Jesus preached to explain his mission. This was his gospel, which means "good news" for all people anywhere. In Mark's account of his life it is said that Jesus began his ministry by talking about the Kingdom of God. "Jesus came into Galilee, preaching the gospel of the Kingdom of God. . . . the Kingdom of God is at hand; repent ye." (Mark 1:14, 15)

This term, so familiar in his life, had a very long history of changing interpretation which led to many misunderstandings. The people thought it meant one thing and Jesus had a radically different idea in his mind. Their country was occupied by foreign powers, one after another, and popular religion had pieced together certain teachings of the prophets into a great expectation that God would send a Messiah who, somehow, would have power enough to deliver the nation and restore the Kingdom of David. When Jesus associated himself with this hope he was a great disappointment for he had no power at all, and just after his death even his disciples thought it was he who would "restore again the Kingdom of Israel." (Acts 1:6) They had never understood in all that time since he began saying: "The Kingdom of God is at hand; repent ye."

Now why did this doctrine stress the figure of a community which was already at hand? The answer is that saving power does not save men, one by one, like taking a "brand" from the fire;

but always in the kind of relationship demonstrated in Christ. The love which wholly possessed him united him with God on one hand and all sorts of people on the other—regardless of age, or class, or race. Here the Kingdom of God was at hand—perfectly. In some degree it is at hand whenever there is any repentance for putting self first, so that love can arouse that inner willingness to assume a little mutual responsibility that allows a freer use to be made of all parties for the common good. To this end Christ taught men to pray: "Thy Kingdom come on earth as it is in heaven." In a sinful world the experience of such a relationship will be only fragmentary, forever interrupted, and forever restored. For we live under a tireless Creator who by judgment sets limits to the success of selfishness, and is ever ready to create new beginnings where there is humility and contrition.

Christian faith in resurrection is quite different from other views of immortality. Most of the familiar arguments for immortality are generally derived, unconsciously perhaps, from what might be called the cocoon theory of life. The butterfly comes to birth out of a worthless wrapping, which had nothing to do with the new creation, and is cast off as useless in the end. The phrase "resurrection of the body" counteracts this view. It takes account of the fact that our bodily life has a part to play in the making of our personality; it is far more important than the outside husk of a cocoon. "Resurrection" implies a transformation of our whole material life and the life of our spirit into the new life of love in union with the Eternal Life of God. (The word "Body" does not mean the physical body, for Paul speaks of a spiritual body that preserves our individuality, and says that "flesh and blood cannot enter into the Kingdom of God.") Paul identified the conversion of his self-centered nature with entrance into Eternal Life. Jesus, when asked how one enters Eternal Life, offered no arguments. He told one rich questioner to give away his wealth and follow a self-abandoned life which, in this particular case, was the only remedy for being obsessed with self. To another man, a lawyer, he told the story of the Good Samaritan who could forget himself for anyone who was in need. To have the ego overcome by the inner willingness to give oneself away was to enter into Eternal Life. The Eternal can be known in part, here and now; we no longer are moving toward it but are in a position to advance in it here and hereafter.

The faith in resurrection is akin to the feeling of many people that Eternal Life is living on in the lives of others. This is a partial truth. At least it suggests that the life of love is lived always in other people even in this earthly existence. Some people seem to live entirely in others without giving themselves a thought, but their individual personality is not lost. Living in the Eternal Kingdom of God would be to know the love that unites us with God and with all people. To have our earthly life, which is a community life, transformed into such a new community would be getting into Heaven, and if a selfish man should by any chance find himself in such a company it would be Hell for him.

In this discussion of salvation, Herberg covers a number of terms that are common to both Christian and Jewish faith. Like many of the Christians we have studied, he is interested in the redemption of this world rather than escape from this world into another world. He sees salvation primarily as the breaking of sinful egocentricity and the acceptance of the rule of God. From what he says about the meaning of the Messiah in Jewish thought it is clear why the Jews do not accept Jesus as the Messiah. To the Jew the coming of the Messiah has roughly the same meaning as the second coming of Christ has for the Christian. Both symbolically express the hope that the believer discerns in the depth of history. It is a way of saying that history moves purposefully toward a fulfillment rather than in endless and meaningless circles. Consider what he says about "resurrection" as opposed to "immortality of the soul." The latter is always associated with those religions which split man into a "di-

vine" soul and an evil body, evil because *it is* matter. *This is*
neither a Jewish nor a Christian notion. Both speak of man as a
"living soul" rather than as a finite body "imprisoning" an immortal soul. This distinction has profoundly important consequences for ethics, particularly sex ethics.

WILL HERBERG

Salvation—individual and social—is oriented to eternity.
But eternity, in the Hebraic view, is not escape *from*, but fulfilment *of* time. It is both "now" and "hereafter." It is *now* because, in fellowship with God, all the vicissitudes of time are
overcome and transcended. Over the man bound to God in
faith, and insofar as he *is* bound to God in faith, time has lost its
mastery. He remains in the world to work within it, for this
world of life and history is, to the Jew, the only field of service to God. But in the new God-centered life of faith, he has
achieved a level of being in which value and meaning are assured
beyond the power of time to destroy. Nothing that time can
bring, neither failure nor defeat, neither sorrow nor calamity, can
separate him from the Eternal; only a resurgence of his own
sinful self-will can do that. But that is precisely the battle of
faith.

The eternity of salvation is also *hereafter*. In the prophetic-
rabbinic vision, "this world"—the world of history, with its per-
verseness, incoherence and defeat—is destined to find fulfilment
and rectification in the "world-to-come," the "new heaven and
new earth" in which justice and power will finally be united in
the kingship of God. The salvation that breaks through vertically into the *now* and redeems us as individual persons from the
vicious circle of sinful egocentricity is the salvation that is *hereafter* to redeem all history in the consummation of the horizontal movement toward the Kingdom of God.

* * *

218

History cannot redeem itself; on the contrary, it proceeds and ends in catastrophe from which it must be redeemed by the hand of God. The coming of the Messiah "at the end of days" is this redeeming act of God. Not that redemption does not enter history at every point and endow it with the partial meanings and fulfilments which it reveals. But these partial meanings and fulfilments ... can sustain themselves only in terms of an ultimate fulfilment to which we look forward in faith. The coming of the Messiah opens the "new age" of fulfilment.

The first phase of the Messianic act is presented to us as the final defeat of the powers of evil in history and the vindication at last of the divine intent in creation. That is why the Messiah means hope and why the pagans who know not the Messiah and do not wait for him are literally without hope.

... The next and culminating phase [is] the resurrection of the dead, the last judgment, and the inauguration of the "world-to-come." ... The teaching of the resurrection affirms, in the first place, that man's ultimate destiny is not something that is his by virtue of his own nature—by his possession of an "immortal soul," for example—but comes to him solely by the grace and mercy of God, who "wakes him from the dead." ... It affirms, in the second place, that what is destined for fulfilment is not a disembodied soul that has sloughed off its body, but the *whole* man—body, soul and spirit—joined in an indissoluble unity. It affirms, in the third place, that the salvation promised of God is not a private, individual affair that each one acquires for himself upon his death, but the salvation of mankind, the corporate redemption of men in the full reality of their historical existence. The whole point of the doctrine of the resurrection is that the life we live now, the life of the body, the life of empirical existence in society, has some measure of permanent worth in the eyes of God and will not vanish in the transmutation of things at the "last day." The fulfilment will be a fulfilment for the *whole* man and for *all* men who have lived through the years and have entered into history and its making. ... It is a doctrine with which we cannot dispense, no matter how impatient we may be with the literalistic pseudo-biological fantasies that gathered around it through the centuries.

Following upon the resurrection of the dead, in the traditional picture, is the last judgment. For the completion of history is not merely fulfilment; it is fulfilment that is also judgment. . . . That in men and their deeds which is found worthy in God's eyes is fulfilled and completed; that which is evil and contrary to the divine intent is purged and destroyed. . . . The culmination of the transfiguration promised in faith at the "last day" is the "world-to-come." But the term in its English translation is misleading; it is not a new "place" that is promised, but a new *time*, a new *age*. . . . To those who have lost the sense of the transcendental, it might help to illustrate, however inadequately, what is implied when we speak of the meaning of history being revealed and completed in a great fulfilment at the "end."

The fulfilment of history is the Kingdom of Heaven. But here again the usual translation is misleading. What is meant is not a kingdom in a kind of superworld called "Heaven," but a new age in which the *kingship* of God is revealed in its fullness and sovereignty. The locus of the Kingdom is the world . . . the world redeemed, transfigured and renewed through the establishment of a new relation to God. . . . The Kingdom may be said to be in power in *this* age wherever and to the degree that men are transformed in love of God and in acknowledgment of his total sovereignty. . . . The Kingdom is here, yet for it we pray. It is the redemptive act of God, yet for it we work.[39]

In this discussion of the meaning of salvation Tillich talks not about deliverance of the self from the world but transformation of the self in the world, a breaking of the bondage of "being-for-self" into the freedom of "being-for-others," death of the old self and resurrection of a new self or as the first letter of John

[39] HERBERG, *op. cit.*, pp. 127, 228–235.

puts it, "We know that we have passed out of death into life, because we love the brethren. He who does not love remains in death." (1 John 3:14) While Tillich rejects the notion of life after death as popular imagination conceives it, he speaks of being "kept in the eternal life before we lived on earth, while we are living in time, and after our time has come to an end." Perhaps some of the notions of science suggest in another way the manner in which each of us is tied permanently into the mysterious fabric of being. More important than what he says about the boundaries of life, where it is best to remain something of an agnostic, is his emphasis on each individual as a bearer of healing and liberating power to his fellows.

PAUL TILLICH

We are in bondage. It is the evil one—the symbol of the distorting and destroying powers in the world—that keeps us in servitude. The saviour, then, is the conqueror of the evil one and of his powers. No one has used this image more impressively than Paul in his great song of triumph in the eighth chapter of Romans, when he says that none of the demonic powers which govern this world can separate us from the love of God.

Saving is healing from sickness and saving is delivering from servitude; and the two are the same. Let me give you an example of their unity. We consider the neurotic or psychotic person who cannot face life as sick. But if we describe his disease, we find that he is under the power of compulsions from which he cannot extricate himself. He is, as the New Testament expresses it, demonically possessed. In him, disease and servitude are the same; and we ask whether, in some degree, this is not true of all of us. In which sense, we ask, do we need healing? In which sense liberation? What should salvation mean to us?

It is certainly not, what popular imagination has made of it, escaping from hell and being received in heaven, in what is badly called "the life hereafter." The New Testament speaks of eternal life, and eternal life is not continuation of life after death. Eternal life is beyond past, present, and future: we come from it, we live in its presence, we return to it. It is never absent —it is the divine life in which we are rooted and in which we are destined to participate in freedom—for God alone has eternity. . . . We are mortal like every creature, mortal with our whole being —body and soul—but we are also kept in the eternal life *before* we lived on earth, *while* we are living in time, and *after* our time has come to an end.

. . . All liberating, all healing power comes from the other side of the wall which separates us from eternal life. Whenever it appears, it is a manifestation of eternal, divine life in our temporal and mortal existence. All liberators, all healers are sent by God; they liberate and heal through the power of the eternal given to them.

Who are these healers? Where are these saviours? The first answer is: they are *here*; they are *you*. Each of you has liberating and healing power over someone to whom you are a priest. We are all called to be priests to each other; and if priests, also physicians. And if physicians, also counsellors. And if counsellors, also liberators. There are innumerable degrees and kinds of saving grace. There are many people whom the evil one has enslaved so mightily that the saving power which may work through them has almost disappeared. On the other hand, there are the great saviour figures in whom large parts of mankind have experienced a lasting power of liberating and healing from generation to generation. Most of us are in between. And there is the one saviour in whom Christianity sees the saving grace without limits, the decisive victory over the demonic powers, the tearing down of the wall of guilt which separates us from the eternal, the healer who brings to light a new reality in man and his world. But if we call him saviour we must remember that *God* is the saviour *through* him and that there are a host of liberators and healers, including ourselves, through whom the divine salvation works in all mankind. God does not leave the world at any place, in any time, without saviours—without healing power. . . .

Nations are saved if there is a small minority, a group of people, who represent what the nation is called to be. They may be defeated, but their spirit will be a power of resistance against the evil spirits who are detrimental to the nation. The question of saving power in the nation is the question of whether there is a minority, even a small one, which is willing to resist the anxiety produced by propaganda, the conformity enforced by threat, the hatred stimulated by ignorance. The future of this country and its spiritual values is not dependent as much on atomic defense as on the influence such groups will have on the spirit in which the nation will think and act.

And this is true of mankind as a whole. Its future will be dependent on a saving group, embodied in one nation or crossing through all nations. There is a saving power in mankind, but there is also a hidden will to self-destruction. It depends on every one of us which side will prevail. . . . Unless many of us say to ourselves: Through the saving power working in me mankind may be saved or lost—it will be lost.[40]

This discussion of resurrection and eternal life follows a more traditional line than most of the theologians presented so far. Yet even in this view there is the emphasis on present reality, on the quality of a relationship rather than on its duration, and the honest confession of being not merely on the outer edge of language but of experience. Essentially this belief springs from the logic of present, though fragmentary, experience as being a foretaste of a final, though hidden, completion.

DAVID H. C. READ

The Christian doctrine of the End is technically known as "Eschatology." Under that heading theologians have usually

[40] PAUL TILLICH, *The Eternal Now* (New York, 1963), pp. 114–116, 119–120.

treated such subjects as heaven and hell, judgment, the Return of Christ, and the end of the world. . . .

The Christian Faith implies that there is a real life for mankind beyond the grave. The invisible world by which this world is conditioned is a world in which death has been vanquished. The victory wrought by Christ is no real victory for the believer unless he can share in the immortality which Christ has won, in the resurrection from the dead. . . .

We take this to mean that when a man or woman is laid hold of by God in this life he is not dropped into non-existence when physical death intervenes. He is raised to a new life, and thus remains forever with God. . . . This, of course, leaves many questions unanswered. Before looking at some of these, it is right to stress again that the Christian hope includes without question or cavil a full personal renewal of life after death in that world beyond where God's will is done. Yet we must also note that there is the utmost reticence in the Scriptures about the nature of such a life. . . . To convey to us the meaning of life free from the limitations of time and space would be more difficult than explaining the meaning of color to one who was color-blind.

The most we have a right to believe in the light of the Gospel is that life beyond the grave is richer and fuller than this one, and that it consists in a continued growth into the image of Christ—together. . . . Eternal life, according to the Bible, is knowledge of God—not endless time. It is a quality of life into which we enter now, and which finds its true flowering in a totally different environment. . . .

We have, however, no grounds for limiting the participation in eternal life to those who have consciously received the Gospel of Jesus Christ. . . . Many who have never heard of his name are nevertheless saved by the same grace of God which finds its perfect expression in him. That is to say that whoever is turned towards God in this life, wherever and whenever they may live, can share in his eternity. On all these questions true wisdom lies in a serious reckoning with our own position and a withholding of judgment upon others. God does not damn us: we damn ourselves. And we cannot assert of anyone else that they are bound for hell. To the multitude of questions that may be asked concerning the fate of hypothetical men and women, and concerning the possibilities in the life to come, we must steadily and soberly answer: I do not know.[41]

Tillich and Niebuhr in these two sections seek to describe what the new being, the "peace of God" is like. The main point to notice is that the new life is beyond religion. We sometimes forget that the purpose of religion is not religion but to reunite man with himself, his neighbor and God. Niebuhr has a good statement on the paradox of self-realization and the law of love, which is a translation of the biblical idea that man finds his life by being willing to lose it for the sake of his brother. Why is the "peace" he speaks of full of sorrow?

PAUL TILLICH

Splits and gaps are in every soul: for instance, we know that we are more than dust; and yet we know also that we are going to be dust. We know that we belong to a higher order than that of our animal needs and desires; and yet we know that we shall abuse the higher order in the service of our lower nature. We know that we are only small members of the spiritual world; and yet we know that we shall aspire to the whole, making ourselves the center of the world.

This is man; and because this is man, there is religion and law. The law of religion is the great attempt of man to overcome his anxiety and restlessness and despair, to close the gap within

[41] David H. C. Read, *The Christian Faith* (New York, 1956), pp. 162–165, 167.

himself, and to reach immortality, spirituality and perfection. So he labors and toils under the religious law in thought and in act.

. . . This is the yoke from which Jesus wants to liberate us. . . . He frees us from religion. . . .

"Take my yoke upon you and learn of me . . . for my yoke is easy and my burden is light." This does not indicate a quantitative difference—a little easier, a little lighter. It indicates a contradiction! The yoke of Jesus is easy in itself, because it is above law, and replaces the toiling and laboring with rest in our souls. The yoke of religion and law presupposes all those splits and gaps in our souls which drive us to the attempt to overcome them. The yoke of Jesus is above those splits and gaps. It has overcome them whenever it appears and is received. It is not a new demand, a new doctrine or new morals, but rather a new reality, a new being and a new power of transforming life. He calls it a yoke; He means that it comes from above and grasps us with saving force; if He calls it easy, He means that it is not a matter of our acting and striving, but rather that it is given before anything we can do. It is being, power, reality, conquering the anxiety and despair, the fear and the restlessness of our existence. It is here, amongst us, in the midst of our personal tragedy, and the tragedy of history. Suddenly, within the hardest struggle, it appears as a victory, not attained by ourselves, but present beyond expectation and struggle. Suddenly we are grasped by a peace which is above reason, that is above our theoretical seeking for the true, and above our practical striving for the good. The true—namely, the truth of our life and of our existence—has grasped us. We know that *now*, in this moment, we are in the truth, in spite of all our ignorance about ourselves and the world. We have not become wiser and more understanding in any ordinary sense; we are still children in knowledge. But the truth of life is in us, with an illuminating certainty, uniting us with ourselves, giving us great and restful happiness. And the good, the ultimate good, which is not good for something else, but good in itself, has grasped us. We know that now, in this moment, we are in the good, in spite of all our weakness and evil, in spite of the fragmentary and distorted character of our self and the world. We have not become more moral or more saintly; we still belong to a world which is subject to evil and self-destruction. But the good of life is in us, uniting us with the good of everything, giving us the blessed experience of universal love. If this should happen, and in such a measure, we should reach our eternity, the higher order and spiritual world to which we belong, and from which we are separated in our normal existence. We should be beyond ourselves. The new being would conquer us, although the old being would not disappear.[42]

REINHOLD NIEBUHR

The "peace of God" for man is partly achieved by the emulation of God's love. Man is not so created that he can live his life in either calm detachment or cautious self-possession and moderation. He lives most truly according to his nature if his imagination, his sympathies, and his responsibilities draw him out of himself into the life of the community, into the needs, the hopes and aspirations of his fellows. But this self-realization through love is not something which can be achieved by taking thought. It is not possible if we regard love as a law which must be obeyed. Love is indeed the law of life; but it is most surely obeyed when we are not conscious of obedience to any law. It is obeyed when the sorrows of others arouse our sympathies, when their needs prompt us to forget our own needs and meet those of our friends and neighbors. We become most truly ourselves when we forget ourselves; for it is preoccupation with self which prematurely arrests the growth of the self and confines it to too narrow limits. The peace of love is thus the ultimate peace of being or becoming what we truly are: creatures who do not live

[42] Paul Tillich, *The Shaking of the Foundations* (New York, 1948), pp. 97, 99–100.

in and for themselves, but find themselves in the life of the community, and finally in God. Obviously, however, this ultimate peace of love is filled with pain and sorrow. It is aware not only of its own pains but also of those of others.[43]

[43] Reinhold Niebuhr, *Discerning the Signs of the Times* (New York, 1946), pp. 184–185.

228

APPENDIX I

An Introduction to Ethics

INTRODUCTION

It is one thing to think out a philosophy of life, a faith, a reason for living; it is quite another thing to live by it and find in it genuine resources of insight and inspiration. It is beyond the scope of this book to deal in any systematic way with ethics. Nonetheless, it is perhaps useful to open up several of the overriding problems of our time so that the points of view (particularly the biblical) discussed in the previous sections of the book may be tested and evaluated for their relevance to these issues. It is important to remember that any ethic (the do's and don't's) is based on assumptions about the nature of man and his place in the universe, assumptions which in the last analysis are matters of faith and commitment and which therefore reveal one's god. In other words, a man's primary interest or loyalty will determine his ethical decisions. Unfortunately, too many people who get involved in arguments about right and wrong refuse to examine the ground of faith out of which their ethics come. Suppose, for example, a person starts his thinking from the assumption that we should love people and use things; another starts from the assumption that we should love things and use people. In such a situation it would be fruitless for these two to argue about the rightness or wrongness of a conclusion which either might reach on any ethical issue.

Let this section, therefore, be a sort of testing ground for the reader's honesty. If he calls himself a Christian, yet resolves every ethical problem in terms of what is expedient for him, let him at least recognize the inconsistency. If he is inclined to the notion that might makes right, then let him gracefully hand over his wallet to the one who has the strength to take it from him.

The trouble with most of us too much of the time is that we simply do not want to face up to our responsibilities as human beings, let alone as Christians, Jews, or humanists. So we permit ourselves the luxury of slogans and gross oversimplifications, careless generalizations, and half truths. We have forgotten that ideas have consequences, that attitudes get translated into actions, that what is right in one context may be dead wrong in another. There are those who see no difference in Patrick Henry's "Give me liberty, or give me death!" in the days of cannon ball and musket and the phrase "Better dead than Red!" in the age of nuclear bombs and guided missiles. "Live and let live" makes good ethical sense among friends who are secure and independent, but it offers little guidance in the face of aggressive evil.

What one believes pretty much determines what one does. Our beliefs and the theories we derive from them are eminently practical, for they suggest to us how we could best fashion our world. It stands to reason, therefore, that a belief which ignores an element of nature will bring ruin on the structures we seek to create. Events of the past fifty years give us many persuasive illustrations of the way in which history refutes all theories that choose to ignore certain aspects of reality. Those who have distrusted the people have discovered they couldn't check a tyrannical government. Those who depended uncritically on the people have been unable to get around ignorance and special interest. Those who have exalted the individual have been unable to deal with the corrupting power of egoism and anarchy. Those who have exalted the state or some other system of organization have been unable to maintain individual initiative and a sense of the value of the person. The perennial temptation of man is thus revealed in the effort to create some final solution, some permanent answer to what is essentially a fluid, ever-changing situation. Ethically, we want to work out a static body of rules, an absolute morality, that would tell us ahead of time what to do. It is this attitude which more often than not leads people to tolerate injustice in the name of "principles," to place states' rights over human rights, to withhold freedom in the name of freedom, to kill people for humanity's sake.

232

Introduction

One of the major problems in the area of ethical decisions is our individual and collective reluctance to notice what is really happening at any present time. There seems to be a general tendency in men to assume too quickly that if they have a goal or an ideal it will somehow actualize itself. They are not interested in examining the means they are presently using to pursue their goals. This is why so many of the writers we have been studying laid such stress on man's incredible capacity to deceive himself, to hide from what is really going on both within himself and in his communal existence. Fromm talks of man's narcissism which leads him to see everything in terms of his own interests and fears, so that his neighbor appears to him only as a threat or a promise, never simply as a person. Berger speaks of the "bad faith" by which we conceal from ourselves our responsibility for our own acts by a variety of social and religious fictions. Tillich describes the resistance in man to his own depth and the depth of his historical situation. Reinhold Niebuhr points to man's pretension and pride, his refusal to accept his creaturely status, his desire to play God—tendencies which cut man off from reality. Buber reminds us of our refusal to listen to what the moments of our daily existence say to us. Each in his own way and in his own vocabulary suggests that the question of ethics is secondary to the question of the salvation and redemption of man. Thus St. Augustine could summarize the Christian ethic by saying, "Love God and do as you please." That is to say, when man is grasped by the power of true being, when his mind, heart, and will are given over to the spirit of love which is God, then what he pleases to do will be what he ought to do. St. John says, "I am writing you no new commandment, but an old commandment which you had from the beginning. . . . Yet I am writing you a new commandment, which is true in him and in you, because the darkness is passing away and the true light is already shining. He who says he is in the light and hates his brother is in the darkness still. He who loves his brother abides in the light, and there is no cause for stumbling. But he who hates his brother is in the darkness and walks in the darkness, and does not know where he is going, because the darkness has blinded his eyes." (1 John 2:7–11)

Let it be said at once, this life of love is not simply a matter of individual, interpersonal relations, though it certainly includes such matters. What is infinitely important for our time is the clear understanding that in our crowded, highly organized, interdependent world our most crucial ethical decisions will have to be actualized through the impersonal structures of society, our response of concern for our fellow man will have to take political, economic, and legal forms. Agape love has little to do with affection. Rather it visits those in prison, clothes the naked, feeds the hungry, cares for the sick. In a simple society this meant face-to-face encounter. In a time when technology has made all peoples conscious of their common membership in the human community, private charity is no longer a sufficient ethical response. It is this growing awareness of the enormous extent of our responsibilities that has led many to reconsider the nature of government. Should it be seen as playing merely a negative role, or should it be seen more positively as a necessary arm of its citizens in doing the work of the world? So too with all the other structures of society. If we are to have a future, if our children are to inherit a human world, then it follows that each collective discipline and professional work of man must be understood as a human enterprise. No longer can we afford to exclude our public activity from claims of conscience and moral accountability. "Business" is not our business; mankind is our business, and if it does not soon become our primary business, there will be little business at all and few to do it.

This is why it is so important for people to recover some real sense of their own worth and regain some measure of the personal dignity and value conveyed in the ancient vision of man as child of God created in His image to have dominion over the earth. Man is neither God nor worm, neither perfectible nor contemptible, neither self-sufficient nor helpless. The Bible tells us it is all right merely to be ordinary, limited, fallible human beings. That is the way the Creator made us and He said Yes to what He made. And all the way through the Bible we get this absurd notion that this Yes, this affirmation of our stiff-necked, rebellious being is not conditional on our being white, or pure, or American, or wise, or successful, or liked by others, or moral, or religious. This fundamental acceptance, this ground of being-for-us is the given of our existence and whenever we are able to believe this, we find that we don't need to use and abuse our fellows in order to establish our worth. We find we are liberated from the compulsive concern to prove ourselves. We find we are free simply to be whoever and whatever we are. Moreover, we then discover—and perhaps this is the final secret of being alive —that we can be liberators of others, we can give real life to others. The truly ethical are not really interested in ethics, nor are they much concerned with building their own characters or saving their souls. They are too preoccupied with the needs of others. Melville understood these two kinds of morality, one kind devoted to self, the other forgetful of self. He met both kinds aboard a man-of-war. He saw the former exemplified in the person of the commodore:

It beseemed him . . . to erect himself into an example of virtue and show the gundeck what virtue was. But alas! when virtue sits high aloft on a frigate's poop, when virtue is crowned in the cabin of a commodore, when virtue rules by compulsion, and domineers over vice as a slave, then virtue, though her mandates be outwardly observed, bears little interior sway. To be efficacious, virtue must come down from aloft even as our blessed Redeemer came down to redeem our whole man-of-war world; to that end mixing with its sailors and sinners as equals.

He met the latter in the person of Jack Chase, a plain seaman.

No man ever had a better heart or bolder. He was loved as a seaman, and admired by the officers; and even when the captain spoke to him, it was with a slight air of respect. . . . there was such an abounding air of good sense and good feeling about the man that he who could not love him would thereby pronounce himself a knave.

...We maintop men were brothers, one and all; and we loaned ourselves to each other with all the freedom in the world.*

A farmer once told William James, "There is not much difference between people, but what difference there is is very important." Because we find corrupt judges, hypocrites in church, scoundrels in government, and perhaps because we discover that we are not much better ourselves, we fall into the habit of thinking that there is no good, no trustworthy moral order, that it is and always has been an outrageous hoax imposed on each generation by those who were in authority and wanted to keep people in line. Yet the farmer is surely right. All people in all times and all cultures have this perplexing mixture of good and evil in them, but there is a spirit that dominates the lives of some which makes a radical difference, a spirit which makes them reconcilers among men, overcoming the estrangement, bringing new life and communion. And because we recognize in them this spirit that has been "from the beginning," we feel able to speak of an eternal and at the same time natural "law" of life which to disobey or ignore is a kind of death. When we encounter it, we may be constrained to say as Ishmael did as the result of his friendship with the savage Queequeg,

I began to be sensible of strange feelings. I felt a melting in me. No more my splintered heart and maddened hand were turned against the wolfish world. This soothing savage had redeemed it.**

Perhaps there is another point to be made here; namely, that the life we face, the world that moves toward us, can be terrifying. To the degree that we open ourselves honestly to all that touches us, we become aware of the throbbing energy of new life that seeks to actualize itself in and through us. We are made to see in such moments that real life is more than we can manage by ourselves. And so, for protection, we move toward

* HERMAN MELVILLE, *White Jacket.*
** HERMAN MELVILLE, *Moby Dick.*

236

one another in collective support of illusion, or we move apart into the false security of self-preoccupation. There is another way, a way not popular with the self-assured or the proud. If we can accept the fact of our humanity, then we may move toward each other acknowledging our mutual need, confessing the partiality of our understanding, seeking together to hear the word spoken to us in our situation, and together letting go of that which is dead in us and in our world so that new creation may take place.

THE NATURE OF THE PROBLEM

In his first paragraph Niebuhr reminds us of the way our self-concern colors the knowledge we have of historical events and the judgments we make of them. Even today, for example, a Southerner and a Northerner could scarcely approach an evaluation of the Civil War from the same point because each has a personal stake in the conclusions that might be drawn. This personal concern is not present when we study the content of a drop of water under a microscope. Why is this distinction so important in any discussion of ethics?

In the rest of the passage, he points to an aspect of the Christian faith which can sustain a person caught in the slow processes of the world. Because the Christian does not look for fulfillment in history, as, say, the Communist does, he is not so likely to swing between unrealistic optimism, on the one hand, and hopeless despair on the other.

REINHOLD NIEBUHR

The difference between the knowledge of nature and the knowledge and estimate of our fellowmen is this: in the knowledge of nature the mind of man is at the center of the process of knowing; and the self with all its fears, hopes and ambitions is on the circumference. In the knowledge of historical events the self, with all its emotions and desires, is at the center of the enterprise; and the mind is on the circumference, serving merely as an instrument of the anxious self.

* * *

238

The Nature of the Problem

Ideally there is a tremendous resource for the accomplishment of immediate possibilities in an ultimate hope. Such a hope frees us from preoccupation with the prospects of immediate success or fears of immanent failure. It helps us to do our duty without allowing it to be defined by either our hopes or our fears. This is a resource which will be particularly required in the coming decades and centuries. We do not know how soon and to what degree mankind will succeed in establishing a tolerable world order. Very possibly we will hover for some centuries between success and failure, in such a way that optimists and pessimists will be able to assess our achievements, or lack of them, with an equal degree of plausibility. In such a situation it is important to be more concerned with our duties than with the prospect of success in fulfilling them. . . .

A sense of ultimate security and ultimate fulfillment may beguile a few from their immediate tasks. But the heroic soul will be the freer to seek for possible securities in history if he possesses a resource against immediate insecurities. The city of God is no enemy of the land of promise. The hope of it makes the inevitable disappointments in every land of promise tolerable.[1]

In the following passage we see how the biblical doctrine of man deepens our ability to come to terms realistically with the problems of social existence. The cynicism and idealism Niebuhr poses against each other demonstrate what happens when the paradoxical tension of man in God's image and man as sinner is broken and one side or the other is selected as the key to man's nature. The maintenance of the paradox lies at the basis of Niebuhr's cogent epigram: "Man's capacity for justice makes democracy possible; but man's inclination to injustice makes democracy necessary."

[1] REINHOLD NIEBUHR, *Discerning the Signs of the Times* (New York, 1946), pp. 5, 92–93.

According to the Scripture "the children of this world are in their generation wiser than the children of light." This observation fits the modern situation. Our democratic civilization has been built, not by children of darkness but by foolish children of light. It has been under attack by the children of darkness, by the moral cynics, who declare that a strong nation need acknowledge no law beyond its strength. It has come close to complete disaster under this attack not because it accepted the same creed as the cynics; but because it underestimated the power of self-interest, both individual and collective, in modern society. The children of light have not been as wise as the children of darkness.

The children of darkness are evil because they know no law beyond the self. They are wise, though evil, because they understand the power of self-interest. The children of light are virtuous because they have some conception of a higher law than their own will. They are usually foolish because they do not know the power of self-will. They underestimate the peril of anarchy in both the national and the international community. Modern democratic civilization is, in short, sentimental rather than cynical. It has an easy solution for the problem of anarchy and chaos on both the national and international level of community, because of its fatuous and superficial view of man. It does not know that the same man who is ostensibly devoted to the "common good" may have desires and ambitions, hopes and fears, which set him at variance with his neighbor.

Our modern civilization was ushered in on a wave of boundless social optimism. Modern secularism is divided into many schools. But all the various schools agreed in rejecting the Christian doctrine of original sin. . . . Through it one may understand that no matter how wide the perspective which the human mind may reach, how broad the loyalties which the human imagination may conceive, how universal the community which human statecraft may organize, or how pure the aspirations of the saintliest idealists may be, there is no level of human moral or social achievement in which there is not some corruption of inordinate self-love.

Whenever modern idealists are confronted with the divisive and corrosive effects of man's self-love, they look for some immediate cause of this perennial tendency, usually in some specific form of social organization.

The children of light must be armed with the wisdom of the children of darkness but remain free from their malice. They must know the power of self-interest in human society without giving it moral justification. They must have this wisdom in order that they may beguile, deflect, harness and restrain self-interest, individual and collective, for the sake of the community.[2]

This is an excellent statement of the dilemma that confronts moral man in immoral society where all choices are ambiguous, equivocal, and partially infected with evil. Too often people define the morally good act as a "pure" act, and therefore are inclined to look at the possible acts available to a businessman, for example, and see only "sacrifice of principle to expediency," or what they sneeringly call "compromise." There are serious questions raised here that go to the heart of ethical decision. They rise around two points: Who is moral, the one who protects the niceties of a "pure" conscience or the one who is responsible in the sense of getting his hands dirty with the effective strategies available to him? Is there not an important difference between a compromise that is merely a balancing of competing interests in order to avoid a deadlock, and a compromise that is an honest attempt to actualize as much of one's ideal as the situation permits? In the first situation one is content if he has kept things moving regardless of the price. In the second, his uneasy conscience reminds him that he did in fact compromise so that he remains in tension with the claim of his ideal.

[2] REINHOLD NIEBUHR, *Children of Light and Children of Darkness* (New York, 1946), pp. 10–11, 16–17, 41.

WILL HERBERG

In its most practical aspect, the dilemma of the moral life we are trying to understand reveals itself in the fact that in the actual course of social existence, the choice we are confronted with is not between a line of conduct that is absolutely good and another that is absolutely evil, but between courses of action all of which are ambiguous, equivocal, and to some degree infected with evil. . . .

The absolute imperatives calling to perfection acquire their potency precisely through the fact that they transcend every actuality of existence. They are regulative, not constitutive, principles of the moral life; they cannot themselves be directly embodied in action but they operate as a dynamic power within it. They serve, first, as principles of criticism of existing conditions. They serve next as principles of guidance in the struggle for better conditions. And they serve, finally, as principles of discrimination and action in the choice among relevant possibilities under any conditions. . . . In no connection is the "impossible" ideal more pertinent, indeed indispensable, than in relation to the decisions that constitute the ongoing process of our moral life. When we are confronted with a number of alternative courses of action, none of which is simply right or wrong—and that is the permanent predicament of human life—how shall we make our choice? Clearly no choice is possible unless we are able to measure the alternative courses against some standard that transcends them. Once we have such a criterion, it becomes possible to say—after a responsible estimate of consequences— that one course constitutes a lesser evil than another. . . . Decision, choice, is always in terms of an ideal standard: that is what the cynics cannot understand. But this standard, though practically operative remains transcendent and ideal; it can never be simply identified with any course of action possible under the circumstances: this the perfectionist utopian refuses to see. Jewish ethics grasps both sides of the complex reality and is thus able to make moral ideals relevant to actual life without falling into sentimentality and illusion. It is able to make pragmatic and utilitarian judgments without taking either pragmatism or utilitarianism as final. It is able to employ all the resources of science for co-ordinating and implementing ends without falling victim to the delusion that empirical science can *set* the ends of human life.... The real moral peril consists not so much in choosing what in our best judgment seems to be the lesser evil, [but rather] in trying to make a virtue out of necessity, in converting the lesser evil we choose, merely because we choose it, into a positive good.... With a heavy heart, we may decide that going to war is the only course open to us in the world of today, but killing does not thereby become right and good....

Allegiance to the absolute imperatives of the moral law is the ethical aspect of the worship of a holy God. It saves us from taking final satisfaction in anything we do in a situation where everything we can do is qualified by the relativities of time and circumstance. It inculcates a wholesome spirit of humility which gives the soul no peace in any achievement while a still higher level is possible.... The resolution of the heart-rending, existence-shattering conflict between that which we know we ought to do and that which in fact we do do is possible only on the religious level, on the level of repentance, grace and forgiveness. At this point, ethics transcends itself and returns to its religious source and origin.[3]

Karl Adam corrects a number of false notions about the Catholic Church. A Catholic is required to follow his conscience even though the Church considers him to be wrong. If he assents to the faith that the Church is the locus of man's encounter with God, and that the bishops are the authentic exponents of God's message to the world, then in this living fellowship he finds the guidance and strength to meet the moral challenges he

[3] WILL HERBERG, *Judaism and Modern Man* (New York, 1951), pp. 109–113.

confronts in the world. Given that fundamental vision of the Church as the premise of faith, Adam is right when he sees it as a service of truth to set free of the Church one who acts on a different premise.

KARL ADAM

The theologians are unanimous in deprecating that spiritual state wherein a man's moral activity is determined only by fear and compulsion. The Catholic recognises in the ordinary and extraordinary teaching of the Church the expression of God's will. He knows that the Church does not make the divine law of faith and morals, but only authoritatively attests it, its contents and its validity. The law is the requirement of God, nor is it as such an arbitrary dictate of the divine will, but the revelation of the divine Wisdom, Sanctity, and Goodness. Its positive ordinances represent the ideal humanity as the eternal Wisdom and Love desire it to be realized, and the new man as God's design would have him. Of its essence, therefore, the law of God does not impose a burden on human nature, but is an enriching, fulfilling, and perfecting of it. It is a life-giving truth and a life-giving law. And therefore the Catholic affirms it in the light of his practical reason and by a free choice of his will makes it his own, so that it becomes his own law, an act of his moral freedom, a determination of his moral conscience. . . .

Nevertheless it is possible that a man's practical reason may sometimes fail, not recognising God's will plainly and clearly as such or being involved in invincible error. In such a case he is not bound to the objective law, but to that which appears to his conscience to be God's will, although the judgment of his conscience be objectively false. No less an authority than St. Thomas stresses this obligation of the erroneous conscience. Even in the case of so vital a matter as belief in Christ a man would act wrongly who should profess this faith against the judgment of his (erroneous) conscience.

... The Church does not compel the Catholic to shut his eyes to the religious problems which arise, nor does she even permit him to do so. The Vatican Council condemns blind faith and stipulates with the Apostle (cf. Rom. 12:1) that the obedience of our faith should be in accordance with reason. So that the Catholic is morally bound to give himself such an account of the faith that is in him as is required by his education and by his circumstances. It may happen, in a time harassed as ours is by problems of knowledge and of biblical criticism, that his studies will lead him to profound conflict of soul. He must wrestle with God until He bless him, and there is no help for him save in grace alone. ...

If a man have little respect for authority and considerable self-confidence, he withdraws his work and his research from the influence of the Church's life and from her blessing, in particular from the influence of the grace of faith, and so his tentative doubts and scruples harden into invincible errors. But it is important to note that Catholic theologians teach plainly and unanimously that the sometime Catholic is bound to follow his new attitude of mind, so long as it is a genuine and invincible conviction of conscience. ...

In the light of this fact it is an unfair and untenable charge —which does not become more tenable by constant repetition —to say that the Church enslaves conscience by requiring an unqualified obedience in matters of faith and by claiming divine authority. As the authorized preacher of the truth, the Church will never cease to give her authoritative witness to it and to oblige all consciences to accept it. Yet she does not seek to overpower conscience, but to convince it. She seeks internal, not merely external assent. And when a man cannot give this internal assent she leaves his conscience to the mercy of God and sets him free. That is not fanaticism or severity, but a service to truth and sincerity. ... And in this she protects the sincerity of [his] conscience as much as she guards the sincerity of her own being.[4]

[4] KARL ADAM, *The Spirit of Catholicism* (Doubleday Image Book), pp. 206–210.

The next passage by a French Catholic is useful for an American. We need to see how we appear to others if we are to get any true perspective on ourselves. It is especially important in a world where we have to take account of what others think we stand for. Notice what he says about the impact of the word "capitalism" on most of the people of the world. To the black man sweltering in the bottom of a South African diamond mine it does not and never will mean what it has meant for most of white America. Notice, too, what he says about the balance of wealth in relation to population and the speed with which newer nations are acquiring the power to challenge the favored position the West has traditionally held.

R. L. BRUCKBERGER

The greatest fault you [America] have, as a matter of fact, seems to be not so much a fault as the inability—an inability of which you may even be proud—to make yourselves known for what you are. Americans, you are not easy to understand, and perhaps for that very reason you are hard to love. But from the moment one begins to understand you, one realizes with a shock that the portrait of America and Americans accepted throughout the rest of the world is not a likeness but a caricature.

You have a keen sense of privacy which, translated into terms of international relations, means isolationism. You love your country, you are always happiest when you are at home and among compatriots, and this is quite natural. Your country is vast enough, rich enough, roomy enough to put you all at your ease. . . . At the same time, you deploy your troops, your planes, and your battleships all over the world, and now and then you use them. You accept this as temporarily unavoidable and blame it on those tiresome Russians who refuse to behave. Deep in your hearts, you look back with nostalgia to the day when America had no world responsibilities. Since you are not imperialists, having all you need at home, you long for the return of a day which for you was so peaceful. But you may as well make up your minds that that day will never come again.

The foundations for unifying our planet have already been laid. They are not of a political or religious nature. The most solid of them is the technological progress that has already changed part of the world and tomorrow will change the rest of it. The spirit in which modern industrial enterprise is undertaken may vary from country to country, but its structure remains substantially the same in America as in Russia, in Western Europe as in China.

Thanks to modern industrial enterprise, America has eliminated the proletariat. Western Europe is on the way to attaining the same goal; so too is Russia; and China, through mass production and mass distribution, will also no doubt attain it tomorrow.

Walter Lippmann makes clear the precise point at which Communist propaganda becomes identified with the hopes of the overpopulated and underprivileged nations. For these nations, the example of America and Western Europe carries no weight. They cannot see a future for themselves in a process as slow as the industrial growth of America and Western Europe has been. By contrast, the industrial growth of Russia and China is taking place with such lightning rapidity that every last nation, no matter how backward, no matter how overpopulated, now sees the possibility of conquering poverty in the span of a single generation.

The imposture of Communist propaganda lies in the fact that Marxism has had nothing whatever to do with technical and industrial progress.... It is not because of Marxism that Russia and China are increasing their industrial power so rapidly and raising their standard of living; it is because they have adopted the industrial methods invented and perfected in the West. Their present pace of industrialization is possible only because the West explored a virgin territory and blazed the trail. In 1912, at the time Henry Ford was launching his assembly line and demonstrating the phenomenal efficiency of his industrial methods, America and America alone embodied, for the poor on every continent, the hitherto inconceivable hope of throwing off the harsh yoke of poverty and achieving a decent standard of living, dignity for the individual, and political independence, all at the same time. Today that hope is divided. Although the underprivileged peoples still want their independence, they are now ready to sacrifice individual freedom to national or racial dignity, even when independence turns out to be illusory. But what they want first and foremost is to escape from the servitude of poverty and achieve a decent way of life.

Russia has mastered the art of revolution. It has succeeded on the one hand in identifying Communism in the minds of the poor and underprivileged with an industrial progress available to the most backward peoples and with immediate victory over poverty, while on the other hand it has succeeded in identifying America with capitalism and all its past but unforgotten and heinous crimes, with war, with imperialism, with the systematic exploitation of the poor by the rich.

You are right to resent the horrible caricature of America and Americans that Communist propaganda has drawn. But alas, resentment leads nowhere; it never solves a problem. To counter this caricature, as to counter every other phase of Communist propaganda, you will have to prove that the dilemma on the horns of which they have impaled you is a false dilemma; you will have to prove that there is a third choice, an "alternative," as Mr. Lippmann calls it, which completely changes the whole tenor of the problem.

... Walter Lippmann is also quite right in saying that it is not enough to answer propaganda with propaganda, that there must be some grandiose, spectacular, and immediate action, and he suggests that America dedicate itself to making India a modern industrial power.

I hold it very much against you that you insist upon using the word "capitalism" to define your economic and industrial structure. You who are the greatest travelers in the world should ask yourselves what people outside America think of the word capitalism. To them, capitalism stands for imperialism, for the exploitation of the poor by the rich, for colonialism. It is a dishonored word, and one that breeds terror. . . . You will ask me why it should be you Americans who have to accept the definition that the rest of the world gives to the word capitalism, why it should not be the rest of the world which has to accept your definition of the word capitalism. But this is not the point. The real point is whether or not you want to win the world's confidence.

Perhaps what the Western world most lacks today is a clear and wholly comprehensible doctrine of man's earthly salvation, a doctrine not opposed to Christianity but inspired by it, a practical doctrine which can be put into practice through some such project as the one Walter Lippman proposed with respect to India. It is, I believe, because Marxism presents itself as a doctrine of man's earthly salvation that it exerts such a powerful attraction.

For man, who has always had to face the question of his salvation in eternity and his personal immortality, must also face the question of salvation here on earth. This question has become more pressing than ever now that mankind is aware of the threat to its survival—the twofold threat of the atom and of hunger. . . . Americans, it is your misfortune as it is the misfortune of the entire West, that you were the first, and until now the only, nation to drop the atom bomb on open cities. It is an added misfortune for you and for the West that you used the atom bomb against a colored race. It does no good to tell us that you were compelled to drop it, and that this terrible act, by shortening the war, saved more lives than it destroyed. The rest of the world remains unconvinced that you were compelled to drop the bomb. . . . I will concede that not all its results were disastrous. It may well be that the memory of Hiroshima restrained the Russians at a time when, with your armies demobilized and Western Europe defenseless, there was nothing to keep them from advancing to the Atlantic coast. But even if true, this still proves that the use of the atom bomb served only the interests of the West. It only confirms the underdeveloped peoples in the belief, implanted in their minds by the Communists, that the West is prepared to go to any murderous extreme to preserve its material supremacy. . . .

Another aspect of the world situation, an aspect which would be less dangerous for the West if the unification of the world were not taking place so rapidly, is the imbalance between the relatively prosperous peoples of North America and Western Europe and the underfed millions of Asia and Africa who spend their lives on the verge of famine. The industrialized nations, primarily the Western nations, which comprise only fourteen percent of the world's population, enjoy fifty-five percent of the world's income. This disparity is constantly becoming greater, as a result of the prodigious increase in population in the underdeveloped countries.

It is only too easy to believe, and most people in the West do believe, that this situation can go on forever, with the comparatively sparsely populated nations enjoying ever-increasing material prosperity while the starving and overpopulated nations —separated from the others by oceans and continents—have no other recourse than to resign themselves to poverty. But this is totally unrealistic, now that continents and oceans no longer separate and distance is abolished. China and India are now our next-door neighbors.

For thousands of years, the world has been underpopulated. Soon it will be overpopulated. Medicine has made such progress that people everywhere now live longer. The world birth rate is constantly rising. Whereas in 1900 the global population was one and a half billion, by the year 2000 it will be almost certainly more than six billion. At the present rate of increase, within a century and a half it will probably exceed thirty billion.

... This phenomenal increase works in favor, if one may so put it, of the colored peoples and the underdeveloped regions of the world. ... Nowhere does the optimism of official statistics come closer to deceiving, more nearly border upon imposture. We are living by assumptions and equations now completely obsolete.

Up to now the white race has maintained supremacy by industrial progress. But it is about to lose the advantage of this monopoly. Western Europe and America took two centuries to reach their present stage of industrial development. Russia has taken only forty years to reach approximately the same stage. China will need still less time. Other nations will follow suit, and those that fail to take part in the vast industrial expansion will not survive, at least not as nations. ... Under these circumstances, nothing could be worse than for the West to be driven, through its own improvidence and folly, into a position where, within one or two generations, it would have to defend itself against the majority of mankind.

If we are to save the world, and specifically the West, the antagonism between poor and relatively rich nations must at all costs be prevented from becoming more virulent; the gap that separates them must at all costs be closed. ... Nor is it any less important, any less urgent, to prevent this world-wide social problem from being further envenomed by racial hatred. That is why I believe it to be of burning import for America to reach an honorable solution of its racial problem and for France to succeed in its effort to construct a European-African community.

If we want to save not only the West but the world, a world in which we are at least free to breathe, we can no longer tolerate anything whatever that might tend to create an irreconcilable rift between the proletarian and the capitalist nations, between the colored races and the white. We must move at once, and with immense determination, toward true solidarity and brotherhood between race and race, between rich and poor nations. We cannot be saved except collectively. Never in history have men so depended upon one another for their temporal salvation; it is all mankind that will be lost or saved. Ours is indeed one world.[5]

---

[5] R. L. Bruckberger, "Letter to America," in *Image of America* (New York, 1959), pp. 262–275.

AN APPROACH TO THE PROBLEMS OF
RACE, ECONOMICS, AND WAR

The following notes on a Christian approach to social policy may be a useful basis for discussion. They are by no means definitive, but they do suggest certain lines of thought which a Christian would have to take into account in making an ethical judgment. The three problems examined—race, economics, war—embrace in one way or another most of the crucial dilemmas that we have to face. Also, decisions made in one of these areas involve elements of the other two. For example, in trying to make relevant decisions on racial matters, we are inevitably drawn into the ethical implications of conflict and force, as well as into many issues that require both knowledge of the current economic situation and a challenge of some business and union policy.

It would be encouraging to report that Christians go to Church in order to ponder problems such as these and to talk together on how best to translate the claim of love into concrete strategies that would extend justice and comfort to their less fortunate brothers. Unfortunately in America the Church has tended to concern itself with the preservation of order rather than the pursuit of justice. It has too often provided rationalizations for maintaining the status quo rather than judgments that would bring it into question. It was for this reason that Marx rejected religion as an opiate of the people just as Jeremiah long ago stood in the gate of the temple and said to a complacent congregation:

Thus says the Lord of hosts, the God of Israel. . . . "Do not trust in these deceptive words: 'This is the temple of the Lord, the temple of the Lord, the temple of the Lord! . . . If you truly execute justice one with another, if you do not oppress the alien, the fatherless or the widow, or shed innocent blood in this place . . . then I will let you dwell in this place, in the land that I gave of old to your fathers for ever. . . . Will you steal, murder, commit adultery, swear falsely . . . and go after other gods . . . and then come and stand before me in in this house, which is called by my name, and say, 'We are delivered!'—only to go on doing all these abominations?" (*Jeremiah* 7:3 ff.)

Lenin once wrote of a Communist ethic the following lines

We repudiate all morality derived from non-human and non-class concepts. . . . We say that our morality is entirely subordinate to the interest of the class struggle of the proletariat. . . . we do not believe in eternal morality.

If we were to remove the words, "of the proletariat," we might be embarrassed to discover the real morality, as distinguished from the professed morality, of a surprising number of churchgoers and an even greater number of so-called "red-blooded Americans." Perhaps the most fruitful way of dealing with the ethical questions in the next few pages would be to see how much more congenial we find a class-centered ethic than we do a Christian ethic.

Some basic difficulties in relating the Christian ethic of love to the concrete problems of society. No clear and specifically Christian blueprint for social action.*

* I am indebted to Dr. John C. Bennett for the several outlines on ethical problems in the concluding pages of this section. Their substance is derived from lectures he gave at Union Theological Seminary in New York, though I have added some comments of my own, particularly on the subjects of race and war. For a fuller treatment of these ideas, see his book *Christian Ethics and Social Policy* (New York, 1950).

1. No generation can start with a clean slate. Evils of the past have accumulated over the years and confront us with vicious circles of hatred, fear, and vindictiveness for which we are not directly responsible. The racial problem and the issue of international tension are obvious examples.

2. Specific moral decisions concerning large groups (nations, corporations, unions, etc.) with whom we have no direct personal relationships are especially difficult because our imaginations are so limited that we cannot fully appreciate the needs and feelings of people we have never met and who in some ways are quite different from us.

3. In addition to the limitations of our imagination, we are also caught between conflicting interests and responsibilities. How far can the individual allow himself to be controlled by the necessities of the group to which he belongs or which he represents? Must he not limit the demands of his own personal moral convictions? Corporation manager is responsible to his family, to the public, to the stockholders, and to labor.

4. Another factor that makes moral decisions in public life difficult is that personal responsibility is in many ways watered down. Each citizen has some responsibility for the policies of his nation but it is shared with so many others that it does not come home to him in full force. In economic affairs a stockholder in a corporation is primarily interested in dividends and perhaps unaware of or indifferent to the methods by which that corporation makes its profit.

5. Weighing of values—efficiency, justice, freedom, equality, order, etc. Difficult to decide where to place the emphasis in many moral decisions. All of the values have a claim and therefore cannot be dismissed. In a complex society, how does one strike a balance between constructive planning and individual freedom? Difficult to know whose freedom has priority.

6. Psychological and political prediction—difficulty of knowing how groups of men will react if a particular policy is enacted. What method should we use to combat poverty or the racial issue? Through what political party should we work? There is no specifically Christian answer to these questions, yet it is on precisely such questions that some of our most fateful decisions depend.

The kind of guidance to look for in Christian ethics as it applies to social problems.

1. The belief that God not man is the Lord of history, implying a recognition of man's finiteness, is a source of judgment on all sorts of idolatry. One form of idolatry is the tendency to take one value and make it an absolute.

2. Faith and love should control our motives and intentions. The dominant motive of groups at best will be enlightened self-interest. However, the people who enact the policy of the group must be motivated by more than enlightened self-interest themselves or the policy will gradually break down. So too must there be a strong element in the national community deeply committed to more than enlightened self-interest.

3. The doctrine of sin gives us a basis for self-criticism. Makes us aware of our own shortcomings when we think we are righteous. Should keep us humbly aware of the subtle ways that we hide our self-interest under the cloak of idealism.

4. The radical demand of the kind of love revealed in the life of Christ should lead to concrete criticism of the status quo and also of the various proposals for changing it. Such an ethic should guide us in determining goals relevant to our time, the next steps on the road to peace and justice.

5. The Christian understanding of sin and love should make us aware that there are limits to legitimate self-interest

but no limits to a concern for the dignity and welfare of all individuals, even our enemies.

6. Distributive justice (giving every man his due) and punitive justice involving coercion are the necessary instruments of love in the impersonal relationships of society. Love, however, remains always in tension with justice and drives it to ever higher levels. Reforms in the penal codes and labor practices are examples. Love goes beyond justice because it forgives men before they deserve it.

RACE

The Problem. The most sensitive interpreters of the racial struggle see it as essentially the white man's problem. James Baldwin, the Negro novelist, warns his fellow Negroes that they cannot be free until white men are free, that the Negro will never be accepted by the white man until white men learn to accept themselves and each other. When that happens—if it ever happens—there will no longer be a Negro "problem" because it will not be needed any longer.

What a tragic irony that so many people in the "land of the free and the home of the brave" should have to sustain their sense of their own value by excluding twenty million Negroes from an equal share in the good life. Whenever a white man seeks to justify the present state of affairs by the argument that Negroes would be happy if it were not for "outside agitators" or Communists, he need only ask himself if he would be willing to trade places with any Negro, rich or poor. Would he be willing to move into any of the black ghettos of the cities or send his kids to the black schools? Would he accept the burden of explaining to his children why so many would judge them alone of all the people in this land by the color of their skin rather than by their character, intelligence, responsibility, or achievement? Would he really want even the guilt-inspired overacceptance accorded some Negroes?

There is little to be gained in any discussion of the racial issue unless this dimension of the problem is honestly faced. For only as we face it squarely can we begin to appreciate the anguish, rage, and frustration that has now erupted into the protests and demonstrations occurring all over the world.

I. CAUSES OF RACE PREJUDICE.

   (a) Prejudice is not inherent in human nature. It is no problem with young children. It is rather something that is learned and developed. Adults have to teach each new generation.

   (b) Some specific causes—economic, political, and social.

      1. Fear of competition from minority groups for jobs, particularly the more desirable jobs.

      2. Fear of being dominated politically and of losing control of the power structure through which an unjust situation is maintained.

      3. Fear of losing social status. This fear hides behind the notion of maintaining racial purity.

II. SOME UNIVERSAL TENDENCIES IN HUMAN NATURE WHICH FIND EXPRESSION THROUGH RACE PREJUDICE.

   (a) The assumption that difference means inferiority. We tend to take our own group as the standard of good and consider those who differ from us as inferior.

   (b) The desire to have some human group to which one can feel superior without the necessity of winning superiority. This emotion is pervasive even among Negroes themselves.

   (c) The desire for a scapegoat on which to project one's hostility or the blame for the failures of society or of the dominant group. Hitler's persecution of the Jews is an illustration.

   (d) The tendency to justify special privileges for oneself on the basis of the inferiority of another group.

   (e) The tendency to have a double standard. We judge

others by a different standard than we apply to ourselves. We judge other groups by their practices and ourselves by our professions.

(f) The racial stereotype. We imagine a racial "type" to suit our prejudice and call the good people in that race the exceptions. Indelibility of color makes it easy to identify the object of our prejudice. The irrationality of prejudice and the arguments that sustain it are revealed in the fact that whenever a Negro passes for white, he acquires first-class citizenship regardless of his education, moral standards, etc.

III. TYPES OF DISCRIMINATION.

Compulsory segregation is humiliating to a minority group. It tends to create arrogance and insensitivity in the dominant group and destroys fellowship. The defense of segregation tends to be self-deceptive about how justice is going to be attained.

(a) Economic: Restricted housing, limited opportunity in jobs, limited access to training programs in many unions, little chance of advancement in many professions.

(b) Political: Abuses in the administration of voting laws, threats and intimidation, effectively restrict the Negro vote in many sections of the country.

(c) Legal: Failure of many communities to give Negroes equal protection of the law. Bias in jury trials, laws interpreted with a double standard, police brutality.

(d) Educational: Segregated facilities tend to be inferior, teachers underpaid and overworked, classrooms overcrowded. Impossible to create separate and "equal" schools.

(e) Social: Clubs, public facilities or private facilities that cater to the general public, churches.

Gunnar Myrdal in his book An American Dilemma, published in 1944, offers an important insight into the nature of the problem in his discussion of what he describes as the scale of discrimination. He lists six types of discrimination and observes that the type the white man worries about most the colored man feels least. He suggests that the white man is maintaining the barriers between the races primarily in order to prevent intermarriage. Out of fear of this hypothetical possibility the white man denies basic freedoms to the entire Negro community. The Negro, on the other hand, is desperately trying to eliminate the barriers in order to pursue the goals that every white man takes for granted; namely, a good job, a good education, a good home, a voice in his own government, equal protection under the law, and decent treatment by those who serve the public. He has human, not Negro, goals. Myrdal's scale, in which he lists types of discrimination in order of their importance to the white man, may be somewhat dated now, but it helps to underline the way in which the white community continues to act on false assumptions.

1. Intermarriage and sexual intercourse
2. Social discrimination
3. Segregation and discrimination in public services
4. Political disfranchisement
5. Discrimination in law courts and law enforcement
6. Economic discrimination

IV. STRATEGIES.

Social. There is no single right strategy. In some situations one may have to further progress within the context of segregation. At the same time a frontal attack on segregation should be supported. Enforcement of laws that protect minority groups and the guarantee of their constitutional rights are also important first steps. Education is important in ridding the public mind of such unscientific ideas as that Negroes are biologically inferior to whites—though one should not be beguiled into thinking that education alone is a cure for prejudice. While it may be true that you cannot legislate morality, it is a fact that new laws or enforcement of old ones can create new types of encounters between the races that serve to allay fears and break down stereotypes which are the soil in which prejudice thrives. When people are thrown together and forced to come to terms with each other as persons, it is infinitely more difficult to maintain the wall between. Witness the countless army and college experiences that attest this truth.

There are significant new tasks for civic groups and churches such as helping to find or create opportunities in jobs and housing, perhaps agreeing to support a realtor who stood to lose financially if he permitted Negroes access to available homes. Most important in the current situation is a demonstration of white support for Negro civil rights groups so that this movement does not degenerate into a power struggle of black versus white.

Personal. The real starting point in overcoming prejudice is in ourselves. The humble recognition that all of us have prejudice against somebody should soften to some degree the present bitterness between North and South. Recent events give neither North nor South an excuse for accepting the status quo. Nor should the Negro be indifferent to his responsibility for helping to create a sense of common interest with his white countrymen. Surely he has had good cause to be bitter, angry, and disillusioned. Yet prejudice and bigotry on his part will only serve to worsen his plight. Only as we allow our faith, rather than our fears, self-interest, and pride, to govern our acts and intentions can we begin to overcome prejudice and move in the direction of real community. We need to recover that biblical way of seeing all men as forgiven sinners who are called to live as brothers before the face of one God.

CHRISTIANITY AND ECONOMIC LIFE

I. WHY SHOULD CHRISTIANITY HAVE ANYTHING TO SAY ABOUT ECONOMIC LIFE?

   (a) Because economics profoundly affects people, the way they live, the way they think, and the way they act toward one another.

   (b) Because the basic ethical principle of love demands that the man of faith show an active and responsible concern wherever men become victims of the economic system through unemployment, discrimination in job opportunities, exploitation by management or by labor.

(c) Because many people make the dangerous assumption that economic life is governed by a set of special rules and laws, and therefore they tend to have one standard of conduct for their private life, another standard in their business.

II. WHAT CAN CHRISTIANITY SAY ABOUT ECONOMIC LIFE?

(a) Its standard of love and justice for all men would be the yardstick for judging all particular economic programs on the basis of how they helped people attain security, happiness, and a sense of responsibility. It would challenge any measure that served special groups in society while inflicting injustice on others.

(b) It would strive for equality of opportunity for all men, while admitting that men are not equal in ability.

(c) It would condemn any policy that treated labor simply as a means to production and ignored the fact that "labor" is not a commodity but human beings who have a right to live and a right to have a voice in the decisions which affect their welfare.

(d) It would seek to avoid extremes of wealth and poverty because they tend to destroy human fellowship. It would insist that we take some responsibility for those at the bottom of society who either cannot or will not help themselves not only because they need our help but also because they stand as a threat to the moral health of the community.

III. WHAT THE CHRISTIAN FAITH CANNOT DO IN REGARD TO ECONOMIC LIFE.

(a) Christianity must never be equated with any particular economic theory or system because all such theories and systems are man-made and therefore contain both good and evil. There is no such thing as Christian economics though some systems embody more Christian values than others.

(b) Christianity offers no blueprint for decision on specific economic problems like taxation, tariff policy, or price support. On such matters the Christian can be a Democrat or a Republican, liberal or conservative.

IV. WHAT CAN THE CHRISTIAN DO IN THE FACE OF CONFLICTING CLAIMS AND DIFFERING OPINIONS AS TO GOALS AND THE MEANS OF ATTAINING THEM?

(a) Because economic problems are so complex and demand such a high degree of technical knowledge, he would recognize that there could be no absolute solutions. Every judgment made in good faith would probably be partly right and partly wrong. Such a premise would tend to keep him sensitive to the need for change and readjustment in the face of new situations and make him tolerant and respectful of the opinions of others.

(b) Such an attitude would compel him to criticize reactionary attempts to maintain the status quo; it would also make him critical of radical schemes to replace the established order. Because he places such a high value on persons, he would recognize that the extremes of both right and left lend themselves to fanaticism, violence, and destruction.

(c) His sense of sin and the pervasiveness of self-interest would make him aware of still another dimension of the problems of economic life. As suggested above, even the best of men are unable to achieve absolute solutions. The doctrine of sin, however, reminds him that no man is as good or as understanding as he thinks he is, and that none of his decisions are as fair and just as they might be. It would remind him that the collective interest of his group (labor union or management), while a dynamic and creative power, tends to go beyond its legitimate claims, and that in the push for power responsibility to the wider community is forgotten.

WAR

I. THE NATURE OF THE PROBLEM.

The problem of war is the problem of conflict, and it is important to realize that war is the violent expression of those conflicts which are always with us in peacetime. Whenever we ignore or fail to resolve the conflicts of peacetime, we increase the possibility of their becoming violent. Ironically, our very success in solving for ourselves most of the problems that have plagued mankind throughout history—hunger, disease, fruitless toil—has generated new sources of conflict. Those who for centuries had accepted their hopeless lot as inevitable have been caught up in what Adlai Stevenson calls "the revolution of rising expectations." They have seen what we have done, and they now are on the move themselves. Their problems are immense. Populations are mushrooming; illiteracy coupled with anti-colonial prejudice creates fertile soil for demagogues; every situation is complicated by the tensions of the cold war and the fears of a hot war which for the first time in history confronts us with the real possibility of total annihilation. The past neglect of human need has brought us a legacy of hatred and suspicion in many parts of the world which will require of us much forbearance and patience. The devastating potential of modern warfare has narrowed the ways in which we can act, raised serious questions about any moral justification of war, and given new strength to the pacifist position. There are few other situations that more clearly illustrate the ambiguity of all Christian ethical decisions.

II. THE CAUSES OF WAR.

(a) From a Christian perspective the essential cause is human sin, the tendency in all men to serve themselves at the expense of others. We cannot simply lay the blame

for war on the Hitlers and the Stalins of the world or upon our collective enemies. Our inclination to do so is an
illustration of sin as self-deception. The first thing we
must recognize in dealing with the problem of war is the
fact that we are all guilty in some respect.

(b) Economic, political, and ideological causes are important, but we should bear in mind that basically they are
expressions of men's desires and needs.

III. THE MORAL DILEMMA FOR THE CHRISTIAN.

His faith confronts him with the uncompromising commands, "You shall not kill; love your neighbor (including your
enemy); resist not evil, but overcome evil with good." Though
these are hard sayings, he might be able to obey them with a clear
conscience if he alone were involved. But when others become
victims of aggressive evil, the individual Christian is faced with a
dilemma to which there is no clearly good answer. The available
options are mixtures of good and evil and involve him in either
doing a measure of evil himself to rescue the victim or allowing
the evil to be done, thereby favoring the life of the guilty to that of
the innocent. There are still other kinds of dilemmas that are
related to this problem. His involvement in the collective life of
his nation through his contribution to its economic, political,
and military strength and his explicit or tacit support of the
nation's policies require some acknowledgment of shared guilt
when that nation decides to go to war. A profound moral dilemma arises from the mere possession of the Bomb with its
implied threat. How long can a dangerous balance of terror be
justified as a means of keeping the peace? Yet unilateral disar-
mament would seem to be not only unrealistic but irresponsible.
So the Christian is faced with ambiguous alternatives, among
which he must make the decision that most nearly meets the
demand of his conscience. That it may seem the only decision
possible under the circumstances should not blind him to the
actual evil in it.

APPENDIX II

Biblical Sources for Parts II and III

[These readings in the Bible may be useful to those who would like documentation for what is referred to in the text as the "biblical point of view." The readings are categorized under the headings and themes that were used in developing this view.]

PART II

The Nature of Man and the Human Situation

SECTION 1

SELF-AWARENESS, FREEDOM, ANXIETY

1. Body and spirit.
   Psalm 8. "All things under his feet."
   Matthew 6:19–24. Anxiety over things.
   Romans 8:13–18. The spirit of man and the spirit of God.

2. Finite in relation to infinite.
   Psalm 145. Man and the unsearchable God.
   See Psalm 8, above.
   Job 38, 39, 40:1–14. Man's final humility.
   I Corinthians 13:1–13. "We know in part."

3. Free and determined.
   Romans 8:1–9. Imposed requirements and the free spirit.
   See also Galatians 5:13–23.
   Romans 8:31–39. Capacity to transcend conditions.
   See also 2 Corinthians 4:6–18. "Perplexed but not in despair."

4. Individual and social.
   Luke 15. Three parables of the value of the individual.
   2 Corinthians 12:11–27. Members of a body.
   Psalm 139. Individual recognized apart from the nation.

5. Man in the Genesis stories.
   Genesis 1:1–31. Image of God.
   Genesis 2:4–7. Man made out of dust plus the spirit of life.
   Genesis 2:8–25. Self-deceit of self-will, and the coming of evil.
   Genesis 6:5–22. The flood, corruption, destruction and recovery.
   Genesis 11:1–9. Tower of Babel—collective pride of nations, and misunderstanding that separates.

269

SECTION 2

MAN AGAINST HIMSELF

1. Sin a religious term.

Psalm 51:1–10. Self-will against God's will.
Genesis 3:1–19. Self-deceit of self-will.
Romans 7:14–25. "What I would not, that I do."
I John 1:5–10. Assumption of innocence.

2. Sin as false loyalty.

Deuteronomy 8:10. Prosperity in place of God.
Ecclesiastes 2, 12:13–14. Man's judgment of existence apart from God's judgment.
Isaiah 40. To whom shall ye liken God?

3. Sin as pride.

Luke 18:9–14. Parable for those who "think themselves righteous."
Matthew 23. Woes to those who outwardly appear righteous.
Matthew 11:28. "I am meek and lowly in heart."
I Corinthians 3:16–23. False pride of worldly wisdom.
Genesis 11:1–9. Tower of Babel and collective pride.

PART III

Whence Cometh Our Salvation?

SECTION 1

THE INESCAPABLE CHOICE

(a) Dependence on supra-human mystery.
Job 28:12–28. Where shall wisdom be found?
Isaiah 55:6–13. My ways are not your ways.

(b) Faith as commitment in contrast to intellectual belief.
Matthew 22:34–40. "With all your heart."
Matthew 4:1–11. The Temptation and the Choice of a final concern.
Hebrews 11:32–40. Heroes of faith in the Old Testament.

(c) Revelation.
In nature: Psalm 19:1–14.
In prophets: Isaiah 1:10–20.
In Christ: John 1:1–18.

Biblical Sources for Parts II and III

THE CONCEPT OF GOD

The Bible's approach—not man finding out God but God encountering man.

1. The experience of Bible personalities.
   (a) Moses. Exodus 2:11–25; 3.
   (b) Isaiah. Isaiah 6.
   (c) Paul. Acts 9.

2. God is love.
   I John 4:7–21. Christ the manifestation of God's love.
   I Corinthians 13. The nature of divine love.
   Acts 17:22. Paul and the Unknown God.
   I John 3:13. God abiding in us.

3. Judgment of God.
   (a) Isaiah 1:2–20. The prophetic view of judgment and mercy.
   (b) Judgment seen in the consequences of action.
       Amos 7:7–9. The figure of the plumb line.
       Matthew 7:24. The house built on sand.
       Matthew 25:31–40. The final test of life.
       Matthew 25:14–30. Talents taken away.
       Matthew 25:1–13. Opportunity missed.
   (c) Judgment as an inner searching of life.
       Psalm 129:1–28. Recognition of each individual.
       Matthew 5, 6, 7. The Sermon on the Mount—the outward life measured
                        by the inner motives.
       Matthew 7:1–5. Judge not that ye be not judged.

4. Saving power of God.
   (a) Picturesque illustrations.
       Luke 19:1–10. "This day salvation is come—."
       Luke 10:25–37. From outer requirement to inner willingness.
       Luke 7:37–50. Forgiveness.
       Luke 15:10–33. New attitude toward persons.
       John 3:1–16. Born again.
   (b) Paul's more complicated language.
       2 Corinthians 5:14–21. New creature in Christ.
       Romans 8:1–27. Justification by faith.
       Romans 5:1–10. While we were yet sinners.
       Ephesians 4:1–16. Growth through community.

271

Galatians 5:14–26. "Life in the Spirit."
Philippians 3:1–14. Paul's personal testimony.
Galatians 2:16–21. Crucified with Christ.

5. God as Creator and Sovereign.

(a) Genesis I. The Creation.
Isaiah 40:12–31. The mystery and continuity of Creation.
Psalm 97.

(b) Providence.
Ecclesiastes 2. The cynical view: all is vanity.
Ecclesiastes 12:13–14. The conclusion of the matter.
Romans 8:31–39. Possibility of good out of evil.
2 Corinthians 4:6–18.

SECTION 3
SIGNIFICANCE OF CHRIST

Mark 8:27–33. Peter's confession of faith.
John 1:1–18. The word made flesh.
John 14:1–6. "I am the truth."
John 12:44–55. "He that seeth me, seeth Him that sent me."
Mark 10:17–22. "Who is good, save God?"
Philippians 2:1–21. "He emptied himself."
2 Corinthians 5:14–21. "God was in Christ."

(a) Crucifixion.

Luke 23:20–49. Account of the crucifixion.
Isaiah 53. Old Testament view of Suffering Servant.
I Corinthians 1:17–31. Christ crucified—the power of God.
Romans 5:1–8. "Christ died for us."

(b) Resurrection.

Mark 16. Account of the Resurrection.
Philippians 3:7–14. Paul and the Power of the Resurrection.
I Corinthians 15:1–26, 35–58. Paul's interpretation of the Resurrection.

(c) Life in the Spirit.

John 14:15–27. The Spirit of truth, The Comforter.
Ephesians 4:1–16. Community of the Spirit.
Romans 8:1–9, 14–19. "Spirit of God in you."
See also 2 Corinthians 5:14–21. "New creature."
John 17:1–4. Eternal Life.
Luke 10:25–37. Inheriting Eternal Life—a quality of life.

Biblical Sources for Parts II and III

BIOGRAPHIES

ADAM, KARL: Roman Catholic theologian, born in Bavaria in 1876. He received his doctorate from the University of Munich and was ordained to the priesthood. From 1919 to 1950 he was a Lecturer at the University of Tübingen. He is now Emeritus Professor of Dogmatic Theology at Tübingen.

BAILLIE, DONALD M.: Educated at Edinburgh, Marburg, and Heidelberg, he was for many years Professor of Systematic Theology at St. Andrews University, Scotland. He died in 1954.

BARBOUR, IAN G.: Chairman of the Religion Department and Associate Professor of Physics at Carleton College, Northfield, Minnesota. He was educated at Swarthmore, Duke, and Yale and received a Ph.D. in physics from the University of Chicago.

BENNETT, JOHN C.: President of Union Theological Seminary in New York. Educated at Williams, Union Seminary, and Oxford University, he was for twenty years Professor of Christian Theology and Ethics at Union Seminary. He has played a leading role in the World Council of Churches and as a member of Economic Life and International Justice departments of the National Council of Churches.

BERGER, PETER L.: Born in Vienna, Dr. Berger came to this country as a young man. He received a Ph.D. in Sociology from the New School for Social Research in New York. He has taught at the University of Georgia and the University of North Carolina. Until recently he was Associate Professor in Social Ethics at the Hartford Seminary Foundation.

BONHOEFFER, DIETRICH: A brilliant young Protestant theologian whose promising career was cut short by the Second World War. Having been forbidden to continue his teaching at Berlin, he joined the Confessing Church in Germany to help train young ministers. Eventually he became involved with the resistance movement and in 1943 was arrested and imprisoned by the Gestapo. He spent the next two years in prison writing and helping his fellow prisoners. He was hanged by the Gestapo in April, 1945.

BRUCKBERGER, RAYMOND L.: Born in France in 1907 he received his Ph.B. at Montpellier University, his STL degree from the Dominican House of Studies, and was ordained in 1934. He was a member of the French commandos from 1939–40, the underground resistance from 1940–44, and the Foreign Legion in the Sahara from 1948–50. Recipient of the Croix de Guerre and Legion of Honor. He came to this country in 1950.

BUBER, MARTIN: Born in Vienna in 1878 he has long been the leading spokesman for the Jewish cultural community in Europe and recognized by leaders

275

of all faiths as an outstanding philosopher and religious thinker. Since the time of Hitler, Buber has been associated with the Hebrew University of Jerusalem.

CHERBONNIER, E. LA B.: Born in St. Louis, Dr. Cherbonnier was educated at Harvard, Columbia, Union Theological Seminary in New York, and Cambridge University in England. During World War II he served in the U.S. Navy as aviator and flight instructor in fighter aircraft. He is Professor of Philosophy, Religion, Ethics, and Theology at Barnard College and Union Theological Seminary.

DOSTOYEVSKY, FYODOR M.: Born in Moscow in 1821, Dostoyevsky was a national hero by the time he died in 1881. One of the great Russian novelists, his books shed a penetrating light on the dark side of man's inner life. Few artists have equalled him in revealing the depths of meaning found in the doctrine of original sin.

EISELEY, LOREN: Educated at the University of Nebraska and the University of Pennsylvania where he received a Ph.D. in Social Science, Dr. Eiseley has taught at the University of Kansas and at Oberlin. He is Professor of Anthropology and History of Science, and Chairman of the Department of History and Philosophy of Science at the University of Pennsylvania.

FRANK, ERICH: Born in Prague in 1883, Dr. Frank was a Catholic philosopher who taught at Heidelberg, Marburg, and Harvard Universities. At the time of his death in 1949, he was Visiting Lecturer at Bryn Mawr College, Swarthmore, and the University of Pennsylvania.

FROMM, ERICH: Born in Frankfurt, Germany, in 1900, Dr. Fromm was educated at the University of Heidelberg where he earned his Ph.D. He was trained in psychoanalysis at the Psychoanalytic Institute in Berlin. At present he is Professor of Psychology at New York University and Professor of Psychoanalysis at the National University of Mexico.

HERBERG, WILL: An influential Jewish thinker, Dr. Herberg has been a keen observer and critic of American religious life for many years. He has lectured and led seminars on religion, philosophy, and social studies at leading American universities and seminaries. He is Graduate Professor of Judaic Studies and Social Philosophy, and Graduate Professor of Philosophy and Culture at Drew University.

LEWIS, C. S.: Born in 1898 in Ireland, Mr. Lewis has gained a wide following for his numerous books on religion. Until his death in 1963 he was Professor of Medieval and Renaissance English at Magdelene College, Cambridge.

MALTHE-BRUUN, KIM: A young Danish seaman who worked in the resistance movement against the Germans, he was executed by a German firing squad at the age of twenty-two.

Biographies

MAY, ROLLO: Born in 1909, Dr. May received his doctorate from Columbia University in 1949. He is a practicing analyst in New York City, a Fellow and member of the Faculty of the William Alanson White Institute of Psychiatry, Psychoanalysis, and Psychology.

NIEBUHR, REINHOLD: Born at Wright City, Mo., in 1892, Dr. Niebuhr studied at Elmhurst College, Eden Theological Seminary, and Yale Divinity School and was ordained into the Evangelical and Reformed Church. From 1928 until his recent retirement, he was Professor of Applied Christianity at Union Theological Seminary, New York. His great contribution to American Protestantism has been the recovery of the biblical and Reformation insights into the nature of man and history, and the demonstration of the relevance of these insights to the political and economic problems of our age.

NIEBUHR, H. RICHARD: Born in 1894, Richard Niebuhr, like his brother Reinhold, received his education at Elmhurst College, Eden Theological Seminary and Yale Divinity School. He also took an M.A. at Washington University and a Ph.D. at Yale. He spent the greater part of his professional career as a teacher at Yale Divinity School and, from 1938 until his death in 1962, was Professor of Theology and Christian Ethics. He is considered by many to be one of the truly great theologians of the twentieth century.

PIKE, JAMES A.: Born in 1913, Bishop Pike has had a remarkably varied career. After getting an A.B. and LL.B from the University of Southern California and a J.S.D. at Yale, he became a practicing attorney, the author of a number of books and articles in the field of federal judicial and administrative procedure, and a lecturer at various law schools. He was a naval intelligence officer during World War II. In 1944 he was ordained into the Episcopal Church. By 1949, he had become Chairman of the Department of Religion at Columbia University. He then became Dean of the Cathedral of St. John the Divine in 1952 and at present is Bishop of California.

READ, DAVID H. C.: Born in Scotland in 1910, Dr. Read studied at Edinburgh, Paris, Montpellier, Strasbourg, Marburg, and in Palestine. Author of a number of books on the Christian faith, he has earned the reputation of being a distinguished preacher as Senior Minister of the Madison Avenue Presbyterian Church in New York.

ROBERTS, DAVID E.: Born in 1911 in Nebraska, Dr. Roberts earned a B.A. from Occidental College, a B.D. from Union Theological Seminary, and a Ph.D. from Edinburgh University. He was a Professor of the Philosophy of Religion at Union Theological Seminary, New York, and was active in college student work. He pioneered in relating the Christian faith to psychotherapy before his untimely death in 1955.

SAROYAN, WILLIAM: Born in Fresno, California, in 1908, William Saroyan is a well-known American novelist.

277

Biographies

TILLICH, PAUL: Born in Germany in 1886, Dr. Tillich taught philosophy and theology in German universities. He settled in this country when Hitler came to power and from 1933–1955 was Professor of Philosophical Theology at Union Theological Seminary, New York. From 1955 to 1962 he was University Professor at Harvard and since then has been Professor of Theology at the Divinity School of the University of Chicago. His great work has been in the area of relating the Christian faith to the disciplines of our culture and the entire history of culture, and in reinterpreting the central symbols of the faith in the language of our time.

UPDIKE, JOHN: Born in 1932 in Pennsylvania, John Updike graduated from Harvard in 1954. He has received wide critical acclaim and is generally considered one of America's most gifted young writers.

WEIGEL, GUSTAVE: Born in 1906, he was educated at Woodstock College. He acquired a Ph.D. and an S.T.D. at Gregorian University in Rome. He taught theology at the Catholic University of Chile and from 1949 until his death in 1964 he was Professor of Ecclesiology at Woodstock. He was instrumental in developing genuine understanding and dialogue between Catholic and Protestant Churchmen in this country.

WREN-LEWIS, JOHN: Assistant Research Controller to Imperial Chemical Industries, Ltd., he is well known in Great Britain as a writer and broadcaster on theological and philosophical as well as scientific subjects.